UNCONFORMITIES IN SHAKESPEARE'S LATER COMEDIES

Unconformities in Shakespeare's Later Comedies

Kristian Smidt

Emeritus Professor of English Literature
University of Oslo

St. Martin's Press   New York

PR2981
S565
1993

First published in the United States of America in 1993

Printed in Great Britain

ISBN 0–312–09099–4

Library of Congress Cataloging-in-Publication Data
Smidt, Kristian.
Unconformities in Shakespeare's later comedies / Kristian Smidt.
p. cm.
Includes bibliographical references and index.
ISBN 0–312–09099–4
1. Shakespeare, William, 1564–1616—Comedies.   2. Comedy.
I. Title.
PR2981.S565   1993
822.3'3—dc20
92–37355
CIP

For my Shakespeare friends in Japan

Contents

Preface

This is the fourth and last volume of a series in which I have conducted an analysis of all the plays in the Shakespeare canon. Only one play partly attributed to Shakespeare has been omitted. *The Two Noble Kinsmen*, whether or not because Fletcher had the smoothing-out of the composite parts, offers relatively little of interest to a study of 'unconformities'.

The term 'unconformities' may be thought more pejorative than I intend, but, as I have explained before and repeat in the Introduction to the present volume, I have found it useful, with some stretching of its original geological meaning, to designate the breaches of continuity or consistency occurring in the play texts for whatever genetic reasons. In many cases, and this is why they may be worth studying, they direct us to thought processes which shaped and inform the plays as we have them, both in major aspects and minor matters, and help us besides to recognise accidental corruptions for what they are.

I do not pretend to be the first to discover all these unconformities. In fact most of them have been observed and pointed out by critics from the seventeenth century on. Dryden mentioned *Measure for Measure* as one of several plays made up, as he complained, 'of some ridiculous incoherent story' (*Essay on the Dramatique Poetry of the Last Age*). And, naturally, editors of the plays, particularly in our own century, have been attentive to irregularities of various kinds, some of which they have amended. Lists of inconsistencies appear in the introductions to a number of modern editions and have occasionally simplified my own survey. Nevertheless, even major unconformities may sometimes have gone unnoticed, and certain types of irregularity, like redundant repetition (often signalling real or intended omissions and additions, as I shall show), have too seldom been identified (see also the Appendix). Some of my observations therefore are new. And at least there may be some merit in bringing them together from all the plays. Seeing the unconformities systematically demonstrated and discussed should help to bring certain prevalent tendencies of Shakespeare's work into clearer view.

What I am basically concerned with are phenomena, not ideas

except as parts of phenomena, and to a great extent I would leave it to others' endeavours to place my objective observations in larger theoretical or evaluative contexts. Phenomena need to be simply described. In any case I am, regrettably or not, incapable of reasoning on the level of abstraction to be found in much recent academic discourse. Further, if my identification of phenomena sometimes may seem indiscriminate, this, I submit, is because it is impossible to fill in the whole background of surprise effects in Shakespeare which are *not* considered as unconformities.

The reproach that I most anticipate and would wish to forestall is that I have too exclusively examined the play texts as literature and have not sufficiently considered their theatrical intentions. It seems to me that bardolatry nowadays is becoming sectarian, and the theatrical sect is especially loud in its denunciation of heretics. Shakespeare has truly become an idol of the theatre. In a recent symposium of essays and interviews, *The Shakespeare Myth* (ed. G. Holderness, Manchester University Press, 1988), Michael Bogdanov says of Shakespeare: 'He wasn't literature; he was theatre. His work became literature later on when people transcribed his plays on to paper.' 'This dreadful tradition', he calls it. And John Hodgson declares: 'The root of the problem is that Shakespeare has become literature. The danger occurs when we forget that Shakespeare was a man of the theatre; he was an actor who also happened to write plays.'

It is time to oppose this increasingly manic denial of Shakespeare's literary significance. Whatever Bogdanov may think, the plays were written before they were performed and, what is more, written by a poet who certainly could not expect his every line to be spoken on the stage, let alone to be fully appreciated on a first hearing. Some of his plays were printed and published in corrected versions after being first 'maimed, and deformed by... iniurious impostors'. And for all we know he may himself have wished to publish them all before he died. Need we believe that Francis Meres had only seen and heard, not read them, when he compared them for excellence to those of Plautus and Seneca; or Gabriel Harvey when he said of *Lucrece* and *Hamlet* that they 'haue it in them, to please the wiser sort'? In any case, we do as a matter of plain fact possess them as literature and are quite capable of enjoying their literary as well as their theatrical qualities.

On the other hand, the Romantics were mistaken, of course, in wishing only to read the plays and to be spared the experience, limiting in their minds, of watching them performed. I am in no way denying that the plays were destined for the theatre. Some of them, probably, were written hastily and for special occasions. And the present study is theatre-oriented, not because it is concerned with the stage histories of the plays or particularly focused on theatrical interpretations at various times but because it addresses itself to problems which directors and actors at any time have to face and solve. It also attempts to determine more precisely than has hitherto been done in all cases the contents of the scripts used for the earliest productions (e.g. what omissions were intended) and in what ways the texts may have been adapted for performance. A large part of my efforts will be directed towards discovering by means of recognisable signs what changes the author made in his notional plots or already-written texts, changes which would frequently have been motivated by his wish to improve the effect of presentation on the stage. It is in ways like this, I submit, that academic critics, so often dismissed or denigrated by theatre people (see e.g. M. Billington (ed.), *Directors' Shakespeare*, Nick Hern, 1990, pp. 114–17) may be of service to practical interpreters of drama.

It had no doubt been a thing worthy to have been wished to have seen a play directed by the author himself in his own theatre. This would have been of immense importance in deciding a great many questions concerning ultimate intentions and in supplementing the stage directions recorded in print. Even in Shakespeare's own day, however, a performance must have been an interpretation which realised some of the play's potentials, but not all. Productions in later times lacking the benefit of the author's supervision are even less definitive but may still be illuminating, not least as regards the viability of particular emphases or inclusions. Analysis of the texts must be open to experiential evidence but cannot be governed by it. Thus it is no doubt possible to make the Jupiter scene in *Cymbeline* seem significant when enacted, but my argument that it is both detachable and expendable is not shaken in principle by the fact that reviewers missed it in a recent production (see Smallwood in *Shakespeare Quarterly*, Spring 1990, p. 104, and Dessen in *SQ*, Fall 1990, pp. 352–3) – perhaps the audience was bemused by the fact that the theophany was given in dumb show only. Some unconformities are also hard to eliminate or disguise. Kenneth Branagh's splendid *Twelfth Night* did nothing to remove (though it did a lot to compensate for) the absurdity of Viola not acting on her realisation that she was taken for Sebastian.

Productions of the plays have opened my eyes to many of the problems and solutions I have touched on in this book, but my explicit references will be chiefly to printed criticism. With regard to particular aspects and questions I have often found them most usefully pinpointed in articles published in scholarly journals like *Shakespeare Quarterly*, while major studies of the comedies, problem plays and romances have been invaluable in providing both matter and perspectives both of a specific as well as a general kind. I have continued to find Bertrand Evans's *Shakespeare's Comedies* stimulating.

My staple source for reference and quotation is the New Arden Shakespeare.

I owe a considerable debt of gratitude to Dr Robert Smallwood of the Shakespeare Centre, Stratford-upon-Avon, who has once again gone through my typescript and offered valuable suggestions for improvement both as to matter and form. His patient criticism is all the more handsome as he is not invariably in sympathy with my views, but his sound scholarship and wide experience of Shakespeare in the theatre have helped me to clarify and modify my statements in many places where I have been insufficiently cogent or circumspect. Remaining faults are all my own.

The chapter on *As You Like It*, 'All Even in Arden?', was published with slight differences in *English Studies*, 70.6 (1989), and I am grateful to the editors for permission to reprint.

My thanks to the Norwegian Research Council for Science and the Humanities for a generous subsidy towards publication.

Kristian Smidt
Oslo

1

Introduction

Post-Shakespearean generations in England and elsewhere are the fortunate inheritors of a body of dramatic masterpieces which by common consent are unsurpassed in the history of European literature at least since the ancient Greeks, and which are preserved in print in editions published during the lifetime of the author or shortly after. The only trouble (which is no problem at all to the vast majority of Shakespeare's admirers but which is apt to worry dedicated interpreters) is that neither the quartos published prior to 1623 nor the great Folio collection of that year are the word of God. They have no absolute authority. Some of the plays have come down to us in variant versions. Some have peculiarities which indicate their provenance from untidy manuscripts ('foul papers') or memorial reports. The texts had an eventful history before reaching print. Transcripts were made for various purposes and by various persons. Stage performances would require adaptation, and special demands were made by court appearances and provincial tours. There was censorship before licence to play. And finally the printing process added its quota of interference. In all of this a great deal happened to the original texts by way of deliberate alteration or accident, particularly on the micro-level (obvious confusions and corruptions of detail have always been noticed), but sometimes on the macro-level too (and these are often harder to trace).

A more insidious problem and one which nevertheless presents itself even to unsophisticated readers and viewers, though they may not admit it to full consciousness, is whether Shakespeare himself always perfectly realised his own creative potentials and the potentials of his chosen material (theme, character, action, expression). This problem is particularly hard to tackle because of the factors extrinsic to the author's own work, touched on above, which tended to obscure bits and features of his original design. Critics from Heminge and Condell on, particularly in the past two centuries, have been unwilling to find imperfections in Shakespeare. But it is a tribute to his humanity and by no means a

1

slur on his greatness as an artist to recognise that even a genius such as he is fallible. It is naive and wishful thinking to imagine that plays in Elizabethan times were born perfect of their limbs. But vision and craftsmanship combined may more than compensate for moments of inattention or flagging inspiration. Shakespeare by all indications wrote happily on, much of the time, without hesitations and back-references. Apparently he often forgot to check back through his growing pile of sheets in the interest of consistency or fulfilment of expectations, and the result is a certain amount of seeming carelessness. Iachimo notes in II.ii that the mole on Imogen's left breast has a 'cinque-spotted' pattern, but only two scenes on he omits this observation in his report to Posthumus, though one might think it the most clinching detail of his treacherous evidence.[1]

Shakespeare's temperament, impatient of small scruples as we may suppose, may have had a say in all this. His circumstances must have been equally important. Writing against time to provide his company with two plays a year on a rough average for his whole output, he would neither have felt the need nor found the leisure for systematic tidying-up. Then again the nature of the plays he wrote would favour inconsistencies. He delighted in complication and multiple plots, often twining main and subsidiary plots into an intricate network. (The one play in which he seems to have subordinated his own shaping initiative to that of John Fletcher, *The Two Noble Kinsmen*, is simple and streamlined in the development of its action, compared to such plays as *Much Ado* or *Pericles*.) He has numerous characters and numerous scenes. In fact Elizabethan plays in general have more and shorter scenes than modern plays, where action is often conveyed by verbal conflict or discussion rather than physical movement. *Twelfth Night* in this respect is characteristic of Elizabethan usage. (*As You Like It* has an unusual amount of discussion, but there, too, the scenes are mostly short if we go by the comings and goings of characters.) Long speeches occur, of course, and in the late plays they tend to differ from the more realistic dialogue of some of the earlier comedies and tragedies in their closely-packed semantic texture, which in itself tends to produce occasional confusion.

It is quite possible, and in fact seems likely, that Shakespeare sometimes composed his plays not in a running sequence of episodes but in separate scenes independently of their final arrangement, and so as to highlight to some extent their autonomous dra-

matic effect.[2] Whenever he followed this procedure it would naturally produce a certain neglect of continuity from scene to scene.
Another theory has it that he structured some of his scenes in an
antithetical pattern. J. R. Price has noticed a dialectic habit, especially in *Measure for Measure*: Shakespeare, he says, 'made it a habit
to alter his characters, moment by moment, or rather, scene by
scene.... Similarly, he learned to set up one scene as if he were
coming out for Isabella ... in the next, he would be quite careful to
undermine her whole argument'.[3] I am not sure this theory accounts
for the contradictions in *Measure for Measure*, but we cannot ignore
the dialectic strain in Shakespeare's treatment of themes and characters or deny that it might produce problems of coherence.

Moving on to matters of planning and inspiration, it would seem
that Shakespeare's mental conception of a projected play was not
always perfectly clear from the start and sometimes remained
equivocal. In any case, new ideas and new insights would certainly
supervene on his initial programme. Inspiration is not an entirely
governable or predictable entity, and in a person gifted with a generous supply would certainly tend to operate continuously so as to
modify and even change an ongoing creative process. In some cases
this would amount to a change of mind and in extreme cases to a
change of direction, which would leave undeveloped beginnings
and arbitrary-seeming transitions in so far as revision was not concurrently undertaken to assimilate the old ideas to the new. We
must imagine Shakespeare sometimes feeling dissatisfaction with
something he had done or was doing. For this reason, too, he
would revise *en route* or after completing his draft. Some passages
he would strike out or mark for omission, others he would interpo-
late. Revision, we must suppose, would mean improvement, but
evidently it was incomplete and sporadic, and sometimes hesitant,
as if Shakespeare contemplated alternative versions of a passage
that troubled him. Frequently it left traces, some of which are
readily recognisable, others less so. We shall try to identify them.

In seeking the causes of unconformities, we must not, of course,
forget the extent of Shakespeare's indebtedness to literary and
dramatic sources of various kinds. These must have supplied
valuable suggestions to ease his creative labours, but there was
always a danger of importing flaws and obscurities from the
rifled stores along with more precious loot; and an even greater
danger of failure to adapt every detail of acquired material to new
and original designs. An appreciable number of unconformities

may have come about in this way. Besides, it would only be natural if the author was sometimes neglectful in clarifying the associations that accompanied his borrowings, so as to leave the reader or auditor puzzled as to the full meaning of certain speeches or incidents. This *a fortiori* applies to modern readers and auditors lacking the resonances familiar to Elizabethans and unacquainted with much of the literature available to the educated members of Shakespeare's society. Carol Gesner and James C. Bulman, dealing respectively with Shakespeare's romances and tragedies, have convincingly shown that a number of passages in the plays which seem anomalous to modern critics are essentially allusive and can be explained, if not necessarily justified aesthetically, by reference to classical contexts. [4]

In the first century after the publication of the great Folio, critics and theatre directors were more intent on adapting Shakespeare's texts to their own tastes than on scrutinising the printed plays in order to answer questions about authenticity and internal agreement. In the eighteenth and nineteenth centuries scholarship more and more focused on explanation and 'emendation' of obscure or obviously corrupt passages – not, of course, to the prejudice of theatrical innovation but for a better understanding of the genius on which all interpretation depended. In our own day we have seen great advances in bibliographical research and have increasingly realised the vulnerability of Elizabethan play-texts to non-authorial interference as well as their exposure to authorial revision. In recent decades traditional assumptions about the Shakespeare canon – that the extant quarto and Folio versions with a little judicious correction give us the author's texts as he monumentally or ideally wanted them – have come under heavy attack. There is a growing scepticism as to whether we have Shakespeare's finished work or not. Did he complete all his plays in the first place? Did he intend one final form, which we may or may not have received? Did he plan or execute alternative versions for particular occasions and places of performance? To what extent did he collaborate with other writers? And did he write to be read as well as for theatrical use? In all of this, how faithful were scribes and printers to his intentions? [5]

We naturally wish to get closer to these intentions, even if we have to admit that we can never fully define them. But there is little help to be found in contemporary Elizabethan and Jacobean material outside the printed plays. There are some brief remarks by Ben Jonson about absurdities in *Julius Cæsar* and *The Winter's Tale* and, as for stage performances, we have some concentrated eye-witness accounts by Manningham, Forman and Wotton. Occasional phrases and lines occur as quotations in other writers. And there are rough sketches of the Swan theatre and of a scene from *Titus Andronicus* as they were seen by playgoers around 1595 or 1596.[6] We are actually confined to the canonical texts themselves if we wish to examine the creative process behind them. And a good deal of work has been, and is being, done which is based on verse and vocabulary tests, on spelling habits and typographical practices. My own approach is by way of what I call unconformities.

Unconformities, as I use the word,[7] are essentially a matter of broken continuity either in the story-line (the plot sequence), the presentation and interrelations of the characters, the general mode of the play with the stylistic and technical means by which it is served, and in thematic focus. Other terms which I use are inconsistencies, incongruities, discrepancies, disruptions, discontinuities, contradictions, all considered under the aspect of anomalies or irregularities, but not *a priori* pejorative.

I include all sorts of semantic and structural anomalies but will concentrate on significant occurrences. We will not be unduly concerned with the more trivial inconsistencies, which abound in the plays. Some of them form patterns among themselves, others may be related to major disturbances. But, on the whole, they are devoid of contextual interest. Editors monotonously repeat their belief that we do not notice them. I believe we notice them more often than these comforters like to think – unless, of course, all irregularities are ironed out in the theatre. But that is not the point. The point that should be insisted on is that small isolated slips simply do not matter. They are too insignificant to be judged by any impression of wholeness, and it is wholeness, unity, coherence, continuity (again a number of words will serve) which must be our criterion.

It is otherwise with the larger unconformities. Here again some critics turn a blind eye and even tend to see faults as virtues. R. A. Foakes maintains that

> beginning with the dark comedies, Shakespeare learned how to liberate himself from a commitment to characters presented with psychological and linguistic consistency, in order to achieve special kinds of effects in his later plays, and particularly as one means of distancing his audience from the characters and preventing identification with them, in the way an audience

identifies with Hamlet. What has seemed clumsy to many readers of *Cymbeline* may be merely a daring new development in Shakespeare's dramatic art.[8]

Thus, according to Foakes, 'the notorious inconsistencies of speech and behaviour in a figure like Cloten appear natural if we accept the basic dramatic conventions of the play'.[9] Foakes in this matter follows in the footsteps of Northrop Frye, who in books like *A Natural Perspective* (1965) and *The Myth of Deliverance* (1983) has probably done more than anyone to make us accept the *prima facie* absurdities of Shakespeare's later comedies as artistic achievements. Frye's point of departure is his objection to coarse realistic standards of criticism. He goes so far as to say,

> it seems clear that no audience of Shakespeare, whether Elizabethan or modern, is allowed to think at all. They have the power to like or dislike the play, but no right to raise questions, as long as the action is going on, about the plausibility of the incidents or their correspondence with their habitual view of life.

'It follows', he says, 'that the criticism devoted to the vividness of characterization in Shakespeare's comedies may get out of proportion if it is not kept in its context.'[10] Frye stresses the inherent requirements of the comic form and the 'illusion of reality' which it is the business of comedy to suggest. 'The drive toward a comic conclusion' he finds to be 'deeply rooted in nature' and 'so powerful that it breaks all the chains of probability in the plot, of habit in the characters, even of expectation in the audience'.[11]

One may admire the critical generosity of Frye's attitude and accept many of his insights and yet reserve the right to demur. It is obviously true that Shakespeare ignored any appeal to everyday reality when it suited his purpose, though it should be borne in mind that life itself is full of contradictions and absurdities. But he hardly expected his audiences not to do any thinking at all while his actions were in progress, and one may disagree with Frye and Foakes about the ease with which unconformities may be experienced as entirely functional. Frye tells us not to look for realistic plausibility, and perhaps it needs to be said that this is not what we shall be looking for in this study, at least realistic plausibility *per se*. We shall not be particularly concerned with conformity to realistic expectations unless it becomes structurally relevant. We must look for conformity within the mode which is established as the dominant convention for each play, usually comprising different degrees or blends of the realistic and the fantastic. Realism itself is certainly not a criterion which can be profitably used to identify unconformities.

The underlying assumption of this book is that Shakespeare ideally aimed at unity of theme, conservation of character and continuity of plot, and I have supported this assumption in my analyses of his histories, tragedies and early comedies.[12] In the introduction to my previous book on the comedies I discussed the background of dramatic theory and theatrical tradition against which Shakespeare's work principally needs to be seen and I shall only briefly recapitulate here.

Shakespeare, it is generally agreed, had a grammar-school education. This would in all probability mean that he studied some of Terence's comedies at school and possibly one or two of Plautus's.[13] Terence's plays were the subjects of detailed commentaries and were referred to as models in a large body of critical and theoretical writings by medieval and Renaissance scholars and humanists. Shakespeare would have acquired some knowledge of the commentaries of Donatus and Willichius and of the structural principles upon which classical comedy was built according to these rhetoricians. He would be familiar with the Horatian five-act formula and with the triple division into *protasis, epitasis* and *catastrophe* introduced by Donatus; perhaps, too, with a four-part system including a *catastasis* (or 'the counterturn which stirs up added difficulties').[14] He would have learnt that a comedy, to be correct, must obey the laws of logic and the proprieties of rhetoric, that it must have a unified 'fable' or plot moving through articulated stages to a desired goal, and that characters must be true to type and consistent throughout in speech and behaviour. Any acquaintance he may have had with Aristotle would have reinforced these doctrines. The double plot which was characteristic of Terentian comedy was seized upon by Italian comic dramatists before Shakespeare and ingeniously developed into multiple actions featuring close interrelations and strong causal connections between the different plot elements.[15] In England Greene and Lyly provided models of comedy showing a high degree of structural tautness.

Greene and Lyly were also influenced by the native tradition of romantic comedy which, as Leo Salingar has emphasised, was still flourishing in England throughout the sixteenth century.[16] This, as we know, was a comedy of a rambling, episodic kind which delighted in improbable adventures and supernatural surprises. Shakespeare would in all probability have witnessed some of these popular plays in his formative years, and though their example is not of paramount importance in the comedies up to and including *Measure for Measure*, with the partial exception of *A Midsummer Night's Dream*, they helped decisively to shape the 'romances' belonging to the final phase of his writing career.

Shakespeare has been credited with a fusion of native and classical dramatic elements which, along with the achievements of Kyd and Marlowe, made possible the great flowering of English drama from the 1590s on.[17] From popular romantic plays he inherited a fascination with love as a serious passion rather than a laughable malady, and a formal freedom which allowed him to develop his plots without too restrictive an economy or undue observance of neoclassical rules. Even so, there is always a firm story-line in his comedies, and a sense of a *telos* which guides his actions to a satisfying conclusion. Northrop Frye, who rejects any 'limiting definition of the essence of comedy' and bluntly declares that 'there has never been such a "thing" as comedy', nevertheless observes that

> In most forms of comedy,... at least the New Comedy with which Shakespeare was mainly concerned, the emphasis is on a teleological plot, usually one with a mystery in it which is disclosed in or near a final recognition scene. The emphasis is not on sequence, but on moving toward a climax in which the end incorporates the beginning.[18]

Frye sees the drive towards a festive conclusion as the distinguishing mark of comedy (differentiating it from tragedy) even though 'the upward turn of the hero's fortunes is often some kind of "gimmick" or concealed device'. In fact 'it is very seldom', he says, 'that a genuinely comic resolution to a play seems the "logical" outcome of the action. There is nearly always something residually perplexing or incredible about it'.[19] I am not very happy about this view of the comic dénouement as applied to Shakespeare's structures, and tend to see any 'gimmickry' involved – if it is 'gimmickry' – as a desperate remedy. But as to the irresistible impetus towards a final resolution, there can be no disagreement, or should be none.[20]

This is a movement which is as necessary to the 'romances' as to the more realistic comedies, though in some of the romances the intervention of supernatural powers to bring about a resolution may seem at first glance decisive. Nor can I discover that Shakespeare in his last plays surrendered his adherence to integrity of story and character portrayal in favour of symbolic action or mere happenings. Even fairy tales have a logic which, of course, comprises the possibility of magic. As in a game of snakes and ladders, the vagaries of fortune do not deflect the player from his settled purpose to overcome the obstacles that are set in his way. In an interesting discussion of *The Winter's Tale*, Carol Gesner shows that though Shakespeare 'recognizes the hand of Fortune' he 'does not make his characters slaves to chance; he employs natural causation frequently where Greene, like Heliodorus, explains an occurrence by a simple attribute to Fortune'.[21] Shakespeare experimented in form and content to the end of his career, and his romances, like his earlier comedies, differ greatly among themselves in the extent to which human enterprise provides the causal connections between the episodes, and the extent to which they are just strung-out in sequence. But there is always, to justify the episodic parts, a logical continuity which becomes apparent when we gather up the elements of the whole play at the end. Or, when the logical pattern is incomplete, we may have good reason to suspect an unintended looseness.

Assuming, then, on good grounds, that Shakespeare usually wished to produce patterns of consistency in the various aspects of his plays and that breaches of consistency are not meaningful in themselves though they can often be justified for other reasons, it will be interesting to see when, where, and why these breaches occur and what justification may be found for them. What I hope to achieve in the first place is a commonsense understanding of many of the puzzling details and features of the plays as being due to unforeseen complications or unplanned changes rather than sophistication. Many of the unconformities have been so understood before, but more can be added and a good deal of pointless speculation about hidden meanings can possibly be saved. Secondly, and what may be more interesting, I think we can approach a closer knowledge of the texts as Shakespeare intended them, especially with regard to passages which were not meant for final inclusion or for inclusion in all performances, or fragments that may have been lost. I shall have some new suggestions to make in an area where little enough can be conclusively decided but where every little clue is valuable. And, thirdly, from our study of unconformities and hypothetical intentions there should emerge a picture of Shakespeare at work, providing, it may reasonably be hoped, an expansion of insight into his methods of composition, his problems of construction and adjustment, and his aesthetic priorities.

The plays I have examined in my previous books belong to different genres and to some extent different periods of Shakespeare's career. But they have a great deal in common as regards the nature and frequency of unconformities. Nor do the later comedies and last plays differ basically from this general pattern. But they form a more heterogeneous group than any of my earlier divisions of the canon, and there is a gap of about four years – when Shakespeare devoted himself to the writing of tragedies – between the appearance of *Measure for Measure*, which temporarily concluded a long series of comedies, and *Pericles*, which inaugurated a new, short series. There is a generally recognised triple distinction between the 'festive comedies' *Much Ado*, *As You Like It* and *Twelfth Night*, the 'problem comedies' *All's Well* and *Measure for Measure*, and the 'romances' *Pericles*, *Cymbeline*, *The Winter's Tale* and *The Tempest*. We will have to take account of this distinction in our assessment of the structural qualities of the plays.

The term 'festive comedies' has been used by C. L. Barber to call attention to the background of popular entertainments which were associated with traditional festivals such as May Day and Twelfth Night, and which helped to give a shape and mood to many of Shakespeare's plays.[22] But Barber and other critics have also used the term in a wider sense to designate the comedies in which a spirit of merriment and cheerfulness is prevalent, and it is in this sense that I am adopting it. Some of these lighthearted plays were included in my book on the early comedies, and those now to be considered – *Much Ado*, *As You Like It* and *Twelfth Night* – may be seen as a continuation and development of the sequence represented by *Love's Labour's Lost*, *A Midsummer Night's Dream* and *The Merchant of Venice*. In *The Merchant* and *Much Ado* there is a darkening of mood which points forward to the problem plays, but even these two comedies are predominantly high-spirited. In *Much Ado*, Claudio is not a very attractive lover and he grows less so. Don John's malice and the repudiation of Hero threaten to turn all to tragedy. But in fact we hardly experience the ruin of happiness too seriously. The proxy wooing and other matter with which the action opens are in a completely comic vein and help to set the tone for what is to come. The jangling of Benedick and Beatrice provides witty amusement all along and even Beatrice's 'Kill Claudio!' is on impact as funny as it is shaking. Before the repudiation scene, which is undeniably harrowing, Dogberry and his crew have already partly allayed our fears, and their broad comedy effectively dispels much of the gloom which might have engulfed the central parts of the play. Moving on to *As You Like It*, we find little to disturb the general gaiety except perhaps a certain feeling of disillusionment underlying some of the discussions of love and society and inspiring Jaques to melancholy utterances. Both in this comedy and in *Twelfth Night* the use of disguise produces sustained hilarity. *Twelfth Night* has a more audible note of melancholy than *As You Like It*, sounded most clearly by Orsino and Feste, and some have felt the humiliation inflicted on Malvolio to be unnecessarily cruel. But there is not much real depth to the characters of the Count or even the jester or much undeserved suffering in the case of Malvolio to cloud the atmosphere, and here again there are characters, Sir Toby and his companions, to provide more boisterous entertainment.

On the whole, characters in the festive comedies, whether good or bad, are uncomplicated. Benedick and Beatrice are interesting, but apart from a few cryptic hints we learn little about their private histories or secret thoughts, or as to why they have assumed their characteristic humours. Hero as a person is quite insipid, Claudio only a little less so. In *As You Like It* the characterisation clearly does not aim beyond the superficial. Only *Twelfth Night* has a certain sophistication, at least in its portrayal of the heroine. In keeping with the psychological two-dimensionality, obstacles to the final happiness towards which the protagonists strive are largely external, again with a certain reservation in the case of Benedick and Beatrice. The machinations of Don John or the enforced disguises of Rosalind and Viola have little to do with internal conflicts.

Love is the theme and marriage the happy ending of the festive comedies. But in the three which rise to the peak of Shakespeare's achievement in comedy a slight change of attitude as compared with earlier comedies may perhaps be discerned. E. C. Pettet sees these three plays as a trilogy and finds in them a 'shift of dramatic gravity away from the love romance'. Thus in *Much Ado* the 'entanglement of Beatrice and Benedick', not the tale of Hero and Claudio, has always been recognised as 'the dramatic heart of the play', and the plot of this entanglement, which is Shakespeare's own invention, 'is one that owes very little to romantic tradition'. In *Twelfth Night* the romantic plot is rivalled for prominence and outdone as entertainment by 'the gulling of Malvolio, Sir Toby's confidence tricks on Sir Andrew, and Sir Andrew's duel with Viola'; and 'there is no courtship between Viola and the Duke or between Olivia and Sebastian, who are all united in a somewhat perfunctory manner'; while *As You Like It* 'contains some of Shakespeare's most withering, though always genial, comment on the central doctrines of romantic love'.[23]

It must be observed that the situation of a lover (Orlando) sighing for a mistress whom he does not recognise or that of a maiden in love and disguise (Viola) sighing for a desired lover who does not recognise her is close enough to traditional conceptions of romantic love. But Pettet probably has a point: the focus on tender passion is blurred in the last of the festive comedies, while the ironic treatment of love, which was noticeable already in some of the comedies of the middle nineties, is correspondingly stressed. And accompanying this change of focus and attitude, there is a growth of realism in the trilogy compared to such playfully patterned comedies as *The Two Gentlemen of Verona*, *The Taming of the Shrew* or *Love's Labour's Lost* and to *A Midsummer Night's Dream* or *The Merchant of Venice* with their magic flowers and deceptive caskets. Beatrice, Rosalind and Viola are down-to-earth heroines always ready to deflate unreal or hollow-sounding amatory protestations.

Realism and fairy-tale jostle in *All's Well that Ends Well*, largely in terms of character, which is realistically portrayed, versus action – the healing of the King and the bed-trick – which derives from folklore and *fabliaux*. There are links with *Twelfth Night*: Parolles, like Malvolio, functions as a butt of contempt and ridicule, and Lavatch has some points of resemblance to Feste. But we are no longer among the festive comedies, and *All's Well* has usually been considered a 'problem play'. This group has been variously defined and delimited since Boas introduced a name for it in 1896.[24] His criterion for inclusion among the 'problem plays' was their treatment of intricate cases of conscience, and he found that four plays in particular met this criterion: *All's Well*, *Measure for Measure*, *Troilus and Cressida* and *Hamlet*. W. W. Lawrence and E. M. W. Tillyard found similar grounds for considering these plays as specially problematic.[25] Lawrence, who also spoke of 'dark comedies' (omitting

Hamlet), found in them a distressing complication of moral issues. He found, too, a failure to suffuse 'formal and traditional plot-elements with naturalness',[26] which points to a technical as well as a moral problem. And, in fact, Tillyard distinguished between the two kinds, maintaining that *All's Well* and *Measure for Measure* qualify for inclusion 'because they *are* problems', whereas *Hamlet* and *Troilus* qualify 'because they deal with and display interesting problems'.[27] Pettet follows up the technical approach. There is a 'cleavage', he says, 'between Shakespeare's mind and art, which is a flaw running through all three of the plays under present review',[28] the three plays being those which critics almost unanimously single out as 'problem comedies': *All's Well, Measure for Measure* and *Troilus and Cressida*.[29]

It is not difficult to agree with the critics and to find these plays problematic both by moral and technical criteria. There are morally unsavoury or dubious characters both in principal parts (Bertram, Angelo, Cressida) and in supporting roles (Parolles, Lucio, Thersites). Between them and such entirely admirable characters as the Countess of Rossillion, Lord Escalus and Hector, there are persons of ambiguous motivation, a category which may be seen to include Helena (in *All's Well*), Isabella, the Duke of Vienna and Troilus. They are made both interesting and puzzling by the fact that the problem plays are in parts fundamentally more probing than the festive comedies in the portrayal of their protagonists and that they introduce in the minds of their characters internal obstacles created by pride, social disparity and religious commitment. In all three plays it may be felt that the pursuit of love is essentially a pursuit of sex. Certainly love as a motivating force is replaced in these plays by lust, most obviously exemplified in the behaviour of Angelo. Additionally there is the need to legitimise social standing, as in the cases of Helena and Mariana. In this last connection the bed-trick of *All's Well* and *Measure for Measure* introduces a moral problem of a very special kind, having to do with historical understanding as well as general moral evaluation. The same may be said of Helena's method of capturing Bertram at first.

The bed-trick solution of the two plays also raises a major problem of dramatic technique in as much as it involves an abandonment in both plays of the serious concern with character and behaviour in favour of pure intrigue. In the case of *Measure for Measure* the switch from emotional intensity to comic relief is also very sudden. In both plays we get frighteningly close to tragedy before the comic reversal, almost as if Shakespeare was contemplating catastrophic conclusions before he changed his mind. It may not be irrelevant to observe that the composition of *Measure for Measure* seems to have been roughly contemporaneous with that of *Othello* and to have shortly preceded *Lear*. It is noteworthy, too, that the third play commonly classified as problematic, *Troilus and Cressida*, is almost indeterminately tragic or comic. I personally consider it as a tragedy and have dealt with it as such in my study of the tragical plays.

Northrop Frye compares the 'problem' comedies (he does not really accept the term) to the later romances and finds that they have in common an action which tends towards disaster until an unexpected reversal brings about a 'deliverance'. He wonders 'whether the typical comic reversal may not transcend the framework of law altogether, as the work of a redeeming or rescuing force opposed to the normal movement of circumstances'. So 'the reversal of action in *Measure for Measure* is not an accident or a stunt, but something deeply involved with Shakespeare's romantic conception of comedy'. And again: 'The purpose of the reversal of action...in *Measure for Measure* is to prevent it from becoming a problem play in the ordinary sense. The reversal forces it solidly and securely into the mould of comic convention.' Frye probably feels, however, that his defence of the trickery which is resorted to in the problem comedies has to overcome strong critical misgivings, for he urges us not to reason about it: 'listen to the story, look at the action, and don't think, at least until you know what you're thinking about'.[30]

A similar rejection of rational assessment is urged by W. W. Lawrence on historical rather than archetypal grounds. Absurdities, he says, were 'usually necessary and fundamental' elements of the narrative tradition which survived in Elizabethan times from the Middle Ages, and reflect habits of thought with which 'the audience in an Elizabethan theatre was thoroughly familiar'.[31] We should therefore, he implicitly argues, endeavour to accept them in the spirit of Shakespeare's contemporaries. As for the sombre aspect of the problem plays, Lawrence largely ascribes it to fashionable influences: 'At just the time when the problem comedies were written, realistic plays of sexual intrigue were occupying the stage, and satirical verse was engaging the attention of poets' ; and Shakespeare 'was deeply affected by what was going on about him'.[32] This sounds a little like finding an intrusive, unauthentic quality in the darkness of the dark comedies, but the sombre aspect of *All's Well* and *Measure for Measure* may also be seen, as Foakes sees it, as an expression of Shakespeare's need to experiment.[33] Foakes accepts both the ominous developments and the surgical solutions in the plays as highly successful dramaturgy in terms of stage performance, and incidentally has little regard for the internal consistency of the text compared to its effectiveness in the theatre.

Everything that may be argued in defence of the abrupt reversals, conflicting moods and disparate modes of the problem comedies must be borne in mind when we come to examine the plays more closely. Some of these arguments will also be relevant to our study of the four romances which represent the last phase of Shakespeare's dramatic output. But, as we shall see, there are serious objections.

It took four years from the completion of *Measure for Measure* before Shakespeare exhausted his inventive genius in tragedy sufficiently to be attracted again to happy endings. Lawrence maintains that he not only wrote the problem comedies under 'the influence of prevailing literary and dramatic fashions' but that 'with the revival of romance under Beaumont and Fletcher, he altered his work once more, while not giving over the gloomy and realistic scenes which had found, and were to some extent still finding, popular favour'.[34] Historical comparisons no doubt help to account in some measure for the genesis of most literary (or dramatic) masterpieces, and the often-noted similarity between such plays as *Cymbeline* and *Philaster* may certainly be taken to suggest, if one wishes, a general indebtedness on Shakespeare's part to Beaumont and Fletcher.[35] Nor can Shakespeare as the leading playwright of a prestigious theatrical company have been indifferent to popular taste. But again Lawrence's explanation is oversimple. Shakespeare helped to form the temper of his audiences as well as observing it, and one cannot read or see his romances, or indeed his plays of any period, without sensing a personal aesthetic motivation for his changes of manner and choices of matter. It will be of some importance to remember this in considering the methodic aspects of his work.

The 'romances' label has, of course, been attached to the last comedies because the old stories in verse and prose which have been traditionally so termed provided much of the material and suggested many of the properties of the plays. Lyly and Greene were inspired by ancient and modern narrative romances, and so was Shakespeare in his early as well as his later comedies. Pettet points to the 'mass of incident' and the 'vigour and excitement of narrative' which is 'characteristically romantic in that it is quite unhampered by any considerations of verisimilitude'. He reminds us of the romance conventions of disguises and mistaken identities, and of 'the quality of movement and of abrupt changes of scene that we find so frequently in the romance tale, as well as in Shakespeare's comedies'.[36]

Comparing the 'romances' to what he calls the romantic and dark comedies, Pettet finds that in the former

> Shakespeare is much more sparing of uneventful, expositionary scenes than he had been in the comedies. Very rare, too, are those static scenes of wit-play and conversation, so frequently found in the comedies; the dialogue is limited, fairly strictly, to the needs of a continuously moving action. Above all, there is much more in the romances of the theatrical and sensational type of scene, much more playing on suspense and surprise.

Pettet is no great admirer of the romances and thinks that 'one important consequence of this emphasis on the surprising and sensational . . . is that the characterisation is thinner, the motivation more deficient, and the emotion more strained and false in the romances than in the comedies'. He finds a 'diminution and transformation of the love-interest' and a 'marked decrease of the comic element', which he obviously regrets. Instead there is a new 'concern with evil, and evil that is, within limits, destructive'. There is also a unique emphasis in the romances on reconciliation, penitence and forgiveness.[37]

This last feature is commented on by most critics. And other distinctive features may be added. F. D. Hoeniger finds that 'what sets the last plays apart from Shakespeare's romantic comedies is primarily their kind of action, or rather actions': there is 'a peculiar kind of double plot' involving parents and children. And besides, 'The action of all the last plays is overshadowed by supernatural forces', which 'have no share in Shakespeare's earlier comedies'.[38]

There is an indication in Hoeniger's statements of a fairly radical break with Shakespeare's earlier practice. A link of some kind between the last plays and the preceding comedies and tragedies by the same poet there must inevitably be. But as to the nature of that link there are various opinions, and some critics emphasise the extent to which the romances represent a new start.

Tillyard sees an organic development of the romances from the tragedies which immediately preceded them.[39] This view is strongly attacked by Pettet, who, in spite of the important distinctions we have noted, traces 'a broad line of continuity' between the comedies and the romances of Shakespeare. Tillyard's contention, he says, 'leads him to make far too much of the themes of reconciliation, repentance (and perhaps regeneration), and it produces considerable distortion, particularly in his excessive reading of symbolism into these plays'.[40] There is no need to dwell on this disagreement or decide the issue in favour of one view or the other. But perhaps we should observe that students of the romances have commonly tended to focus on their relation specifically to the problem comedies, notwithstanding the gap of years between the two groups of plays. Frye mentions a variety of ways in which 'the "problem" comedies anticipate the romances of Shakespeare's final period', for instance 'the very long and elaborate recognition scene ... in which a great number of mysteries of identity are cleared up' and the 'disconcerting mixture' in the action 'of the inevitable and the incredible'. *Measure for Measure*, in particular, he says, anticipates the romances 'in the way that it contains, instead of simply avoiding, a tragic action. What we are seeing is a myth of deliverance.' By climbing to these heights Frye is able to see a continued growth in Shakespeare's achievement both technically and spiritually, and to praise the romances as his 'final articulations of craftsmanship'.[41]

Hoeniger, as I mentioned, indicates that there was a break in Shakespeare's dramatic practice when *Pericles* inaugurated a new type of play. He maintains, in fact, that 'as the first of Shakespeare's Romances, ... *Pericles* represents a completely new experiment in drama on the Elizabethan stage'.[42] The romances are not only tragi-comedies but, according to Hoeniger, tragi-comedies of a special kind, containing, as was partly quoted above, 'the most characteristic structural element of the Romances: the double plot involving parents and children'. Another critic who has insisted on the romances being seen as a genre apart is Barbara Mowat. She thinks that 'to call these plays "expanded tragedy" or "expanded comedy, " ... is to overlook the very careful blending of tragic and comic effects in the plays'. Mowat, too, sees them as a special kind of tragi-comedy, because, in her view, they 'focus on tragedy as it verges on the ludicrously overstated, on comedy as it reaches out to involve the tragically painful'.[43] And not only do they blend tragic and comic effects but also the presentational modes of narrative and drama. The audience is carried along by 'the power of story', helped by the use of chorus, 'expository and commentary monologues' and other narrative devices, and is ushered *'in* and *out* of the illusion of reality' by the open display of the dramatist/narrator's craft. It is sporadically engaged in the action and disengaged from participation. All this eliminates the need for the usual mid-play climax and for a dénouement which brings the action to a full conclusion – in fact, the romances are what Mowat calls 'open form drama'.[44]

Mowat finds it possible to assert that 'untruths and illusions provide the bases for most of the actions in these plays' and that they lack 'the normal Shakespearean curve of expectation–fulfillment '.[45] There may be something to be said for this assertion, and her views in general provide valuable insights into the nature of the romances. But her emphasis on the storyteller's privilege of arbitrary audience manipulation goes too far. Untruths in the romances were not necessarily intended as untruths when they were written down, and though the normal 'curve' of expectation–fulfilment, whatever it is, may be ignored in Shakespeare's last plays, no story which reaches completion as finally as do the romances in spite of what can be said about their open-endedness, can do without some pattern of expectation and fulfilment. We may have to decide that some of the phenomena which Mowat interprets as signs of a new freedom from dramatic conventions are simply lapses or enforced solutions.

Pericles and *Cymbeline* have a particularly rambling structure. In *The Winter's Tale*, as well as in *Pericles*, there is a time-jump which defies ordinary dramatic continuity. *The Tempest* introduces a world of magic and spirits alongside the rationally human. All four plays are set in distant regions or distant times, or both. Happenings are often attributed to Fortune or the gods. But however different they may be in some respects from Shakespeare's earlier comedies (and his tragedies, for that matter), the romances have the same basic need for consistency of characterisation and for a teleological direction of events. They are concerned with the nature and causes of things that happen to certain characters and with the consequences of their actions, though the consequences may be surprising. We must only guard against applying too rigid criteria of consistency or conformity.

Grouped together as the plays which 'remain' after my previous studies of Shakespeare's unconformities, the three great 'festive' comedies, the 'problem' comedies and the romances form a somewhat mixed assemblage, but one that is exciting because of its diversity and which offers opportunities of comparison and developmental exploration not equally presented by the more homogeneous groups of plays.

With regard to quarto/Folio comparisons, however, there are fewer opportunities. In fact, among the plays examined in the present study only *Much Ado* and *Pericles* were printed in quarto before 1623 (in 1600 and 1609 respectively), and *Pericles* was not included in the Folio collection. With only single substantive texts of all but one of these plays to work from, the assessment of unconformities is both simplified and constricted – simplified because a great number of problems due to variant readings do not arise, constricted because in a great number of cases of apparent irregularity the clues that might have been provided by variant readings are non-existent.

It seems likely that a more systematic control was imposed on the safekeeping and copying of play manuscripts owned by the Chamberlain's Men soon after their removal to the Globe. Whereas no fewer than four of Shakespeare's histories and comedies were printed in 1600, after that year the quarto publications, mostly of tragedies, were few and far between. Both Shakespeare and his fellows, we may plausibly guess, would wish to preserve their literary capital for the theatre, where the growing reputation of Burbage and Shakespeare would ensure success; and with the acquisition of Blackfriars in 1608, audiences composed of literate spectators could be more easily catered for collectively than under former conditions.

This does not mean that Shakespeare necessarily opposed any reading of his works by patrons of the arts. The texts of the plays we are to consider here were hardly identical with those eventually heard from the stage and might even be considered fitter, particularly as to length, for private perusal than for communal entertainment. It is generally thought that most of them are fair transcripts by Ralph Crane or other scribes of Shakespeare's 'foul papers',[46] to use the common term for the untailored final or semi-final authorial versions. The transcripts could have been made for licensing, for the preparation of prompt-books, as copy for printing – or for reading by the chosen few. But the dramatic products of Shakespeare's mind and pen, which is to say all that he wrote for the theatre, were necessarily created with a consciousness of their effects in performance, and this consciousness became more and more acute with the accumulation of experience.

Shakespeare's rate of production slowed down after *Hamlet*, and instead of two or three plays on an annual average he wrote only one a year after about 1600. The great tragedies would have taxed his powers and his energies to an unusual degree. It has been suggested that after the exertion of the tragic years he suffered a certain fatigue[47] and that this partly accounts for the relative laxness of form of the final romances, and their abandonment to marvels and surprises. But it seems more likely that – external influences and pressures apart – he wrote in his later years with a greatly increased knowledge of what would work in the theatre. Things that a reader may question need not be questioned by an audience, and improbabilities which disturb a studious mind will often add to the delight of a spectator. A recent production of *The Winter's Tale* in Oslo clearly demonstrated that the abrupt fits and glaring contradictions, the tremendous jumps in space and time, all of which involve major unconformities in the play, may be successfully absorbed in the excitement of a good performance.

Here, however, it is necessary to enter a *caveat* against too much enthusiasm. I am not thinking chiefly of the fact that directors are at liberty to change not only the details but even the whole atmosphere of a play to make it conform to an interpretation of their own. Nor of the fact that actors by their mere physical presence add a dimension of continuous reality even to the most discontinuous action. But of the fact that, if we attend to a performance which has strong persuasive qualities, we tend to be carried away on a tide of suspense and admiration, and there is no time for reflection. We may have an exhilarating, moving, shattering theatrical experience, but it may be a superficial experience compared to what the play potentially offers. We may lose some of the dialogue, or at least its nuances and inflections. We may be caught up in the show and the story so as to be unaware of the profundities which critics rightly or wrongly imagine we discover (or exhort us to discover) even as we watch a performance.

There is still in these days something to be said for reading and pondering Shakespeare's plays if we wish to see them fully. And there is a great deal to be said for recognising the hesitations and veerings which often illuminate the author's concerns more clearly than does a regular unfolding of a dramatic tapestry. Certainly directors and actors as well as 'ordinary' theatregoers can only profit from a close study of Shakespeare's printed words.

The comedies and romances examined in this volume will be

observed with due regard for their peculiar qualities. And I trust they will not appear the worse, or less individually distinct, for a scrutiny of how they cohere or in what ways and for what reasons they defy the expectations they set up. The reasons are not always admirable, but they may be.

2

Against the Bridal Day

The title of *Much Ado About Nothing* is a poor mnemonic by which
to remember this rich comedy. 'Much ado about nothing' may or
may not have a particular reference to the impression produced by
the main plot. The charge of unchastity which is brought against
the heroine and which causes all the 'ado' may perhaps be said to
be 'nothing' in the sense that it is false. But in any other sense it is
of weighty importance. And if, as some critics think, 'nothing' is a
pun on 'noting' (since the two words were apparently homo-
phones) we can only guess at this rather feeble witticism by hind-
sight. In any case the title is more humorous than descriptive. It
may even be said to be deceptive. But then the whole play is a
string of deceptions. And not only do the characters continually
plot to deceive one another, but one is soon made to feel that
Shakespeare may be playing a game of deceptions with his audience, making us believe one moment only to disbelieve the next,
masking and unmasking his characters both literally and figura-
tively, and in the beginning of the play feeding us as well as them
with conflicting and unreliable information. One has to be particularly wary, therefore, in analysing the unconformities of *Much Ado*,
for they may not be accidental as often as they would normally be
in other plays. Shakespeare may have created them by design to
emphasise a basic theme of this comedy.[1]

There is the added complication that the play as we have it is
obviously in an unrevised state, so that one cannot be certain as to
what alterations may or might have appeared in a hypothetical fair
copy or in the prompt-book. It is generally agreed that the text of
Much Ado represented by the 1600 Quarto and without much difference by the Folio version which was printed from it exhibits a
number of the features characteristic of incompletely finished work.
As A. R. Humphreys puts it in his Arden Introduction, 'what Q
reflects is his original invention little revised as to inconsistencies or
to ideas varying as the play evolved' (p. 77). Stage directions are
misleading, insufficient or imprecise, and characters are identified

in directions and speech headings in a sometimes bewildering variety of ways.[2]

Particularly, Shakespeare seems not to have arrived at a final decision with regard to the inclusion or function of certain minor characters. Leonato's family and relations remain somewhat obscure. His wife, Hero's mother, appears in stage directions at the openings of the first two acts. In the former of these she is named Innogen, but she has no further textual existence, and in fact Leonato's facetious reply to Don Pedro's enquiry whether Hero is his daughter – 'Her mother hath many times told me so' (I.i.97) – could plausibly be taken to imply that Innogen is not only absent but perhaps dead. Leonato's brother is most of the time just 'old man' or 'brother' in stage directions and speech headings as if he is merely a *commedia dell'arte* character, and is given a name only in two brief passages of dialogue, once as 'signior Anthonio' (II.i.103) and twice as 'brother Anthony' or 'Anthonie' (V.i.91,100). He is peripherally useful in the plot on only three occasions, in Act 1 when he reports a report of Don Pedro's conversation with Claudio and in Act V when he challenges Claudio to a duel and poses as Hero's father. And he is conspicuously absent from some of the central scenes, particularly the wedding scene.[3] Antonio was perhaps included to provide, with Leonato, a parallel and contrast to the princely half-brothers Pedro and John. But as Humphreys observes (p. 78), 'one would think Leonato's brother qualified for more recognition'. Antonio has a son in I.ii, where the young man is asked to provide music, probably for the dance at Leonato's house, though he is not mentioned on that later occasion. He is perhaps identical with the 'kinsman' who appears in the stage direction for II.i. But this posterity seems to be denied in V.i, when Hero, parading as Antonio's daughter, is given out as Leonato's and Antonio's only heir. The son, incidentally, can hardly be conflated with Balthasar, as some critics suggest, for Balthasar is quite clearly one of Don Pedro's men.

Balthasar is named early on in a stage direction (I.i.87) and may have been intended for a larger part than we see him in, since two speech headings identify him as Margaret's partner in the masked dance of II. i and since he is to provide music for a serenade 'at the Lady Hero's chamber-window' (II.iii.84–7), a scene which seems to have been planned and subsequently cancelled. But there is reason to think that Margaret's unsavoury friend Borachio should have been her partner in the dance scene, which has a very odd initial stage direction.[4] And in fact Balthasar could have been introduced as an afterthought, when a singer was found to be wanted, perhaps in lieu of Antonio's son. He entertains Don Pedro and his companions with the thematically appropriate and charmingly cynical 'Sigh no more, ladies, sigh no more, Men were deceivers ever', and most editors give the dirge for Hero, sung as it may seem by an anonymous Lord in the original texts (V.iii.12–21), to Balthasar. But Balthasar has no concern with the plot.

There is a surprising bit of information at the very beginning of the play regarding an uncle of Claudio who is apparently resident in Messina (though Claudio is a Florentine). This uncle is a person of sufficient importance to receive intelligence from the battle front before the Governor of Messina gets his despatches, and we are told that he broke out into tears 'in great measure' at the news of Claudio's bravery and safety. We may well wonder why, after such an introduction, this uncle never appears in the play and is never referred to again. But there is good reason to believe that his appearance in the first place was an inheritance from Bandello, whose story in *La Prima Parte de le Novelle* was Shakespeare's main source. In Bandello's story Sir Timbreo (Claudio) falls in love with Lionati's daughter Fenicia and determines 'after much inner debate to ask her father for her hand in marriage'. We are then told that

> he sought out a nobleman of Messina with whom he was on the friendliest of terms, and told him his purpose, instructing him in what he wished him to discuss with Messer Lionati. Off went the match-maker, and fulfilled the commission . . . .[5]

Shakespeare turned the friendly nobleman into Claudio's uncle and perhaps intended at first to use him as the go-between. But the Prince may eventually have seemed preferable, and we shall see why (pp. 33, 39).

There are other anomalies with regard to the characters,[6] but these are the most important. It may be further noticed, however, that titles and forms of address are variable, as they tend to be in a number of Shakespeare's comedies. Don Pedro is consistently spoken of by that title and name in the long first scene of Act 1 (with a solitary exception when Leonato, addressing Don John, calls him 'the Prince your brother'), and he is merely Pedro in speech headings till towards the end of II.i. He is frequently addressed at first as 'your Grace' (as well as 'my Lord'), possibly

suggesting ducal rank,[7] though Claudio on one occasion exclaims
'My liege, your Highness...' (I.i.270). But from I.ii.7 on in the dialogue and II.i.307 in speech headings he is the Prince throughout
the rest of the play. It rather looks as if Shakespeare was initially
undecided as to Pedro's precise title and settled for the Prince after
first contenting himself with a Don.[8] There is a similar unexpected
promotion in *The Two Gentlemen of Verona*, where Silvia's untitled
father becomes a Duke, in *Love's Labour's Lost*, where the Duke
becomes the King, and in *The Merchant of Venice*, where Signior
Bassanio becomes Lord Bassanio after his lucky dip in the caskets.[9]

Don John is likewise promoted, though stigmatised as the
Bastard in early stage directions and in speech headings from III.ii
on.[10] He is 'sir Iohn the bastard' in the entry direction for I.iii and is
spoken of as 'counte Iohn' three times in II.i. But he is one of 'the
princes' in the speeches of the Friar at IV.i. 85–202 and of Leonato at
V.i. 262, so he apparently followed his brother's upward rise. As for
Claudio, he is fairly consistently a Count and it may be through
mere inadvertence that he is once addressed by Don Pedro as
'signior Claudio' (I.i.136) and that twice later on he is included
along with Don John among the princes.

There may be only a change of style and no change of conception
behind most of these formal differences and we have to make the
best consistency we can in the play as we find it. But it does look as
if Shakespeare at first thought of sticking closer to the story of
Claudio and Hero as *he* found it in Bandello. In the Italian *novella*,
Fenicia (Hero) has a mother, who helps to revive her from apparent
death, Sir Timbreo (Claudio) has recently been made a Count, and
he employs a friend in Messina as a go-between. We have seen that
this last detail could have suggested Claudio's uncle. As Joan Rees
remarks, 'a near relative for Claudio might well have appeared to
be useful if Shakespeare was thinking initially of developing more
of the source material for the Hero/Claudio story'.[11]

A number of the irregularities mentioned above could also be
consonant with the theory that Dover Wilson put forward: that
behind our version of *Much Ado* there was an older play by
Shakespeare himself, which he revised so as to give a larger place
to the Benedick–Beatrice business, originally a merely subsidiary
plot element.[12] The old play was in verse and the revised matter
in prose, according to Wilson, leaving only about one-quarter of
the resultant text in verse. Undoubtedly some of the verse bits
in the extant play stand out as lacking in Shakespeare's later

sophistication, particularly the rhymed passage in abridged sonnet form spoken by Beatrice after being duped in the arbour (III.i.107–16). On this Dover Wilson comments very scathingly:

> 'Taming my wild heart to thy loving hand'! The Beatrice we *know* is incapable of such a thought even in soliloquy: it is some primitive puppet who speaks.... And – 'No glory lives behind the back of such'! What a line! It is inconceivable for Shakespeare in 1598. Indeed, I find it hard to believe that he can ever have been capable of it. The speech is patently from a drama of the early nineties.... [13]

I see no reason to reject Wilson's theory out of hand. It will explain a good deal, among other things perhaps the seemingly truncated impression of the Borachio–Margaret relationship, which may once have been more fully developed. But it will not account for all anomalies. In fact most of them could have arisen in the process of writing a quite new play. And in this process Shakespeare's main concern, perhaps his overriding concern, must inevitably have been the blending and fusion of the two main plots – where to emphasise and how to effect a satisfactory integration. He had already experimented several times with the mingling of heterogeneous plot elements. The wooing and the bond stories of *The Merchant of Venice* are one kind of example. In *The Taming of the Shrew* he had successfully divided a complex wooing intrigue into a burlesque and a romantic component and forefronted the burlesque action. In *Much Ado* he was faced with a similar but more difficult problem: that of grafting an anti-romantic comedy of courtship on to a near-tragic romantic plot which remains structurally dominant. In both *The Shrew* and *Much Ado* a wedding is at the centre of the action, but in the one case the farcical wedding of the comic couple (though the church 'ceremony' is only reported) makes a fitting watershed; in the other case the broken nuptial of the romantic couple threatens to upset the whole balance of the comedy. It is natural to ask whether the combination of anti-romantic realism represented by the Benedick–Beatrice plot and the romantic melodrama represented by the Claudio–Hero plot really works. E. K. Chambers thought it did not:

> it is the atmosphere of Benedick and Beatrice, not the atmosphere of Claudio and Hero, which is predominant in the play,

and...the incidents of the melodrama are inevitably forced out of their own plane and into the plane of comedy. Now the plane of comedy...is far nearer to real life than is the plane of melo-drama. The triumph of comedy in *Much Ado About Nothing* means therefore that the things which happen between Claudio and Hero have to stand the test of a much closer comparison with the standard of reality than they were designed to bear.... Before Beatrice's fiery-souled espousal of her cousin's cause, the conventions of melodrama crumble and Claudio stands revealed as the worm that he is, and that it should have been the drama-tist's main business to prevent the audience from discovering him to be. The whole of the serious matter of the last act neces-sarily fails to convince.[14]

Critics who undertake a general discussion of *Much Ado* seldom, indeed, fail to raise the question of unity actualised by the two plots, but it is rare to find a concurrence with Chambers's negative judgement. Dover Wilson answered his strictures point by point in his *Shakespeare's Happy Comedies*.[15] Alexander Leggatt, while agree-ing 'that the reality of the subplot in some way "shows up" the melodrama of the main plot', contends that 'In the end, the formal-ity of the Claudio plot brings its own kind of satisfaction.[16] And A. R. Humphreys emphatically declares that 'the notion that two disjunct stories split the play is quite misguided'. He proceeds to a detailed and able demonstration of parallels and contrasts, thematic links and structural connections.[17]

There is no need to discuss this compositorial problem further in the present analysis. Shakespeare found excellent ways of exploit-ing or obviating the unconformities involved in the combination of the heterogeneous plot elements. We will turn instead to his treat-ment of the two main stories considered separately, and it may be said at once that we shall find the Claudio–Hero story most in need of examination.

Much Ado, as has been said, is a play about deceptions or, to use Bertrand Evans's phrase, about 'practices'. A great deal depends upon overhearing, whether accidentally or intentionally: there is certainly much ado about 'noting'. All the practices succeed more or less, or succeed at first, and expectations once aroused are gener-ally fulfilled. Don Pedro succeeds in his proxy wooing of Hero and in the gulling of Benedick and Beatrice, Don John succeeds in his villainous trick to ruin everyone's happiness and the Friar succeeds ultimately, thanks to the fortunate intervention of the Watch, in his ruse to restore that happiness.

An illogicality may appear to lie in the stated aims and the actual results of Don John's and Borachio's practice against the bridal party. One would expect it to be directed against Claudio mainly, if not exclusively, since it is Claudio who has recently exacerbated Don John's congenital bitterness: 'that young start-up hath all the glory of my overthrow. If I can cross him any way, I bless myself every way' (I.iii.62–4). And again: 'I am sick in displeasure to him, and whatsoever comes athwart his affection ranges evenly with mine' (II.ii.5–7). What Borachio proposes, however, and Don John accepts, is to fabricate 'proof enough to misuse the Prince, to vex Claudio, to undo Hero, and kill Leonato' (II.ii.28–9). And in fact what they both achieve is almost to kill both Hero and Leonato, while the Prince and Claudio, after their first outburst of indignation and up to the discovery of the imposture, go scot-free, as far as we can observe.

Don John is Shakespeare's invention. There is not much explanation of his villainous bent, and critics hold different opinions as to whether he has been overcome by Claudio in battle before the play begins or has simply been displaced by him in the Prince's favour; and as to whether or not his bastardy is the original cause of his misanthropy. 'Q' wishes we had been 'given some more particular motive for Don John's scheming than a certain degree of moroseness at having been born a bastard'.[18] But J. D. Huston thinks such speculations irrelevant: 'What in fact really matters about Don John's villainy', he says, 'is that it *is* essentially unmotivated, mere motiveless malignity.'[19]

We are reminded of the villain of a later play, whom Coleridge accused of 'motiveless malignity' and who also dragged a virtuous woman who never hurt him into his manic revenge. But Iago is a self-styled villain of tragedy while John is in a comedy; and there may be some point in the objection that a villain merely devoted to evil fits awkwardly in an action which is marked by a certain degree of comic realism. The only explicit support in the play for John's complete depravity is his admission to Conrade that he knows himself for 'a plain-dealing villain' (l.iii.30). And it still remains strange that Don John's malignity should injure those whom he has no cause to hate rather than those he deeply hates. If we are meant to feel this strangeness as an example of the unpredictable consequences of motiveless malignity, we should perhaps have had more guidance, or Borachio's plan for general destruction should perhaps have been omitted.

It is Borachio who invents and engineers the plot to scandalise Hero, and in his case it is even more difficult than in that of Don John to defend such boundless malevolence as is demonstrated in the early scenes. Borachio's villainy is too all-encompassing to be satisfied with a limited attack on Claudio and far exceeds the service he may be said to owe to his master. Nor is he obviously instigated by love of gain, though he boasts to Conrade of the thousand ducats he has earned of Don John (III.iii.106–7). His repentance after the execution of his plot may be no more incredible than the sudden conversion of Proteus in *The Two Gentlemen of Verona*, or Oliver in *As You Like It*, or Angelo in *Measure for Measure*. But it is Don John , not Borachio, who would be the nearest parallel to these wrongdoers, and John chooses to abscond rather than repent. What chiefly raises questions as to the consistency of Borachio's portrayal is his devotion and loyalty to Margaret – unless, of course, she is held to be as depraved as he is. There is no need to overemphasise these questions, but some critics obscure them unduly, tending to see Borachio in the light of his later rather than his earlier behaviour. Thus John A. Allen admits that 'Borachio is a curious anomaly': 'Although he both conceived and executed the device which temporarily blackened Hero's reputation, he is by no means indifferent to moral values; and, as his generous exoneration of his friend Margaret suggests, he is not without a certain magnanimity.' Allen further finds him 'a thoughtful chap, satirically inclined', who has deceived the 'very eyes' of his dupes 'not because he is a dedicated villain but because, human nature being what it is, villainous deeds are easily accomplished and well paid'.[20] This is in part a paraphrase of Borachio's self-vindication in his conversation with Conrade just before their arrest by the Watch, and it may be comforting and even useful to arrive at this sort of summing-up of his character. But there is no support for it in the first two acts.

Margaret's character and her role in the deception practised against Claudio and the Prince have naturally been much debated. Margaret is certainly both 'fresh' and vivacious enough, if this should make her a fit companion for a villain. She first appears in the masked dance, where it seems possible that her partner should be Borachio, though the stage direction and the speech headings have become confused.[21] She is next mentioned by Borachio as one he can count on to assist him in his wicked charade (II.ii.12–14). She appears briefly with Hero in III.i, though it is Ursula who accompanies Hero into the garden for the fooling of Beatrice.[22] In the scene of the arrest Borachio tells Conrade about Margaret's part in his conspiracy (III.iii. 139–54). Then in the very next scene, on the morning after, we may be surprised to find her good-humouredly teasing Hero about fashions and marriage and exchanging bawdy talk with Beatrice. Borachio includes her as an accomplice in his confession of guilt to the Prince (V.i.232–3) and Leonato, who enters just after the confession, has been briefed by the sexton (V.i.248) and accuses Margaret of complicity in the fatal deception. Though Borachio exonerates her from blame (294–7), Leonato remains decided to question Margaret and we subsequently learn that he has found her 'in some fault' (V.iv.4). Before this last information we find Margaret in a flirtatious sparring-bout with Benedick, as if she is quite unaware of any suspicion of her.

There are thus three slightly different explanations of the waiting-woman's part in the window deception. Leonato at first believes that she 'was pack'd in all this wrong, Hir'd to it by your [i.e. Don Pedro's] brother' (V.i.292–4). Borachio replies, 'No, by my soul she was not, / Nor knew not what she did when she spoke to me' (294–5). And finally Leonato, having examined her, declares that

> Margaret was in some fault for this
> Although against her will, as it appears
> In the true course of all the question.

It is this last verdict that we must accept, but if we can trust the stage directions of the concluding scene, in which it is spoken, Margaret has obviously been forgiven, for she takes part in the final celebrations though she becomes uncharacteristically mute. It remains that Leonato's judgement does not remove all blame from the lady, and we may still wonder whether she is an innocent tool or a woman of conflicting loyalties and principles, basically two Margarets.[23] I think we can only note that the inconsistencies are there.

We are cheated of 'the crucial scene under Hero's chamber-window',[24] and the omission has been as often deplored as defended. There are in fact two events prepared for this famous window, and neither is staged. Before Borachio's spying scheme is broached to Claudio and Don Pedro, the latter asks Balthasar to 'get us some excellent music', since he intends to serenade the bride-to-be on the following night (II.iii.84–7). There is no serenade, and there is only a report by Borachio of the mock lovers' meeting, which he calls a wooing (III.iii.140). Bullough finds it 'truly remarkable that Shakespeare does not present the scene in which the hero sees his "rival" climbing to his betrothed's window; for such a scene is found in all the analogues'.[25] And undoubtedly we are led to expect this scene. Borachio outlines it in advance when he tells Don John that the victims of the conspiracy 'will scarcely believe this without trial', but with their own eyes they will 'see me at her chamber-window', they will 'hear me call Margaret Hero, hear Margaret term me Claudio', 'there shall appear such seeming truth of Hero's disloyalty that jealousy shall be called assurance' (II.ii.40–9). And when Don John persuades his brother and the bridegroom to witness the fatal spectacle he stresses the importance of ocular proof, to use Othello's term:

> Wonder not till further warrant: go but with me tonight, you shall see her chamber-window entered, even the night before her wedding-day.

> If you will follow me, I will show you enough; and when you have seen more, and heard more, proceed accordingly.
>
> (III.ii.100–3, 109–11)

The window scene is such an important part of the intrigue that the ocular proof might have been afforded to the theatre audience as well as to Borachio's pair of gulls. It seems not very likely that Shakespeare thought it hard to stage the scene convincingly, as Parrott suggests.[26] He would have been quite capable of creating a remarkable illusion and as a consequence making the Prince's and Claudio's reaction more credible. It may be (and has been) argued that Margaret has to be kept out of sight in this deed of wickedness since she is to be disculpated later, but her involvement in Borachio's plot is never denied, as we have seen. Another suggestion is that the scene was omitted in order that attention might be focused more on Benedick and Beatrice than on Claudio and Hero. But perhaps the most satisfactory explanation when all is said and done is that of Geoffrey Bullough:

> I cannot believe that if ever there were a scene so dramatic, so central, it would have been omitted even to make room for Beatrice and Benedick to manoeuvre. Shakespeare refused to use

it, I suspect, in order to draw attention to his major theme of hearsay and false report.[27]

Exactly how things are managed by Borachio is not important either. There is no point in asking how he got Hero out of the way or why she does not later produce an alibi, as Lewis Carroll thought she easily could and obviously should have done.[28] Eyebrows have been raised over Borachio's plan that the disguised Margaret should be heard to call him 'Claudio' (II.ii.44), since this would seem to give the game away, especially as the real Claudio would be listening.[29] And even if Claudio was briefed beforehand as to this part of the deception it is hard to see why Borachio should not be identified by his own name.[30] Possibly Robert Graves is right in supposing that 'something has clearly dropped out in the text – perhaps: "She will call me [what she wills, save only] Claudio"', [31] but I prefer to side with the editors who emend 'Claudio' to 'Borachio'. It should be noticed that Borachio instructs Don John in advance to tell the Prince and Claudio that Hero loves him, i.e. Borachio (II.ii.34–5), though John does not follow this instruction. No matter: Claudio believes what he thinks he sees, which is sufficient for the plot.

And so to Claudio, the young nobleman of Florence, who is introduced as a war-hero, turns into a romantic lover, and proves a fool and a cad. He has been vehemently abused, confidently excused and (rarely before but often more recently) eloquently enthused over as a model of honour.[32] What sort of person did Shakespeare wish to depict? And is there an incompatibility between his nobility and his love of Hero on the one hand and his brutal repudiation of her on the other? Is there perhaps just a lack of explicitness and clarity which gives rise to the different interpretations of Claudio's character, without necessarily implying an unconformity in the presentation?

Though Don Pedro has to be introduced to Hero on his arrival in Messina (I.i.95–6) it seems that Claudio met her and liked her before he went to the wars (I.i.276–85), and his conversation with Benedick in the opening scene suggests that he fell in love with Hero at first sight (I.i.150–82). We are shown his desire for the young lady, his jealousy when he thinks he has lost her (II.i.270–9) and his happiness in winning her. This naturally helps to prepare us for the violence of his disappointment when he thinks she is false. And perhaps when Shakespeare let the Friar foretell the consequences of Hero's pretended death, he had it in mind to show us Claudio's grief. On the other hand, it is hard to believe in a deep passion, seeing how dutifully he gives up Hero to Don Pedro after all when he is deceived into thinking that the latter has won her for himself. And it is legitimate to wonder whether he has been mainly interested in her material prospects. His first question to Don Pedro after the latter has been apprised of his interest in Hero is 'Hath Leonato any son, my lord?' We must suppose the answer to be reassuring: 'No child but Hero, she's his only heir' (I.i.274–5). And to comfort him further Leonato welcomes him as a son-in-law with the words 'Count, take of me my daughter, and with her my fortunes' (II.i.284–5). If we come to think of it, it is surprising, too, that, although Claudio is eager to be wedded and bedded as soon as possible – 'Tomorrow, my lord: time goes on crutches till love have all his rites' (II.i.334–5) – he is quite willing to accompany the Prince to Aragon immediately after the wedding (III.ii.1–4).

It is no doubt important to see the marriage as an arranged affair and Hero as being at Leonato's disposal. Antonio expresses the assumption that she will be ruled by her father (II.i.46–7). And since there is to be a negotiated match, if the conventions are to be observed Claudio needs the Prince to arrange the marriage for him. Don Pedro has enough authority to assure Claudio of success even before the undertaking (I.i.307).[33]

Social differences are important in this play as in Bandello's story. Claudio and Benedick, a count and a signior (as we are continually reminded), may appear to be on an equal footing in their badinage and companionship. But their consistent use of 'thous' and 'yous', Claudio saying 'thou' to Benedick, Benedick saying 'you' to Claudio, reveals their sense of rank.[34] There is no explicit debate of Claudio's social superiority to Hero, but it seems implicit in Don Pedro's confident assumption that he will prevail with Hero's father, and it surely underlies Claudio's and Pedro's discussion of Hero's 'worthiness' (I.i.204–12).[35] This social inequality may account for some of the callousness of Claudio's rejection of Hero. And the whole rejection business is as much an expression of social shame as of emotional shock on the part of Claudio and the Prince. The Prince at least has no thought but for his own dignity:

I stand dishonour'd, that have gone about
To link my dear friend to a common stale.
                                        (IV.i.64–5)

It only enhances the theatrical effect to stress the social implications of this scene.

The Friar's prediction concerning Claudio's remorse when he shall hear of Hero's death raises an expectation which actually startles us by not being fulfilled. Only when Claudio learns that Hero was innocent does he grieve, but even then he shows no repentance. 'Yet sinn'd I not / But in mistaking', he complacently declares (V.i.268–9). It may be said that both Don Pedro and Claudio are more to blame for their later coldhearted indifference than for their cruel denunciation of Hero, which after all, to them, has a subjective justification.[36] Nothing is harder to reconcile with any impression of true nobility than their levity in the exchange with Benedick after they have just learned of Hero's death:

> D. *Pedro.* Welcome, signior; you are almost come to part almost a
>   fray.
> *Claud.* We had like to have had our two noses snapped off with
>   two old men without teeth.

> (V.i.113–16)

And nothing could be in worse taste in the circumstances than Claudio's quip to Benedick:

> What, courage, man! What though care killed a cat, thou hast mettle enough in thee to kill care.

> (132–3)

We, the audience, are not to forget that Hero's death is a pretence, and there may suitably be a release of comedy when the stratagem is put to the test (as there is even in *Romeo and Juliet* in a similar situation), but not so as to make the characters who are responsible for the near-tragedy too despicable. Shakespeare never cared much for 'the most exquisite Claudio' (Don John's description at I.iii.47), who was probably rigged out on the Elizabethan stage as a complete fop and was the recognisable target of Borachio's diatribe on that 'deformed thief' fashion in the night-watch scene (III.iii.114–34).[37] Beatrice's scornful description of Claudio must have some basis in Claudio's appearance and character:

> Count Comfect, a sweet gallant surely! O that I were a man for his sake, or that I had any friend would be a man for my sake!

But manhood is melted into curtsies, valour into compliment,
and men are only turned into tongue, and trim ones too: he is
now as valiant as Hercules that only tells a lie and swears it.

(IV.i.315–21)

Shakespeare did not care much, either, to prepare this sweet gallant
for redemption. He grudgingly gave him Hero but no speech in the
conclusion to restore him to a semblance of dignity. So if at first we
thought him a dashing romantic hero, the worse for us and perhaps
the worse for the play, but plot requirements and the decorum of
comedy forced the playwright's hand.

Hero has a shadowy existence at first and hardly speaks in the
first two acts except for a few quick exchanges at the masked ball,
where Harry Berger feels 'a pleasant surprise to hear an unexpected
surge of spirit in her dialogue with the Prince'.[38] In the gulling
scene (III.i) she is uncharacteristically loquacious; and as she
dresses to go to church (III.iv), she shows a 'nervous
irritation...unlike her normal behaviour', perhaps 'quite believ-
able in a bride on her wedding morning, with everyone fussing
about her' (this is Leggatt speaking),[39] but she leaves the wit-
combat with Beatrice to Margaret.

Berger finds Hero 'a much more interesting character than she
has been made out to be'. She is a conventional young woman who
'thinks it wrong to rebel against fathers and husbands' but who is
divided between disapproval and 'grudging admiration' of the
unconventional Beatrice. In the gulling scene,

the game of make-believe is a self-justifying blind, an altruistic
mask, from behind which she can stalk Beatrice with 'honest
slanders' (III.i.84), letting her know what she really thinks of her,
what she really feels, without (for once) being interrupted or put
down.[40]

There may be some truth in this analysis. But one must not indulge
in too much thought-reading, and we may still see Hero as rather
one-dimensional. Benedick's disparagement of her in the opening
scene (150–87) is hardly very serious, being part of his baiting of
Claudio, and in any case it has to do with looks rather than character, but it helps us to take a neutral attitude. Throughout the play
there is not a word of her love for Claudio except for Beatrice's
assertion, confirmed by Claudio, that she whispers words of love in

his ear at their engagement (II.i.296–8). She even tells Margaret on the wedding morning that her 'heart is exceeding heavy' (III.iv.23–4). This may be meant as a premonition of disaster on her part and as a bit of dramatic preparation for our benefit, but it certainly does not express joyful anticipation. As we see and hear her in the third act, she is more concerned with dress than with love, and her only reference to the bridegroom on her wedding morning concerns the gloves he has sent her.[41] Perhaps Borachio's odd digression on fashion [42] was also meant to underscore Hero's concern for it, for Hero's demonstration of vanity follows close on Borachio's little diatribe. David Ormerod has counted the word 'fashion' nineteen times in *Much Ado* and contends 'that fashion, in its guise of Deformed, the vile thief, is the real villain of the play'. Claudio and Hero, he says, are both 'entirely creatures of the eye, not of the mind'.[43] There is a lot to be said for this view. It is all too easy to associate Hero with some of Shakespeare's other romantic heroines and to attribute their qualities to her. There are many similarities between *Romeo and Juliet* and *Much Ado*, but Hero, despite her Count and her interrupted bliss, her kindly Friar and her pretended death, is no Juliet. Nor is she a Viola or a Helena. But as in the case of Claudio, Shakespeare may have relied on the staging to make clear what he did not make unequivocally explicit in the text: the extent to which the principal characters, all but Beatrice, are ruled by worldliness.[44]

We have considered the problematic features of the plot which is hatched and executed by Borachio and Don John and have gone on from there to analyse the characters of the chief persons involved in the plot as instigators, assistants, or victims. We will now turn back to consider the accounts of the wooing which precede the machinations of the villains.

The Prince in the opening scene (288–308) offers to court Hero disguised as Claudio and then speak to her father. Why the disguise should be expedient in itself, as distinct from being necessary in order to prepare for subsequent dramatic developments, is not explained, since there is no indication that Claudio is particularly bashful or tongue-tied, but we are free to assume that it has to do with Don Pedro's love of play-acting. The long first scene is continuous, and it is natural to suppose that the Prince and Claudio, when they discuss the wooing of Hero, are still somewhere before the entrance to Leonato's house where Leonato first received them.[45] If the original stage direction is correct Don John is present to hear the conversation. But it is probably wrong, and nothing is said about other hidden listeners.

Immediately after this tête-à-tête, however, Antonio reports to Leonato a conversation overheard by *his* man in *his* orchard. The prince, he reports,

> discovered to Claudio that he loved my niece your daughter, and meant to acknowledge it this night in a dance; and if he found her accordant, he meant to take the present time by the top and instantly break with you of it. (I.ii.10–14)

Leonato then decides to prepare his daughter for the Prince's proposal, and in the beginning of the next act, before the dance takes place, it appears that Hero has been instructed accordingly (II.i.61–2).

Meanwhile Borachio brings another, slightly less garbled, version of the original conversation to Don John (I.iii.42–60). This time it is said to have taken place in 'a musty room' and to have been overheard by Borachio himself, who for the occasion was 'entertained for a perfumer'. The Prince, according to Borachio's account, 'should woo Hero for himself, and having obtained her, give her to Count Claudio'.

Thus there are three versions of the conversation between the Prince and Claudio: one witnessed by us, one reported at secondhand by Antonio, and one witnessed by Borachio. They differ both as to locality and substance, and the strange thing is that they are all well-attested. *We* obviously must believe what we see and hear at first hand and there is no reason to disbelieve what Borachio says he has himself seen and heard. As for Antonio's story, which seems the least trustworthy, the old man vouches for the reliability of his informant: he is 'a good sharp fellow' (I.ii.16). Attempts have been made both to bring the different stories into agreement and to persuade us that the Prince and Claudio planned the wooing strategy three times over in different places.[46] But the three versions remain obstinately contradictory and, as Humphreys remarks, 'In real life three discussions might be needed, but within the play surely not'. Humphreys goes on to propose the standard explanation, 'that Shakespeare scattered these references without troubling over consistency; an audience will hardly notice'. He may be right in suggesting that if it should notice, 'the variations enhance that prevalence of hearsay and guesswork in which the play abounds'.[47] But as I have pointed out there is no question here of merely unreliable reports: the details of each are specific and deliberately certified. Rather I would suggest that Shakespeare at first was undecided as to which version he would eventually prefer and that in revision he would (or at least would mean to) either align the reported versions with the scene that we witness or else (which is more likely) make the sources of the reports more suspect. The latter solution, preserving contradictory accounts, would be most in harmony with the general tendency of the play to highlight the slipperiness of reported speech.

Antonio's story is that which gives rise to the imbroglio that follows. There can be no doubt that Shakespeare wanted to introduce the idea of Don Pedro wooing for himself and to put that idea into the heads of Leonato, Hero and, not least, of Claudio. Somehow Don John comes to believe this too, though Borachio has told him that Pedro intends to give Hero to Claudio after he has 'obtained her' (I.iii.59–60). 'Sure my brother is amorous on Hero, and hath withdrawn her father to break with him about it', says Don John after the dance (II.i.145–6) and proceeds to impart this information to the disguised Claudio. (It is interesting to notice that the misunderstanding is not created by Don John, as one might have expected, but only exploited by him.) Even Benedick is fooled, as it turns out (II.i.179), though we are not told how. No wonder if we, too, begin to doubt the Prince's honourable intentions. But why should Shakespeare want to lead us and everyone else on this wild-goose chase? The proxy wooing – in planning, rumour, execution and immediate consequences – takes up a lot of space and leads to expectations of a major comic showdown or even a serious flare-up. Bertrand Evans, who is an expert on the use of 'practices' in Shakespeare's plays, comments as follows:

> midway through Act II, everything indicates that the main plot of *Much Ado about Nothing* will grow from the misunderstanding that has occurred. Act I and more than half of Act II have been used to bring about this situation. Every principal person has become involved in an error of which it appears that the inevitable consequence must be conflict between two friends.... It can scarcely be other than startling, therefore, that after another flurry of exploitation, Shakespeare suddenly destroys the error that he has taken nearly two acts to make general;... and momentarily the play, two acts nearly spent, is left without the beginning of a plot.[48]

There were unquestionably possibilities for dramatic exploitation in the rivalry of Don Pedro and Claudio. In *The Two Gentlemen of Verona* Shakespeare had centred his plot on an attempted theft of love by a faithless friend, and in *1 Henry VI* he had shown the King's proxy wooer, Suffolk, gaining the favour of the French Princess Margaret.[49] Greene, too, in *Friar Bacon and Friar Bungay*, had dramatised a similar theme: Lacy is deputed to court another Margaret, 'the lovely maid of Fressingfield', for Prince Edward but wins her for himself. It would not be surprising if it occurred to Shakespeare to develop a similar conflict in *Much Ado*. He chose instead to deflate the whole issue and create an anti-climax. Evans toys with the idea 'that Shakespeare changed his mind while writing the opening acts', but decides against it:

> the best evidence that he did not change his mind, but intended from the outset to drop the Claudio–Don Pedro conflict and to make the slander of Hero his principal matter is, first, the very excessiveness of his initial emphasis on the alacrity of persons to perpetrate practices and to be deceived by others' practices; and, second, the fact that these are precisely the human conditions out of which the slander of Hero rises and is taken for truth.[50]

We may wholeheartedly agree that the double theme of readiness to deceive and readiness to be deceived is introduced very effectively in this prelude to the main plot. Apart from making us sceptical of hearsay, the useful function of the incident from the point of view of audience preparation is fourfold: (1) to show the ease with which Claudio is hoaxed; (2) to show the Prince's fondness for games of deceit; (3) to show Don John beginning his attack on Claudio and Hero; (4) to introduce a pattern of disguises, which will include another impersonation of Claudio, though in the event it is only reported (Borachio's in the window scene with Margaret masquerading as Hero), as well as Hero posing as Antonio's daughter. But we may still feel disappointed with the tameness of the dénouement in this prelude: Claudio giving up his amorous aspiration in eleven dry lines of gnomic blank verse (II.i.160–70), Don Pedro concluding his mission with a perfunctory handing-over of its unprotesting object (278–83),[51] and everyone left unenlightened as to the origin of the misunderstanding.

Shakespeare also cheats us of Don Pedro's actual proposal to

Hero, as if to keep us as well as his characters in the dark as to Pedro's intentions. The Prince was to have impersonated Claudio, but there is nothing to suggest the actual use of this disguise. And the little dialogue between the Prince and Hero, or the part we are allowed to overhear (II.i.79–91) tells us nothing as to how he woos or whom he woos for. 'The episode as a whole never comes properly into focus,' says Leggatt, 'perhaps because the crucial interview between Don Pedro and Hero takes place off-stage.'[52]

Altogether there is much in the wooing plot which remains mysterious, whether it was meant to be so, or because the work as we have it is unfinished. But the prelude, as I have called it, does provide an opening which is entirely comic, and this is important for our continued appreciation of the play. The light-hearted beginning insulates against pity and terror and, together with the broad comedy of the Watch, helps to keep a balance of pleasant anticipation even when the Claudio – Hero plot almost slips into tragedy. Otherwise Benedick and Beatrice become responsible for the main comic action and the sophisticated fun of the play.

Unlike the wooing and wedding plot, the ironical romance of Benedick and Beatrice which is grafted on to it is handled with great forward-moving confidence. There is only one interesting area of obscurity and one case of unfulfilled expectation which probably involves no serious disappointment.

Benedick is a confirmed bachelor whose cynical comments on women and marriage point to a misogynic obsession if not merely a pose. Beatrice is an equally confirmed spinster who values her independence above everything else, or so she thinks. Both are witty and, biased as they are, naturally clash. We sense, however, that there is a strong underlying element of attraction in their quarrel, and this is where the obscurity comes in. There are hints of an earlier love affair, which for some reason has been broken off. Beatrice on three occasions obliquely refers to and speaks of Benedick's behaviour with bitterness:

he wears his faith but as the fashion of his hat, it ever changes with the next block.

(I.i.69–70)

You always end with a jade's trick, I know you of old.

(I.i.133–4)

> D.*Pedro.* Come, lady, come, you have lost the heart of Signior
> Benedick.
> *Beat.* Indeed, my lord, he lent it me awhile, and I gave him use for
> it, a double heart for his single one. Marry, once before he won
> it of me with false dice, therefore your Grace may well say I
> have lost it.
>
> (II.i.259–64)

Benedick never refers to this aborted match, so we have only
Beatrice's scraps of information. But these agree well enough with a
central motif of the play. Sexual faith is at issue. The comedy is lit-
tered with 'horn' jokes and practically opens with innuendos concerning the heroine's legitimacy (I.i.95–106). The bastardy of Don
John is not just a matter of emphasising his villainy but is thematically of some importance. And all the talk of horns and cuckoldry
helps to establish an atmosphere of mistrust. We may safely infer,
therefore, that Beatrice has once been betrayed by Benedick, this
being the 'jade's trick' she throws in his face. But whether Benedick
was then less deeply engaged emotionally than Beatrice ('I gave
him ... a double heart for his single one') or whether it was that
then, as now, he could not 'endure my Lady Tongue' (II.i.257–8),
this we have no means of knowing. Shakespeare may have felt it
sufficient to cast a slur on Benedick without making it too explicit.

The major unfulfilled expectation in the Benedick–Beatrice story
is that of a great scene in which the newly-converted lovers would
confront each other for the first time with all the other characters
present. As Don Pedro whispers to Claudio after the gulling of
Benedick:

> The sport will be when they hold one an opinion of another's
> dotage, and no such matter: that's the scene that I would see,
> which will be merely a dumb-show.
>
> (II.iii.207–10)

We must surely agree with Don Pedro: that is the scene that we
would see. We do get a warming-up for it when Benedick, but not
yet Beatrice, has been brainwashed and she is sent 'against my
will', as she says, to bid him come in to dinner (II.iii.238–54). On a
later day, when Beatrice has also been taken in hand, the Prince and
Claudio are still looking forward to the expected meeting
(III.ii.68–70). But Benedick and Beatrice do not next meet till they

see each other in church at Hero's wedding and do not speak to
each other till all the others have departed and the recent calamity
overshadows their own concerns. John Palmer has well described
what happens:

> There were possibilities of excellent fun with these two professed
> misogamists if Shakespeare had brought them to a mutual con-
> fession of love as an immediate result of the trick played on them
> in the orchard, but he preferred to wait until they could meet
> upon an issue in which their feelings were more deeply engaged.
> He gives us just a sample of the sport he might have had with
> them when Beatrice calls Benedick to dinner, and, in two sym-
> metrical scenes, he shows us Benedick chaffed by his friends and
> Beatrice teased by her cousin for their altered demeanour. But he
> artfully postpones their confrontation until he can use the plot
> against Hero to reveal them as 'human at the red-ripe o' the
> heart'.[53]

The church-scene was probably planned from the start as the
central scene of the drama, and it is allowed to remain so. But the
sensational climax leads continuously into a duologue which is
even more stirring than the repudiation scene in the brilliance of its
wit and the warmth of its humanity, and it may be said that the
conversation between Benedick and Beatrice after the abrupted
wedding, one of the most superb pieces of imaginative psychology
and dramatic wording in all Shakespeare, does ample duty for the
confrontation scene we have expected. But of course this conversation is not witnessed by the other *dramatis personae*. And it looks as
if Shakespeare still felt that he owed it to the Prince and the other
plotters to participate in the amusement of seeing the reformed
lovers engage. He gives us one scene (V.ii) where they once more
converse alone and hover on the point of returning to their old
bickering. Then in the final scene Benedick appears with 'a
February face' (V.iv.41), as if he and Beatrice have not yet discovered one another. The discovery comes at the conclusion of the play,
which is perhaps what answers most exactly to the original intention, except that it is not 'merely a dumb-show' as Don Pedro
expected. In fact part of this scene (V.iv.74–97) has a slightly repeti-
tive look:

Bene. Soft and fair, friar. Which is Beatrice?

Beat. [*Unmasking*] I answer to that name. What is your will?

Bene. Do not you love me?

Beat.   Why, no, no more than reason.

Bene. Why then, your uncle, and the Prince, and Claudio
        Have been deceiv'd – they swore you did.

Beat. Do not you love me?

Bene.   Troth, no, no more than reason.

Beat. Why then, my cousin, Margaret, and Ursula
        Are much deceiv'd, for they did swear you did.

Bene. They swore that you were almost sick for me.

Beat. They swore that you were well-nigh dead for me.

Bene. 'Tis no such matter. Then you do not love me?

Beat. No, truly, but in friendly recompense.

Leon. Come, cousin, I am sure you love the gentleman.

Claud. And I'll be sworn upon't that he loves her,
        For here's a paper written in his hand,
        A halting sonnet of his own pure brain,
        Fashion'd to Beatrice.

Hero.   And here's another.
        Writ in my cousin's hand, stol'n from her pocket,
        Containing her affection unto Benedick.

Bene. A miracle! Here's our own hands against our hearts.
    Come, I will have thee, but by this light I take thee for pity.

Beat. I would not deny you, but by this good day I yield upon
    great persuasion, and partly to save your life, for I was told
    you were in a consumption.

Bene. Peace! I will stop your mouth.

(V.iv.72-97)

This episode would have been more independently effective, and Shakespeare might have worked it out with more comic abandon, if Benedick and Beatrice had not already revealed their feelings to each other in the church-scene. But it fits perfectly into the festive conclusion of the play.

There remains one more oddity to comment on, and it has to do with the time-scheme.[54] The action begins on a Monday and on that day the first part of the plot is completed, taking us through most of Acts I–II; and the marriage of Claudio and Hero is fixed for the following Monday, 'which is hence a just seven-night' (II.i.336–7). The next day sees the gulling of Benedick. There is to be a serenade on the ensuing night, but we do not witness it, and there is now a time-gap till the day before the wedding, Sunday, when Beatrice is tricked, Borachio's plot is hatched and Borachio and Conrade are arrested. On the Monday there is the denunciation of Hero and all that follows from it until the conspiracy is revealed and the ceremony at Hero's supposed tomb is conducted. Finally, the Tuesday sees the two pairs of lovers united.

A great deal happens on the day when Don Pedro and his company arrive in Messina, but there is a leisurely attitude to coming events. Don Pedro will stay 'at the least a month' (I.i.138) and the wedding is to be in a week. Then at the end of III.i, on the eve of the wedding, there is a sudden increase in urgency. There is frequent talk of 'tomorrow', and in the beginning of III.ii Don Pedro intends to depart from Messina immediately after the wedding.

One wonders why Shakespeare should want to leave four days, Wednesday to Saturday, unaccounted for when his usual practice is to concentrate the duration of his stories as much as possible. Claudio as soon as he is betrothed wants to marry next day, and even if time has to be interposed for the gulling of Benedick and Beatrice this could all have been done in a day – as it is, they are gulled in sequent scenes though there are four ghost days in between. On the other hand the wedding-day becomes unreasonably crowded, with Hero supposedly buried only hours after her rejection by Claudio (V.i.69).

When Shakespeare postponed the wedding for a week he must have had something in mind for that period. He may have thought at that point that he would fill the interval with the completion of the Benedick–Beatrice plot, or he may have had other matter, possibly something to do with Borachio and Margaret. When the interval proved unpractical or unnecessary he deftly telescoped the gulling scenes and jumped the days between but omitted to adjust his calendar. A certain impression of carelessness therefore lingers over the time scheme.

This and other carelessness could easily have been repaired, and some of the unconformities of *Much Ado* are such as could have been eliminated by changing a few words here and there: making the credentials of the divergent reports of Don Pedro's confidential conversation with Claudio less definite or bringing forward the wedding date by a few days. It is tempting to see the unrevised state of the copy as the reason for some of the discrepancies. Others were undoubtedly due to modifications of the author's original plans as he went along. Thus Shakespeare at first introduced three characters whom he eventually found no use for: Leonato's wife, Claudio's uncle and Antonio's son. Antonio himself remains something of a cipher. And there are four cases in which expected scenes are not staged or are not staged in expected ways: Don Pedro's wooing of Hero, the serenade which he asks Balthasar to arrange, the confrontation of Benedick and Beatrice after their love-cure, and above all the night-scene at Hero's window. We might add the scene which the Friar leads us to expect, that of Claudio's grief at the news of Hero's death. None of these omissions, however leads to disruption or contradiction in the action, and only the omission of the window-scene may be actually felt as a disappointment.

There remain the inconsistencies in characterisation which we have noticed in the cases of Claudio and Hero, Borachio and Margaret. With regard to the two former the seeming contradictions in behaviour may be due in part to our stock responses: we tend to see the hero of romance as a perfect gentleman and the heroine as a model of sweetness and modesty. But if we see Claudio and Hero from the start as somewhat more affected by worldliness and vanity than our predispositions suggest, we may be able to reconcile the admirable qualities we impute to them with their less admirable manifestations. As for Borachio and Margaret, even if we could fill in the picture of their relationship with guesses about lost matter, we would still probably have to see them as creatures ruled by dramatic convention and convenience rather than by psychological probability. This just has to be accepted. And all characterisation is enlivened at one extreme by the broad humour and at the other by the sophisticated wit which go into the portraits of Dogberry and of Benedick and Beatrice.[55] The two professed adversaries and wit-combatants may be deprived at first of the great avowal scene which everyone expects, but they are given instead a scene of unforgettable poignancy and humour.

3

All Even in Arden?

In *Much Ado About Nothing* some of the unconformities may have been deliberately introduced to suggest the deceitfulness of appearances and of report. In *As You Like It*, it has been maintained, most of the improbabilities are also deliberate and meant to suggest the role of the miraculous and providential in life.[1] Certainly the instant ardours both of the Rosalind–Orlando and the Celia–Oliver pairs, as well as the quick conversions of the wicked brothers, may be seen in the light of miracle. Shakespeare actually makes a point of disarming criticism and disbelief by letting his characters express their wonder at the precipitateness of affection. 'Is it possible,' asks Celia of Rosalind, 'on such a sudden, you should fall into so strong a liking with old Sir Rowland's youngest son?' (I.iii.24–6). And when it is Celia's turn to fall into a liking with Sir Rowland's oldest son, Rosalind pithily remarks to Orlando, 'There was never anything so sudden, but the fight of two rams' (V.ii.28–9). In fact one main theme of the comedy may be summed up in the well-known couplet spoken by Phebe:

> Dead shepherd, now I find thy saw of might,
> 'Who ever lov'd that lov'd not at first sight?'
> (III.v.81–2)

Although Phebe's sudden infatuation with the disguised Rosalind also turns a satiric eye on providential incendiarism we would do well to generalise Oliver's admonition not to 'call the giddiness of it in question' (V.ii.5). As for the moral and religious conversions, these, as we have already touched upon in the case of Borachio, are so much a conventional part of comic solutions that there is no need to challenge their conformity as occurrences *per se*. And while *Much Ado*, in spite of its floutings of likelihood, is anchored in a ground of realism and constantly reminds us of the need for realistic judgement, *As You Like It* floats freely in a makebelieve world. Above all, the dependence of its plot on an impenetrable disguise

46

for the greater part of three acts determines a more fanciful mode of belief than is required by *Much Ado.*

Another peculiarity about *As You Like It* is its delight in discussion. Time, love, nature and society are anatomised in verbal encounters and commented upon in the action. And one main question is never resolved: whether or not life in the 'forest' is preferable to life in the city or life at court. The return to court of the banished Duke and his followers at the end of the play gives only a conventional happy-ending kind of answer, for we cannot forget the Duke's satisfaction at being 'exempt from public haunt' (II.i.1–17), or Corin's content-ment with the shepherd's life (III.ii.11–75) or Celia's willingness to 'waste' her time in Arden (II.iv.92–3), followed by Oliver's decision to 'live and die a shepherd' (V.ii.12). It is remarkable that whereas Thomas Lodge describes the whole of his Forest of Arden as an extremely pleasant region, Shakespeare is obviously in two minds about it. In Lodge's *Rosalynde* Ganimede and Aliena arrive in a pas-toral Arcadia, where they find two shepherds seated in a 'glorious Arbour' 'playing on their pipes many pleasant tunes'.[2] The 'groves and wilde Forrests', too, are both beautiful and friendly, full of 'the melodie of the sweete birdes'. When Saladyne (Shakespeare's Oliver) turns up in Arden, Rosader, we are told, 'tooke his brother *Saladyne* by the hand, and shewed him the pleasures of the Forrest'.[3] In Shakespeare there is also a pastoral idyll (whatever Touchstone may think of it), though it is not so rapturously described as Lodge's. The remainder of Arden, on the other hand, in spite of its running brooks and greenwood trees, is an 'uncouth forest' and a 'desert' in the view of Orlando and a 'wild wood' in that of his second brother (II.vi.6,17; II.vii.110; III.ii.122; V.iv.158), while the inclemency of the 'winter's wind' and the 'rough weather' is stressed both in the Duke's comforting proem at the beginning of Act II and in two of the songs (II.v.40–2, II.vii.174–9). Shakespeare even adds a snake to the fauna of the French forest, where Lodge is content with a lion. The snake seems a gratuitous addition, since it contributes nothing to the heroism of Orlando in saving Oliver from it (IV.iii.107–13), but it is possible to interpret it symbolically, and this may be the reason why Shakespeare wanted it: in its biblical associations the snake is satanic, and chasing if from Oliver's neck is an act of redemption. Thus there is evil in Arden as well as good. It is a place of contradictions, but the contradictions simply reflect a con-scious ambivalence which belongs to the questioning nature of the play.

The basic appeal of *As You Like It* lies in its central comic situation, the mock-serious wooing, and in the exploration of moral–philosophical themes. Since the whole disguise situation is too unrealistic for any very serious treatment of character and the amorous adventures accord to the formula of love-at-first-sight, the lovers are individualised only as far as is required by the plot (her love of teasing, his dim-wittedness), and unlike Benedick and Beatrice, whose emotions are complex, they are mainly interesting for their parts in a complex, half-ironical, enactment of an ideal romance.

The underlying conflict throughout is the one between the usurping and the exiled Duke, and this is reflected in the conflict between the de Boys brothers. The central and most important plot element, however, is the courtship of Rosalind and Orlando, reflected in the Silvius–Phebe and Touchstone–Audrey courtships. The connection between the usurpation and courtship plots is tenuous and throughout practically all the Arden scenes they are determinedly kept apart. There are strong clashes in the beginning of the play, but most of the scenes take place in Arden after a kaleidoscopic turn at the end of II.iii, and it has often been remarked that they are relatively static. In the main part of Act II there is just enough action to establish the princesses in the shepherd life and to bring Orlando and Adam into the forest. Rosalind subsequently retains her disguise, and from a commonsensical point of view one might find an absurdity in the fact that she does not immediately seek out her father and make her presence known to him, which was the purpose of the cousins' flight (I.iii.103). Harold Jenkins has pointed out that the basic fairy-tale story of the youngest of three brothers overthrowing the giant to win the princess suffering under a wicked uncle is mostly over by the end of Act I. Thenceforward the comic situation is provided by a disguise only used after 'the practical need for the disguise is past'.[4] One is not allowed to stop for such irreverent reflections, however. And actually there is a fair amount of conflict in the central scenes, but of a thematic rather than an overtly dramatic kind (true love versus blindness and separation, simple versus refined living). Also, of course, there is a continuous preparation for the grand recognition-scene. A good deal of suspense hangs on the uncertainty as to how long Rosalind will be able to keep up her disguise and what silliness Orlando will be led into. And at the back of our minds there remains the question of how long the exile in the forest will last.

The action becomes fast again in the climax and dénouement. It may, no doubt, be said that the conflict between the two pairs of brothers with which the whole play began is terminated in a very perfunctory way by the convenient conversions of both Oliver and Frederick. Things are not quite so painlessly effected in Lodge's *Rosalynde*, and we might have expected Shakespeare to develop the dramatic conflict somewhat more fully. But we must accept it as a frame for the romantic matter, and there is no denying that the contrived solution of the love problems, in which Rosalind is very much the key figure, is neat and amusing. It makes for a festive conclusion.

So far it may be said that the surprises and contradictions and disjunctions attending the larger movements and themes of the play carry their own justification. But *As You Like It* also has its quota of needless irregularities, mostly minor, it is true, but with certain major implications. It is thought to have been set from a tidy manuscript possibly prepared to serve as printer's copy but, since it did not appear in print till 1623, a few changes may have been introduced from early productions without being completely assimilated into the text. There are also details and general features which point to trial-and-error and perhaps to different stages of revision.

Shakespeare actually began, it appears, by trying out two expository scenes and possibly deciding to scrap the former of them. For the dialogue between Orlando and Oliver which follows the opening conversation between Orlando and Adam largely repeats what the young man has told the old servant and offers all the information we need in order to understand the relationship between the two brothers. This is Orlando's complaint to Oliver:

> My father charged you in his will to give me good education: you have trained me like a peasant, obscuring and hiding from me all gentleman-like qualities. The spirit of my father grows strong in me, and I will no longer endure it. Therefore allow me such exercises as may become a gentleman, or give me the poor allottery my father left me by testament....
>
> (I.i.66–74)

He complains at greater length to Adam but of the same grievances and partly in the same words:

> it was upon this fashion bequeathed me by will but poor a thousand crowns, and ... charged my brother on his blessing to breed

me well...he keeps me rustically at home, or, to speak more
properly, stays me here at home unkept; for call you that keeping
for a gentleman of my birth, that differs not from the stalling of
an ox?... He...mines my gentility with my education.... The
spirit of my father, which I think is within me, begins to mutiny
against this servitude. I will no longer endure it....

(I.i.1–24)

Shakespeare would hardly have meant to retain the verbal repetitions in any case, and in fact the dialogue with Adam is
uneconomical and superfluous as well as undramatic. There is
nothing corresponding to it in Lodge. It would be a reasonable
guess to suppose that Shakespeare first wrote that opening passage
as we have it, then thought it a clumsy expository device to have
Orlando explain things to Adam which the old man must have well
known, and wrote a quarrelling scene with Oliver to replace it. In
so doing he would have discarded Orlando's mention of his second
brother (incidentally making the sudden appearance of that person
in the last act even more unprepared-for than it is in the surviving
text) and left himself free to use the name of Jaques for another
character.[5]

Other irregularities in the first act and the beginning of Act II
seem to be connected with a break in the composition of the play at a
point well on in the wrestling scene. Commentators usually remark
on the anomaly of both the usurping Duke and the banished Duke
seemingly being called Frederick and on the contradictory indications we get concerning the date of the usurpation. There is evidence
of a structural relationship between these inconsistencies.

In the latter part of the wrestling-scene Orlando refers to the
usurping Duke by the name of Frederick (I.ii.223) and the same
person is called Duke Frederick by the second brother in the final
act (V.iv.153). But in the early part of the wrestling-scene
Touchstone tells the story of a certain knight who swore a false oath
by his honour but was not forsworn because he had none. And
there follows this exchange (I give the Folio reading):

Cel. Prethee, who is't that thou means't?
Clo. One that old *Fredericke* your Father loues.
Ros. My Fathers loue is enough to honor him enough; speake
    no more of him, you'l be whipt for taxation one of these daies.

(I.ii.75–9)

It is usually thought that 'old *Fredericke*' refers to Celia's father and that the epithet 'old' is mistaken. If so, the speech heading '*Ros.*' is another mistake and editors frequently emend this to '*Celia*'.[6] But suppose on the contrary that only the speech heading '*Cel.*' in the first line quoted above is wrong, and that Shakespeare, after writing these lines, decided to give the name of Frederick to the younger rather than the elder Duke. It may be too fanciful to guess that the knight whom old Frederick loves is Sir Rowland de Boys, since Sir Rowland is dead and Touchstone uses the present tense. But at least it is suggestive that Rosalind tells us in two places (I.ii.224, I.iii.27) that her father loved Sir Rowland and that this is confirmed by Duke Senior when he welcomes Orlando to his company (II.vii.198–9). And we would sooner associate loving friendship with Rosalind's father than with Celia's. Rosalind's indignation at Touchstone's disrespectful joke is understandable. Celia's would be without a point of reference.

As regards the date of the usurpation, it is made quite clear in Oliver's conversation with Charles the wrestler in the first scene that the banishment of the rightful Duke is recent. It is news to Oliver that the Duke 'is already in the Forest of Arden' (115) and that Rosalind has not been banished with him (110). By the time he wrote the end of the first act, however, Shakespeare had decided on a much longer period of exile, for Celia and Rosalind were only children when the usurpation took place (I.iii.67–72), and in the forest the banished Duke feels that 'old custom' has sweetened his simple life (II.i.2–3).

An apparent unconformity which accompanies this chronological contradiction is the abrupt change in Duke Frederick's attitude to Rosalind. After Charles has reported to Oliver that Rosalind is 'no less beloved of her uncle than his own daughter' (I.i.110–11) there is nothing to indicate other feelings than love till we move into the latter part of the wrestling-scene where Le Beau confides to Orlando that 'the Duke is humorous' (I.ii.256) and informs him that 'of late' he 'Hath ta'en displeasure 'gainst his gentle niece' (267–8). In the next scene Duke Frederick comes storming in to order Rosalind away from his court on pain of death. Shakespeare may have had an idea of introducing the Duke's displeasure at the point in the early part of scene ii where Touchstone has been sent to fetch Celia to her father (55). No reason is given for this message then or later, and when the Duke himself enters he asks pleasantly enough, 'How now daughter and cousin? Are you crept hither to see the wrestling?' (144–5). As it is, the only preparation we have for Frederick's transformation is Le Beau's observation to Orlando just quoted,[7] but this may be another of those sudden emotional upheavals in the play which actually require no explanation. 'On my life,' says Le Beau, 'his malice 'gainst the lady/Will suddenly break forth' (272–3). The suddenness is characteristic.

A detail which may simply have to do with the stature of the boy actors available at various times for the roles of Celia and Rosalind is the information we get concerning the relative heights of the two girls. In answer to Orlando's questions 'Which of the two was daughter of the Duke...?', Le Beau replies that 'the taller is his daughter', i.e. Celia (I.ii.259–62). But at the end of the following scene Rosalind says she will dress as a man when they run away, 'Because that I am more than common tall' (I.iii.111). Both these statements occur after the point in the wrestling-scene where a break in composition may be suspected. But the contradiction does add one more item to the list of irregularities in Act I. Phebe's odd remark about Rosalind/Ganymede later on, 'He is not very tall, yet for his years he's tall' (III.v.118) need not be taken seriously.

The contradictions I have here discussed are probably insignificant in themselves, but it is interesting to see that apart from the statements about the relative heights of Rosalind and Celia the inconsistent elements occur on either side of a transition from verse to prose. Up to near the end of the second scene the play is entirely in prose. Then at I.ii.207 there is an abrupt switch to blank verse when Duke Frederick enquires, 'How dost thou Charles?' and is answered by Le Beau, 'He cannot speak my lord.' The dialogue continues in blank verse to the end of the scene, including speeches by Celia, Rosalind and Orlando as well as Duke Frederick and Le Beau; in fact, from then on until the middle of the play, the scenes are mostly in blank verse. The few exceptions are a short exchange between Celia and Rosalind in I.iii, one between Orlando and Adam in II.vi, and passages where Touchstone and Jaques appear in II.iv and v. The second half of the play, on the other hand, that in which the wooing-game occurs, is chiefly in prose, the main exceptions being scenes featuring Silvius and Phebe, where an artificially heightened style is appropriate.

Dover Wilson characteristically proposed a theory that Shakespeare first wrote *As You Like It* in verse and at a later date revised parts of it in prose, including the opening and middle sections of the wrestling episode.[8] It seems to me that if there was a change in the choice of style in the beginning of the play it was from prose to verse. At least it looks as if Shakespeare began writing the play in prose and when he got to the point of emotional ignition, so to speak, thought that verse would be in keeping with the importance of the occasion and the dignity of the characters and then tended to prefer metre for a long stretch of writing. It is possible, of course, that a certain amount of revision of pages already written was involved, but there is no sound evidence for this theory. On the other hand it seems distinctly possible that a little time intervened between the completion of the beginning of the play in prose and the continuation in verse and that this would help to account for some of the inconsistent details on either side of the divide in the first act, whether because Shakespeare forgot what he first wrote (which is Wilson's suggestion)[9] or because he changed his mind about certain things (which seems a preferable explanation).

There appears to be another break in the composition in the middle of III.ii, the long scene composed of many incidents in which Orlando's love verses are discovered and the principal lovers first meet in the forest. It is marked by interesting changes in the speech-habits of Rosalind and Celia.

It has been noticed by Angus McIntosh that until the middle of III.ii Celia regularly uses the familiar pronoun 'thou' in addressing Rosalind, while Rosalind uses the more formal and somewhat more deferential 'you' in addressing Celia.[10] The exceptions to this practice in fact are very few. In the conversation between Celia and Rosalind at III.ii.160–75 we still find Celia saying 'thou' and Rosalind 'you'. Then from line 176 on the pattern is suddenly reversed: from now on Celia habitually says 'you' to Rosalind and Rosalind 'thou' (with its oblique forms 'thee', 'thy', etc.) to Celia. And this continues to the end of the play, again with only a few exceptions, and barring the last scene of Act IV, where both cousins say 'you'.

As far as I know it has not been noticed that the change in the use of pronouns coincides exactly with a change in the use of expletives and apparently in the referential ambience of the cousins' speeches. Rosalind and Celia are not as pious as Orlando and Adam nor as the banished Duke. In fact the princesses in the beginning speak the same courtly and classical idiom as the characters in Lodge's *Rosalynde*. Cupid, Juno, Jove and Diana are frequently invoked, and Rosalind chooses the name of 'Jove's own page' for her disguise. In the early part of the play the girls even exclaim and swear by the ancient gods (as Lodge's girls do not): 'Cupid have mercy' (Celia, I.ii.1), 'O Jupiter' (Ros., II.iv.1), 'Jove, Jove! (Ros., II.iv.57), 'O most gentle Jupiter' (Ros., III.ii.152). But from the middle of III.ii on the girls speak of God, not the gods (III.ii.202, 205), Rosalind invents 'an old religious uncle' (335–6), and their expletives are monotheistic: 'O Lord, Lord!' (Celia, III.ii.181), 'I thank God' (Ros., III.ii.340), 'God warr'nt us' (Ros., IV.i.73–4), 'God mend me' (Ros., IV.i.178), ''Od's my will' (Ros., IV.iii.17), 'God save you' (Ros., V.ii.17). In one of these places Rosalind actually has what looks like an excuse for innocent profanity: 'By my troth, and in good earnest, and so God mend me, and by all pretty oaths that are not dangerous...'. This last suggests that Shakespeare was anticipating and trying to obviate censorship.

There can be no direct logical connection between the pronominal and the invocational changes, however. The thou/you usage, at any rate, has no religious significance and can have nothing to do with censorship. Its function is to indicate a certain social relationship, as in the case of Benedick and Claudio in *Much Ado*.[11] It is not strange, perhaps, that while at court where her father is the *de facto* ruler, Celia is held to be superior to Rosalind (Celia is the 'Princess' to Le Beau at I.ii.92 and 154, though Orlando not surprisingly addresses Rosalind as 'fair Princess') and that this relationship changes in Arden where Rosalind's father is supreme. But in that case the change in social attitudes should have come earlier than in the middle of III.ii, where it creates a definite incongruence.

It may be relevant to observe that III.ii is also the scene in which the play reverts to prose. This is natural enough as long as Touchstone takes part in the dialogue, since episodes including clowns are commonly in prose, but the prose continues in the dialogue between Rosalind and Celia alone. And even if this bit of dialogue begins a little before the line (176) where the reversal in speech patterns occurs there could quite conceivably be a connection between the latter and the switch from verse to prose. Shakespeare was certainly deliberate about his use of metrical and non-metrical styles in *As You Like It* and even lets Jaques call attention to Orlando's lapse from prose on one occasion: 'Nay then God buy you, and you talk in blank verse!' (IV.i.29–30).[12] The reorientation occasioned by the use of prose in III.ii may well have prompted the other changes.

McIntosh proposes that the thou/you reversals are determined

by the transient moods of the girls, and his explanation is supported with some modifications by Robert Hapgood.[13] Hapgood
also points to a general change in what he calls 'verbal modes',
explaining Celia's switch from 'thou' to 'you' as consistent with the
atmosphere of mockery which pervades the latter part of the play
as compared to the cruel and kind emotions which conflict in the
first half. There may be some truth in this observation, but I am not
convinced by the argument for variable moods. Chiefly the coinci-
dence of different kinds of changes around one point in the play
suggests a break and a new spate of writing on Shakespeare's part.
As it happens, III.ii.176 is just about the middle of the play as well
as near the middle of this long scene. One may actually wonder
whether Shakespeare handed in half his play to his company for a
start and wrote on without having this part of his manuscript at
hand. And if the first half could also have received preliminary censorship there might be an explanation of the Joves and Jupiters in
this part and the Christian invocations in the possibly uncensored
second half of the manuscript.

Shakespeare may also have changed the idiom of the princesses
to accord with the Christian tonality of the play as a whole. Unlike
Lodge, Shakespeare is at pains to create a Christian atmosphere
from the very beginning. Lodge's narrative abounds in allusions to
pagan gods and goddesses and to classical mythology. Only once is
there an invocation of God in the singular, when Saladyne is
imprisoned by King Torismond and begins to feel twinges of conscience:

> And holdes not God a ballaunce in his fist, to reward with favour,
> and revenge with justice?... *Rosaders* wrongs...cries for
> revenge, his youth pleades to God to inflict some penaunce upon
> thee.[14]

The general paganism seems to be a matter of courtly style rather
than philosophical intention and has not much to do with the
serious beliefs and attitudes of Lodge's characters. For at the end of
the story all the couples go to church to be married, though we are
not told how there comes to be a church near the forest retreat.

This is all very different in *As You Like It*. In the opening scene
Orlando and Adam both speak of God (31, 83) and Orlando compares his condition to that of the prodigal son in the biblical parable
(37–9). When Adam offers his savings to Orlando to enable him to

fly the hatred of his brother, he trusts that 'He that doth the ravens feed,/Yea providently caters for the sparrow' will be a comfort to his age (II.iii.43–5). And when Orlando in search of food for his old servant comes upon the banished Duke and his party at their 'banquet' in the forest he first threatens them but then appeals to their Christian charity:

> If ever you have look'd on better days;
> If ever been where bells have knoll'd to church;
>   (II.vii.113–14)

The Duke, who has just chided Jaques for his sinful life (64–5) (unexpectedly, it must be admitted),[15] replies that they have indeed

>   with holy bell been knoll'd to church,
> And sat at good men's feasts, and wip'd our eyes
> Of drops that sacred pity hath engender'd;
>   (121–3)

On his first appearance the Duke spoke of 'the penalty of Adam' and of 'sermons in stones' (II.i.5, 17). He is himself a picture of Christian patience, unless we choose to see him as something more divinely exalted. His wicked brother, who gets his deserts by being slain in battle at the end of Lodge's story, is converted in Shakespeare's play by his 'meeting with an old religious man' (V.iv.159).

It has to be emphasised that all save the two princesses mentally remain in a Christian climate throughout the play. This even applies to Touchstone and Jaques. The latter gives 'heaven' thanks for his abilities (II.v.33) and rails against 'the first-born of Egypt', he advises Touchstone to get 'to church, and have a good priest that can tell [him] what marriage is' (III.iii.75–6) and he goes off at the end to seek the converted Duke Frederick, for 'Out of these convertites,/There is much matter to be heard and learn'd' (V.iv.183–4). Touchstone jokingly declares that he will 'bear no cross' in bearing Celia (II.iv.10), he belabours Corin with his mock admonishments ('Wilt thou rest damned? God help thee, shallow man! God make incision in thee', III.ii.69–70), he has a 'God 'ild you' for Jaques (III.iii.67) and one for Duke Senior (V.iv.54) and he takes leave of the singing pages with a 'God buy you, and God mend your voices' (V.iii.44–5).[16]

Like everything else in the play, sin and damnation are made the subject of ridicule on at least one occasion. Touchstone's bid to prove by false logic that Corin is damned leaves the old shepherd unruffled, however (III.ii.34–49), and the little episode is merely another example of the religious colouring of the comedy.

The Hymen-scene at the end is all the more remarkable in view of this. There are actually three wedding scenes in *As You Like It*. The first is that of Touchstone and Audrey, whose marriage by Sir Oliver Martext is interrupted by Jaques (III.iii), the second is the mock nuptial of Rosalind and Orlando conducted by Celia (IV.i.116–37) and the third the final quartet of unions. The little game devised by Rosalind in Act IV is innocent of any suspicion of profanity. The Martext scene is introduced by Touchstone's learned talk of Jove and 'the gods' and Audrey naively echoes his classical polytheism: 'Do you wish then that the gods had made me poetical?', 'I pray the gods make me honest', etc. (19–20, 29–30, 33, 41). The most surprising thing about this wedding, however, is that it does not take place. When Jaques first appears he is willing to give the bride: 'Proceed, proceed. I'll give her' (65). In his next speech he has turned around:

> And will you, being a man of your breeding, be married under a bush like a beggar? Get you to church, and have a good priest that can tell you what marriage is. This fellow will but join you together as they join wainscot.... (74–8)

There seems to be nothing wrong with Martext's credentials, though his name must have invited ridicule and perhaps topical contempt – unless, of course, a Roman Catholic jibe at the Protestant form of marriage is intended.[17] He is introduced as 'the vicar of the next village' (37), which ought to be good enough, as Audrey stubbornly maintains (V.i.3–4). But Shakespeare may have decided at this point to include the marriage of Touchstone and Audrey in the massed celebration at the end.

In that celebration there is neither church nor priest in spite of Jaques's insistence on decent ceremony. Whether Shakespeare ever intended to have something more like a Christian marriage rite we cannot tell. Lodge, as I pointed out, sent his bridal couples to church. A playwright could not, of course, profane a religious ritual by putting it on the stage. The wedding ceremony in *Ado* is aborted before it really begins. But Shakespeare often leads up to a wedding and leaves the rest to our imagination, as he does in *Romeo and Juliet*. And in the last speech of *As You Like It* we learn, not surprisingly, that the rites are still to be performed. The Duke commands (incidentally contradicting his call for a dance a moment earlier and amusingly repeating Jaques's words in the Martext scene):

> Proceed, proceed. We will begin these rites,
> As we do trust they'll end in true delights.

The author left it at that. The ending of a comedy was not the right place for religious solemnities even if the risk of profanity could be avoided. But there might well have been a priest or friar present.

It has been debated whether Hymen is to be thought of as a real god or an actor in a charade. In the latter case it has been suggested that his part may have been taken by the honeyed singer Lord Amiens, who has an entry in the scene but is strangely mute.[18] Rosalind prepares both her companions and us for supernatural surprises when she speaks of having 'conversed with a magician' since she 'was three year old' and even declares that she is herself a magician (V.ii.60–1, 71). Celia and we know that this is not true, and so will everyone else when Rosalind throws off her disguise. This may not prevent us from taking her at her word, but what really matters is that Rosalind is no Prospero and that supernatural beings paradoxically have no place in this world of wonders. It is more in the established character of Rosalind and in keeping with the general ethos of the play for her to pretend that she was brought up by 'an old religious uncle' than to explain that she has conversed since childhood with a magician.[19]

There can be no god Hymen, therefore, and the Hymen-episode has to be seen even by the audience in the forest as a masque or charade, though it is hard to understand why Rosalind should want one and the heathen spectacle is out of place in proximity with the news of Duke Frederick's conversion by 'an old religious man' (a real one this time, we must suppose, unlike Rosalind's fictitious uncle, and perhaps one who might have officiated at the marriage rites had he been called for).

Even before Jacobean fashions prevailed there was a courtly taste for mythological shows and masques which may have induced the author to include one in *As You Like It*. And we would like to think everything in the play is Shakespeare's. But it seems just as likely that the masque was introduced by an anonymous reviser at a later date, perhaps at a time when divine and quasi-divine apparitions were being brought into the late romances. However they came to be there, the Hymen episode and what leads up to it look superimposed on a wedding-scene differently conceived.[20] The appearance of Hymen may be said to give a festive heightening to the conclusion, but even without Hymen it would have been possible to fulfil Rosalind's promise of making 'all this matter even' (V.iv.18, a phrase which she awkwardly repeats a few lines later and which is echoed by Hymen, line 108). And this is the main business of Act V, where sudden changes and reversals of fortune secure everybody's happiness and prosperity.

This last act, with which may be included the arrival of Oliver at the end of Act IV, brings all the characters of any importance together,[21] combines the usurpation- and wooing-stories and knits up the threads of the plots and subplots. But it has to bear the burden of the sudden conversions which have been commented upon, as well as of the most unpredictable of the love-matches, that of the once villainous Oliver and the admirable Celia.

The actual circumstances of Oliver's conversion are recounted in narrative, and since both a snake and a lion are involved, the scene would obviously have been hard to stage. The lion is in Lodge's *Rosalynde* and one cannot blame Shakespeare for wanting to re-establish the manhood of Orlando, after his sentimental moonings, by having him vanquish this fierce beast which has somehow strayed into Arden. But the 'green and gilded snake', as I have said, is superfluous from the story point-of-view. Doubts may actually be raised as to the authenticity of Oliver's versified narrative as far as Shakespeare's authorship is concerned, and these doubts are strengthened by the mediocre style in places: 'Lo what befell! . . . And mark what object did present itself', 'When that the sleeping man should stir', 'it was his brother, his elder brother' (I.iii.98–120).[22] If authors, like painters, let apprentices put in a few brush-strokes one might suspect some such procedure here, but there is no substantial evidence for another hand.

The report of Duke Frederick's conversion is linked with the arrival of the 'second brother', whose presence in the forest is not only unexpected but seems completely unnecessary, whether or not the mention of this Jaques in the opening scene was meant to be included in the final version of the play. Since a pattern of three brothers is usual in folklore there have been guesses that the second brother was at first lined up for a larger part but, even after his appearance at the wedding party, no notice is taken of him save for his message.[23] Before hearing that message, Oliver estates his father's house 'and all the revenue that was old Sir Rowland's' on his youngest brother (V.ii.10–12), and if we have guessed this final outcome of the quarrel between the two brothers the expectation is now fulfilled.[24] In addition, the Duke apparently abdicates from his dukedom in favour of Orlando, if this is what his somewhat cryptic words addressed to the second brother should be taken to mean:

> Welcome young man.
> Thou offers't fairly to thy brother's wedding;
> To one his lands withheld, and to the other
> A land itself at large, a potent dukedom.
>   (V.iv.165–8)

Seldom can a dukedom have been handed over more casually. But we are in a festive mood and a more formal abdication could have added hints of future care and burdens of responsibility.

What is left for brother Jaques is left untold,[25] but the generosity which pervades the conclusion is reassuring. We like to think that everything can be put right even in our own more trivial lives, and the play is aptly named.

The holiday spirit of *As You Like It* suggests that Shakespeare found the composition of this comedy a far from onerous occupation. It would perhaps be the less surprising if he allowed himself to be distracted at times from his work or if he once or twice put it aside to attend to other business. There is also the possibility that he delivered it in parts for perusal by his colleagues or for preliminary approval before completing the whole play. Or he may simply have decided in the middle of writing that a few minor things should be altered. What is certain is that there are two places where clusters of details occurring before and after a point of transition are inconsistent. In one case a slight emendation (making Frederick consistently the name of the younger Duke) will eliminate the discrepancy, and producers will no doubt see to it that Rosalind is always the taller of the cousins. In no other instances will the discrepancies give rise to confusion, and most of them (I agree for once with the generality of critics), will pass unnoticed when reading or watching the play for pleasure. They are mainly interesting for the light they shed on the author's process of composition. A more serious objection may be raised as to the apparent change of intention which led at first to the aborted marriage of Touchstone and Audrey and above all to the intrusion of Hymen in the recognition scene at the end, where, if four marriages were to be solemnised and a celebrant was wanted, the presence of an ecclesiastic would have been more in harmony with the religious assumptions of the comedy as a whole. However, there, too, Shakespeare's audiences probably got it the way they liked it. And where Shakespeare is concerned, modern audiences usually like what they get.

4

Or, What You Will

Orsino's reflections on the spirit of love in the opening speech of *Twelfth Night* prepare us for a romantic sequel but are teasingly ambiguous. For what is he really saying about love – that it is an all-devouring passion, as capacious as the sea, or a fugitive obsession that wilts 'even in a minute'? Nor do his later speeches contribute much clarity to a general view of love between the sexes, for he contradicts himself first once, and then once again. If he rejects the sea image in the opening speech, he returns to it with positive emphasis in the dramatically ironic and emotionally tense discussion with Viola/Cesario on the nature of love in II.iv. And whereas he speaks of the *in*constancy of love in the opening speech, he insists in the beginning of the later scene on the constancy of all true lovers in the one thing that counts:

> For such as I am, all true lovers are,
> Unstaid and skittish in all motions else,
> Save in the constant image of the creature
> That is belov'd.
>
> (17–20)

No sooner has he said this, however, than he goes back on it:

> For boy, however we do praise ourselves,
> Our fancies are more giddy and unfirm,
> More longing, wavering, sooner lost and worn
> Than women's are.
>
> (33–5)

Having thus praised the superior constancy of women he shortly afterwards denies it indignantly:

> Alas, their love may be call'd appetite,
> No motion of the liver, but the palate,

That suffers surfeit, cloyment, and revolt;
But mine is all as hungry as the sea,
And can digest as much. Make no compare
Between the love a woman can bear me
And that I owe Olivia.

(98–104)

We may be meant to see Orsino as a hopeless waverer, but his words do not necessarily express his complete character or even his deeper feelings as distinct from his moods. Certainly Orsino is not the whole play; in fact his business with the other characters apart from Olivia and Viola is very limited. If we look at the structure of the comedy and the physical proportions of the parts, he actually plays a minor role.

There are two distinct plot strands to invite a preferential choice on our part: that centring on Viola's love of Orsino and that centring on the taking-down of Malvolio. We may go on, if we wish, to distinguish minor sub-plots in Sir Andrew's aspiration to the hand of Olivia and the adventures of Sebastian, but these do not greatly affect the general structure. There is remarkably little connection between the two main plot-strands. Viola and Malvolio have practically nothing to do with each other. But Olivia is important to both, and in fact the wooing of Olivia under various colours, in person or by proxy, by no fewer than four suitors (including Viola but not Sebastian), and the rivalries generated by her attraction, are a central motif on all levels. The Fool, too, is a unifying influence, not only as a general commentator but by the fact that he moves between Olivia's residence and Orsino's and, at one time or another, like Touchstone, meets all the main characters of the comedy. Analysis would show that there is an ingenious arrangement of scenes representing the different conjunctions, and altogether the play is marvellously well-organised. In Parrott's judgement 'it is certainly the most finished of Shakespeare's comedies'.[1]

One of the fascinating things about *Twelfth Night* is that it is open to various interpretations and can be experienced as different kinds of comedy according to the focus we direct on one or other of the characters and the direction of our emphasis on its built-in thematic concerns.[2] You can make of it almost 'what you will'. We may see it as a light, carefree romance, including saturnalian revels, perhaps Shakespeare's most festive invention. In this view all the characters are a little ridiculous, and love itself is a kind of Twelfth Night excess or, to use Olivia's different seasonal term (III.iv.55) 'midsummer madness'. This would essentially be Viola's play and probably the most obvious interpretative choice of readers and directors, since Viola is the only person who has a key to the entanglements of the plot and we, the readers and spectators, the only people (after the Captain disappears) who share her secret. But we may also choose to interpret *Twelfth Night* as high romance, full of poetry and deep feelings. In that case Olivia would be at the centre. A third possibility would be to see it as an ironic, bitter comedy with hints of tragedy. This would be Orsino's play. And if we take it a step further to interpret it as satire we would have the play of the knights and servants primarily. Certainly Malvolio could be put in the centre and often was, it seems, in the early days.[3] Or even Feste.

As for themes, there is a wide choice of priorities: the fantasticality of 'fancy'; chance, time, and fortune; greatness and fortune; appearance and reality; the fool, the wise man, and the madman; to name the probably most important. It might be amusing to pursue the matter of interpretation at greater length rather than discuss the unconformities of *Twelfth Night*. But there is a clear connection. For two of the unconformities we shall consider, Orsino's demotion from duke to count and the irruption of Feste into the play, are not merely of local and technical interest but affect our feelings about the comedy as a whole.

A number of difficulties arise from the fact that the second scene of Act I was apparently left unrevised when changes were made in the continuation of the play. To take the simplest problem first: the rank of Orsino. Orsino is 'a noble Duke' and ruler of Illyria according to the Captain in I.ii, and Viola accepts this information (24–5, 46, 55). He is again called a duke by Valentine in the first line of I.iv. He remains a duke in the stage directions and speech headings of the Folio throughout, i.e. whenever he actually appears. But with the one exception at I.iv.1, he is a count in the dialogue after the sea-coast-scene. Apparently Shakespeare changed his mind about Orsino's title.

There are clear indications even in the later parts of the play that Orsino continues to be regarded as the ruler of Illyria. He has a court, to which Sebastian says he is bound (II.i.41–2), and a fleet of galleys which Antonio has encountered in a sea-fight (III.iii.26, V.i.55). Olivia, who is the daughter of a count and herself a countess (I.ii.36, II.ii.1, V.i.95) is said by Sir Toby to think Orsino above her degree in estate and years, and, as Toby surprisingly suggests, even in 'wit': 'She'll none o' th' Count; she'll not match above her degree, neither in estate, years, nor wit' (I.iii.106–7). In a later scene, it is true, Olivia contradicts the imputation of advanced years: she knows Orsino to be 'of fresh and stainless youth' (I.v.263), and this must modify our general impression of Orsino's age. There are nevertheless hints of his seniority scattered about the play, and they enforce the idea of superiority in rank.[4] Orsino talks like a man of some experience, even if he has not learnt much from life. At V.i.39–42 he more or less summons Olivia to his presence and she actually obeys (99), though admittedly both his and her behaviour in this instance are uncharacteristic. For what it is worth, too, Feste on one occasion tells Orsino, 'Put your grace in your pocket, sir' (V.i.30), where a pun on the honorific usually accorded to a duke may or may not be intended.

On the other hand, in support of the idea of Orsino's being of lesser rank than a ruler, we may notice that Antonio is arrested 'at the *suit* of Count Orsino' (my italics) rather than at his command (III.iv.335–6). And Olivia is on two occasions considered as the wealthier of the two noble Illyrians. For Orsino speaks contemptuously of 'quantity of dirty lands' (meaning Olivia's) as being no temptation for his love (II.iv.82–3); and in the final scene, surely to our astonishment, he accepts her invitation to celebrate his marriage to Viola at Olivia's house and at her 'proper cost' (V.i.417–19).[5]

Some critics hold that Shakespeare made no distinction between dukes and counts,[6] but this is an example of wishful thinking. To avoid seeing Shakespeare as inconsistent one makes him ambiguous. It may be that Elizabethans in general were not particular about the distinction, but to say that Shakespeare was indifferent is to fly in the face of evidence. In *Romeo and Juliet*, *Much Ado*, and *All's Well*, a duke is a duke and a count is a count and it could hardly be otherwise.[7] Robert K. Turner, I think, has the right answer, and the right explanation both of the change of mind on Shakespeare's part and of the discrepancy between stage directions and speech headings on the one hand and the dialogue on the other: 'As the action of *TN* began to develop,' he says, 'it must have become clear to Shakespeare that Orsino would be primarily a lover rather than a ruler.... His role as a youngish man involved in a romantic situation makes Orsino more count than duke... The one [sic] reference to Orsino as a duke in I.ii (251) appears to be simply an authorial lapse.' The author himself was not responsible, however, for the discrepancy between 'count' in the text and 'duke' in the controlling apparatus, says Turner: this 'is much more likely to have arisen from a copyist's normalizing subsequent directions and prefixes after having determined from those in I.i that Orsino was intended to be a duke'.[8] It should also be remembered that there are inconsistencies about ranks and titles in three of Shakespeare's early comedies, too: *The Two Gentlemen of Verona*, *Love's Labour's Lost* and *The Merchant of Venice*.[9] And perhaps we may add *Much Ado*.

If Shakespeare changed his mind to make Orsino 'primarily a lover rather than a ruler' one may feel that this makes him a more likely mate for Olivia and, in the end, for Viola. The eligibility of suitors and the compatibility of lovers is a theme of major importance in this play, and we need only remember Malvolio to be reminded that social equality is assumed to be a condition for marriage. To see Orsino as a count rather than a duke also helps to make the comedy one degree more lighthearted than it might have been in a higher political dimension. Shakespeare inconsistently retained some of the ducal characteristics of Orsino which he had at first envisaged and which he found still useful, but he primarily wished us to accept him as a count, as the dialogue amply testifies. Most modern editors, however, perpetuate the duke.

Another and considerably more important problem arising from the unrevised state of I.ii and in part of II.iv concerns the role of Viola in Orsino's court and the substitution of Feste for Viola as the singer in II.iv.

In the early scene Viola decides to seek service with the 'Duke', pretending to be a eunuch and relying on her ability to sing. It can hardly be doubted that Shakespeare meant at this point to exploit the vocal talent of the boy actor he had in mind for Viola's part. Then in II.iv Orsino asks Viola/Cesario for a song. 'Come,' he pleads, 'but one verse' (7). There is no hint that anyone but Cesario is requested to sing it, but most unexpectedly Curio butts in to inform his master that 'He is not here ... that should sing it' but that he happens to be 'about the house' (8–13). Curio even has to identify the singer to Orsino by name and occupation, although Orsino, we are to suppose, heard him 'last night'. This is the only time Feste is named in the play and called a jester.[10] And the passage of dialogue in which this information is given is exceptionally in prose, wedged into a verse sequence. There is repetition, too, in the request for the song, addressed to Cesario in line 3 ('That old and antic song we heard last night') and to Feste in line 42 ('O, fellow, come, the song we had last night'). This ought to alert us to the possibility of a textual disturbance, as we should by now be aware.[11] Furthermore, Orsino's description of the song which he wishes to hear again in no way answers to the funereal lament which Feste actually sings. 'Come away, come away death' possibly interprets the Count's melancholy mood but it cannot be said to be either 'old and plain' or 'silly sooth', and it certainly does not '[dally] with the innocence of love, / Like the old age' (43–8).

There can be no reasonable doubt, then, that Feste and his art-dirge were substituted for Cesario and the popular ditty he was originally supposed to repeat.[12] Attempts to prove the contrary, such as S. L. Bethell's, are notably weak. Bethell perhaps makes a small point in suggesting that 'if Cesario had sung the song' (sc. 'last night') Orsino 'would hardly refer to it as "That . . . song we heard"',[13] supposing 'we' to mean Orsino and Cesario, but otherwise Bethell's argument that everything is perfectly natural in the scene as we have it simply denies the oddity (1) of the Count's plea being addressed to Cesario, (2) of Curio's interruption, (3) of Feste's presence at Orsino's house, and (4) of the description of Feste's song. We may be almost as enthusiastic as Bethell about the revised scene without refusing to recognise that it is visibly patched and that Feste was put into it without his part being completely integrated with the existing scenario.

Did Feste also partly supplant Fabian? There would at least have been no difficulty in making this substitution, since Fabian is a pretty colourless character. Even his social station is doubtful. The Arden editors point out that 'Sir Toby calls him "Signior" (II.v.1, III.iv.261) and Olivia calls him "sirrah" (V.i.300) . . . He addresses Sir Toby familiarly as "man" (II.v.6), and, speaking to Olivia, he calls him plain "Toby" (V.i.358). Rowe calls Fabian a "servant", Wilson a "gentleman".'[14]

Fabian makes a remarkably late and totally unexpected entry into the play in the letter scene, but from then on he seems to be the constant companion of Sir Toby and Sir Andrew, and their coadjutor. Most critics seem to think that he was a later invention than Feste – that Feste was always in the carousing scene (II.iii) and originally in the baiting scene (II.v) as well, but that he was replaced by Fabian in the latter, either because it was found 'necessary to lighten Feste's part' (Dover Wilson) or to prevent the Fool from upstaging Malvolio.[15] I suggest it was the other way about and that Feste ousted Fabian from the carousing scene. It seems reasonable to suppose that Fabian was at one time introduced with the merry knights in II.iii. He may even have been presented originally as a fool, though this is no necessary assumption. He would have participated in the noisy 'catch' and have been scolded by Malvolio, to whom he bears a grudge, as he reveals later. Maria would have planned that Fabian, and not Feste, should 'make a third' in the baiting of Malvolio, which of course is what he does. But subsequently a lyric, 'O mistress mine', was added to the scene and a Fool with a fine voice to sing it replaced Fabian. This person is praised for his 'excellent breast' (19) as well as his fooling (22–31).

It is interesting to notice that the Fool surprisingly appears just as Sir Toby calls for Maria (14), that Maria turns up only about sixty lines later, and that Toby repeats his demand to her for 'a stoup of wine' (14, 119).[16] This in itself suggests interpolation. A more revealing repetition, however, is the call for a catch both before and after the lyric interlude which interrupts it. 'Now let's have a catch,' cries Sir Toby as soon as the Fool appears, but Sir Andrew begins to praise the newcomer's voice and wants a solo performance: 'Now a song!' (31). Then, after the Fool has complied, Sir Toby returns to his proposal:

> But shall we make the welkin dance indeed? Shall we rouse the night-owl in a catch that will draw three souls out of one weaver? Shall we do that? (58–61)

Beginning with Sir Andrew's praise and ending with Sir Toby's comment after the song, 'To hear by the nose, it is dulcet in contagion' (19–57), there seems to be a clear textual insertion centring on the romantic song. Then at some point after his defiance of Malvolio, the singing Fool disappears from the stage without a marked exit and with an awkward lack of motivation, as if Shakespeare after getting him into the scene failed to get him properly out of it. Maria moots her gulling stratagem in his absence, although, in the version we have, the Fool is to take part in it. The adjustment after the ousting of Fabian is not altogether successful.

In the continuation of the Malvolio intrigue it is Fabian who plans the locking-up of the hapless steward in conspiracy with Sir Toby and Maria (III.iv.134–42). Fabian, however, is not allowed to witness the execution of this plot, while the Fool impersonates Sir Topas and sees to all the fun, instructed by the other two conspirators (IV.ii). It may be remarked that if Toby is available in this scene although fresh from his encounter with Sebastian, Fabian might also have been available if wanted.

Feste and Fabian have few appearances together in the play. They are both present, briefly, in the beginning of IV.i, where Fabian has an entry (24) but has nothing to speak. Feste serves in this episode as Olivia's messenger (sent to fetch 'Cesario'), a duty one might sooner have assigned to Fabian. The latter's one and only conversation with the Fool is in a very short passage at the beginning of V.i. where Feste is now Malvolio's postman, carrying a letter to Olivia which he refuses to show to his companion and about which we naturally become as curious as Fabian. After three remarks Fabian is silent and unnecessary,[17] while Feste is once more made a messenger, this time for Orsino. He is sent to summon Olivia and promises to return for more tips, but in the event he neither fetches nor returns. In what follows there is an extraordinary mix-up of parts. In fact it is probably Fabian who returns with Olivia at V.i.95 as one of the anonymous 'attendants' of the Folio stage direction, and the indications are that he was the original messenger sent to fetch her. Feste only returns much later with the wounded Toby, whom he probably conducts off-stage almost immediately (there is no exit for him in the Folio), and only after everything has been cleared up between the principal lovers does he reappear with the famous letter, which, he now says, should have been delivered 'to-day morning' (284–5).[18] He is not allowed to read it, however; instead Fabian is asked to. And Fabian finally confesses that

> myself and Toby
> Set this device against Malvolio here,
> Upon some stubborn and uncourteous parts
> We had conceiv'd against him.
>
>   (358–61)

Which would be right if it refers to the revenge against Malvolio discussed by Fabian, Toby and Andrew at the beginning of the box-tree scene and to the hatching of the madman plot (III.iv.134–42), but not if it refers to Maria's plans in the carousal scene, for which, in what we may now consider as the revised version, Fabian had no responsibility.[19] On the other hand, Feste remembers Maria's decoy-letter and quotes from it (V.i.369–70), though we have not been given to understand that he has previously seen or heard it.

(Fabian's assertion that Maria wrote the letter 'at sir Toby's great importance' does not either, of course, agree with the facts as we have them but may perhaps be considered as a lie which Fabian makes up in order to shield Maria.)

On the whole, Feste is dispensable as far as the action is concerned, with the possible exception of the Sir Topas scene. This is natural enough if he was introduced into the play subsequently to its completion and its early staging. With regard to two episodes, those containing the lyrical songs, there are clear textual signs of interpolation in the passages where he appears.[20] Both in the former of these scenes and in several others, his practical functions could just as well have been performed by Fabian, whom to some extent he actually duplicates, and the conclusion seems inevitable that some of the Feste episodes were originally Fabian's. One may wonder whether the original version even had a scene showing Fabian plotting with Sir Toby as, at the end, he confesses he did,[21] and whether it was the revision, leaving out Fabian in the conspiracy scene, which made Maria the chief plotter. There is no reason why Shakespeare should want to add Fabian if he already had Feste, but he might have wanted to add Feste even if he initially had Fabian. He may also have decided that the Fool should not be too much involved in the action but stand apart as a commentator, rather like Touchstone and Jaques. I cannot accept the idea that he was once engaged in the letter plot. Molly Mahood thinks the box-tree scene was revised to exclude him: 'The box-tree episode was Malvolio's big scene, and the Fool's popularity with the audience might have detracted from the effect Shakespeare was aiming at here.'[22] If anything, this argument tells in favour of Fabian always having been the spectator in the box-tree. The Fool's popularity, on the other hand, especially if the Fool in *Twelfth Night* was played by Robert Armin, would make it natural to feature him from the start as a special attraction, to let him exercise his wit and singing voice without too much relevance to the other business of the play, and to highlight the qualities of the fool and the merits of fooling. So Shakespeare introduces him as a professional jester, provides him with commendations and repeatedly has other characters remark on the virtues and wisdom of folly.

Thus the professional fool and his credentials are themselves a theme of the comedy. When Feste arrived in *Twelfth Night* he continued a discussion which was begun by Jaques and Duke Senior in *As You Like It* concerning the value of fools. This is what his scene with Olivia and Malvolio is about (I.v.30–98), after he has been scolded by Maria for truancy.[23] In II.iii, Sir Andrew commends him both for his sweet breath and his fooling (19–25). In III.i, Feste's conversation with Viola (19–25) is patently redundant from a dramatic point of view. (Viola asks 'Is thy lady within?' as an excuse for the dialogue, but she is then met by Toby and Andrew, who answer her question by inviting her to enter.) Feste, however, gets a chance to deploy some of the stock-in-trade of the professional clown (he lives by the church because his house stands by the church, etc.), to exhibit his characteristic appetite for 'gratillities', and to justify his presence at Orsino's palace. And Viola at his departure praises his wit in terms which, as Wilson remarks, read 'like an official diploma'.[24] In V.i even the morose Orsino is taken with his wit; 'Why, this is excellent'(23).

However interesting and entertaining these passages may be, and some of them are more interesting than really amusing, they are of no intrinsic importance to the progress of the play. But Feste is important in other ways.

The personality of Feste and his effect on the comedy as a whole have been much discussed. He should possibly be seen as an unhappy person, as many critics seem to feel. I am not sure there is a great deal to build on for a portrait in depth,[25] but his effect on our experience of the comedy can hardly be overestimated. It is not mainly that he contributes vocal and verbal entertainment – his songs fit the moods of the moment and may sound exquisite when sung, but his patter is not outstandingly funny. What he chiefly performs is to mediate between the audience and the protagonists and to allow us to enter sympathetically into the emotions of the characters without relinquishing our consciousness of absurdity. His songs, which stress the shortness and cruelty of love, are a sentimentally ironic comment on the romantic love theme itself, and his unabashed glibness of repartee helps to dramatise the quandaries of the lovers by opposing their seriousness. He evokes a wry sense of pity which mingles with and enriches the comic happiness at the end, and he himself, rebuffed by his mistress both at the first and at the last, tempts us to laugh with a catch in our throats. There could have been a *Twelfth Night* without him, but it would not be the same, and the revision which brought in Armin and Feste was no doubt amply worth the unconformities it caused.

What emerges from all this is that when Shakespeare first wrote the play he had a boy with a good singing voice in the company and wrote Viola's part for him. The boy actor probably sang the 'old and antic song' which Orsino calls for, but which was later exchanged for a more fashionable courtly air. Whether his voice broke, as some have speculated, or whether he became unavailable, or whether Robert Armin was simply preferred in the singing role, this we do not know. But what seems certain is that Armin was brought into the cast after the play was first finished, that the role of Feste was created for Armin and that he took over some of the functions both of Viola and Fabian. The romantic songs in the second act are obvious additions (signalled by characteristic repetitions) and so perhaps are the doggerel rhyme at the end of the madman scene (IV.ii.125–32) and the song at the conclusion of the play, 'When that I was and a little tiny boy'. The Topas scene may have been rewritten for the Fool. And Fabian may have been turned into a more ordinary fellow than he would have been without a Feste in the play.

While still on the subject of revision it may be convenient to raise a minor point having to do with the avoidance of profanity. There are a few speeches in the play where Jove is invoked rather than God or the Lord. On the other hand, there are much more frequent appeals to the Christian deity or to Heaven. It could be supposed that the pagan invocations preserve remnants of revision in compliance with the statute of 1606 against profanity, but the number of times we find 'For the love o' God' and 'God comfort thee' and similar phrases seems to make at least systematic elimination of profanity unlikely. It should be noticed that out of the eight Joves in the text six are spoken by Malvolio and one by the Fool, who just as readily appeals to Mercury. The eighth is Sir Toby's 'Jove bless thee, Master Parson', which is meant for the ears of Malvolio. Unlike some of the other characters, Malvolio has no invocations of God, and conceivably the devotion of this strait Puritan to Jove may have been meant for a laugh.[26] But his fervent exclamations – 'Jove, I thank thee, I will smile' (II.v.178), 'but it is Jove's doing, and Jove make me thankful' (III.iv.75), etc. – strike the present writer as more incongruous than funny. The evidence would suggest that Malvolio's part was the only one to be purged of profanity, whether or not it was subjected separately to censorship. We have already seen that partial censorship may have been exercised in *As You Like It*.

It remains to take a brief look at Act V, in which the difficulties of bringing everything to a satisfactory conclusion in a play as full of independent characters and as rich in imbroglios as *Twelfth Night* are fully demonstrated. There is little, it is true, to disturb our general impression of a play cleverly organised from first to last with a great deal of movement on different levels meshed with moments of meditation and poetry, all concentrated in an easily verifiable time-scheme of merely two days (not counting the hypo-thetical time-gap before Viola puts in an appearance at Orsino's court).[27] But there is no reason why we should not recognise certain imperfections. There is one glaring inconsistency even with regard to the time-scheme, for Orsino declares (97) that Cesario has tended on him for the same length of time that the supposedly same youth has kept company with Antonio according to the latter (92–4), namely three months. If this represents an intentional use of double time on Shakespeare's part, in order to create the impression that we have witnessed a much more protracted martyrdom of love than the rapid events which we actually observe, we have an exceedingly daring use of this time-device. But, taken together with other anomalies in the last act, the contradiction would seem to be just one more sign, in a dénouement crowded with endings, of incomplete attention to premises contained in the play.

One thing is almost too improbable even for willing suspension of disbelief. Like *As You Like It*, *Twelfth Night* is based on a disguise we simply have to accept, and in this case it includes the assump-tion that brother and sister are identical twins.[28] This being admit-ted, it is natural that Viola's 'imagination', as she calls it, should suggest to her at III.iv.384–5 that Antonio has mistaken her for her brother, who must consequently be alive. But her complete forget-fulness of this perception when Antonio is haled before Orsino in V.i ('He... put strange speech upon me,/I know not what 'twas, but distraction'), followed by her slowness in believing Sebastian to be more than a spirit when he finally turns up (230–4), makes us query Shakespeare's own memory of what he had written.[29] We may be tempted to do so again when Sir Andrew and Sir Toby, newly battered and bleeding, irrupt into the stormy *quid pro quo* of the Count and the Countess. They greatly add to the hilarity of the scene as they suddenly confront the supposed author of their injuries and Olivia demands to know what has happened. But it seems quite unlikely that they should have thought Sebastian a coward and engaged with him a second time having once had experience of his swordplay. And on that first occasion serious casualties were prevented by Olivia's timely appearance. There is a palpable unconformity, but whether brought about by revision or adaptation, as Dover Wilson thought,[30] or caused by lack of revision, as I personally incline to believe, can hardly be decided.

We may feel unprepared for Orsino's jealousy bursting out (115–29) even before he learns that Cesario has apparently married Olivia. His discovery that Olivia is in love with his page (123) has to be made plausible by the acting since it does not depend on the text. I have mentioned the strangeness of Orsino's agreeing to be wedded at Olivia's house and at her expense, and in fact the passage in which this offer is made and accepted (315–25) is in such poor verse that one may suspect it of being non-Shakespearian. I have also mentioned the discrepancy between Fabian's confession and the facts of the Malvolio case as we know them, as well as the Fool's erratic comings and goings in the last act. There are further loose ends and improbabilities connected with the secondary and minor characters. Maria is conspicuously absent from Act V, which is particularly odd if she is Olivia's 'gentlewoman'.[31] The information provided in a single line by Fabian that she has married Sir Toby (363) perhaps brings these unlikely lovers into a final haven, but one could wish for something more than Fabian's casual report to mark their union.[32] Nor is it possible to see when there could have been the slightest interval for such a marriage. Antonio is left dangling. There is no care to have him freed from arrest either in stage directions or dialogue, though one has to assume that he is released in dumb show.[33] His last speech occurs 165 lines from the end of the act and he is not remembered again. As for the Captain who brought Viola ashore and was to present her to Orsino, he is entirely ignored throughout most of the play, although he is Viola's only potential confidant. Mahood observes that 'Viola's remarks about the Captain's reliable appearance are so pointed that we expect him to have a fairly influential part in the plot'.[34] Only when she wants her woman's clothes at the end is she suddenly put in mind of him and tells Sebastian: 'I'll bring you to a captain in this town,/Where lie my maiden weeds' (252–3). No one would suspect from these lines that the captain is in jail, but such is the weak excuse which Shakespeare shortly afterwards invents to account for his non-appearance. Viola is now able to state that

> The captain that did bring me first on shore
> Hath my maid's garments; he upon some action
> Is now in durance, at Malvolio's suit,
>
> (271–4)

The 'action' is not disclosed; we are only assured in the Count's final speech that Malvolio will be questioned.

The last act has accumulated too many concerns to achieve fulfilment in every particular. Even Malvolio's history is left open-ended. Sir Toby and Sir Andrew are dismissed in disgrace 180 lines from the curtain, with Sir Toby repudiating his recent drinking companion.[35] But the main action is decisively terminated, and the great recognition scene, however improbable to a sober eye, is excellent theatre. Jack has Jill and Jill has Jack and the villain is turned out in the cold, at least for the present, while the Fool finds consolation in song. We can make of it what we will. R. A. Levin thinks 'the end includes a movement towards exclusion as well as towards inclusion'. In his final view, 'only Feste inspires awe. For the rest there is only sorrow.'[36] But *Twelfth Night* is usually staged as something basically festive, and this, too is probably how most readers will experience it. If we feel the merriment to be laced with a certain sadness and even bitterness, it is not so much due to the unkind fates of some of the characters, as to the melancholy reflections of the principal lover and above all to the songs of the Fool. Feste is a disturbing presence in this play in more than one sense.

5

Dark Doings in Tuscany

After quoting Coleridge's praise of the heroine as Shakespeare's 'loveliest creation', Bertrand Evans concludes his analysis of *All's Well that Ends Well* by graphically presenting his own version of Helena: Bertram, he says, 'has been scratched deep by the longest and stealthiest nails in Shakespeare'.[1] This opposition of superlatives will point the way to the most worrying problem in *All's Well*: is Helena a lovely and loving woman capable of the greatest self-sacrifice, with healing powers for physical and moral ailments, or a secretive and calculating husband-hunter who cares nothing for the means by which she attains her personal ends? And is there a compositional fault in the difficulty of deciding?

Evans holds that Helena systematically deceives the other characters, as well as us, the onlookers to the play. From point to point, as the action unfolds, she pretends and lies and preserves silence concerning her intentions and strategies. Only gradually and belatedly are we initiated into her real designs. Shakespeare certainly has something to gain from this deviousness: he saves his heroine from the worst constructions we could put on her behaviour. As Evans expresses it, 'Helena's motives and means are such that it is expedient to leave them obscure until the goal is won; in retrospect they will not look so bad.'[2] But she still does not emerge in the end as a particularly attractive character.

Perhaps her most admirable quality is her singlemindedness. From the first Helena is set upon one thing, the winning of Bertram. At the end of the opening scene we find her determined to follow him to court and deploy her resources to capture him: 'my project may deceive me,/ But my intents are fix'd, and will not leave me' (I.i.224–5). The King's illness and her ability to cure him will be her excuse for going. When questioned by the Countess she confesses her love of Bertram but affirms that she has no hope of satisfying her passion:

> O then, give pity
> To her whose state is such that cannot choose
> But lend and give where she is sure to lose;
> That seeks not to find that her search implies,
> But riddle-like lives sweetly where she dies!
> (I.iii. 208–12)

Questioned more closely as to her reason for wanting to go to Paris, she first swears 'by grace itself' that it is in order to offer her miraculous medicine and curative powers to the King; then, however, she has to admit that

> My lord your son made me to think of this;
> Else Paris and the medicine and the king
> Had from the conversation of my thoughts
> Haply been absent then.
> (I.iii.227-30)

This is less than completely honest, though the shrewd Countess sees through her evasions.

Married to Bertram by the King's command and against the young Count's will, and sent packing back to Rossillion, Helena shortly afterwards departs for the very place where the French lords have informed her that her truant husband is soldiering (III.ii.51). This time she pretends that she is going on a pilgrimage to Saint Jaques le Grand, whose shrine, as we are perhaps meant to be aware at this point, is at Compostella in Spain. But it is presently made clear that the shrine in question must be on the road beyond Florence, since pilgrims to Saint Jaques customarily lodge at the Widow's house in that city (III.v.35–6).[3] Actually the geographical location of the shrine is of little importance, and if Shakespeare was making a blunder it is no worse than giving Bohemia a sea-coast. In William Painter's *Palace of Pleasure*, which was probably Shakespeare's direct source for the story of Bertram and Helena, originally told by Boccaccio, Helena tells no one where she is going, but simply declares that she has

> determined to spende the rest of her time in Pilgrimages and
> devotion, for preservation of her Soule, prayinge theim...that
> they would let the Counte understande, that shee had forsaken

his house, and was removed farre from thence: with purpose never to returne to Rossiglione againe.

But she has secretly made up her mind to 'recover her husband', and setting out with a maid and a kinsman and well-furnished with silver and jewels, as Painter has it, she 'never rested till shee came to Florence'.[4] There she herself seeks out the mother and daughter whom in Shakespeare she meets fortuitously. It is hard not to believe that in Shakespeare's play, as in the source story, the true and original purpose of her journey is to recapture Bertram.

Helena also wants badly to get into bed with Bertram, while he is determined not to 'bed' her (II.iii.265–6, 269). She is quite clearly a very sensual woman. Her bawdy conversation with Parolles in I.i which has raised so many eyebrows reveals its motive in the question how a woman may lose her virginity 'to her own liking' (147), and in her regret 'that wishing well had not a body in't / Which might be felt' (176–7). If Lavatch's desires may be taken to reflect in a clownish mirror those of his betters, his wish to be married to Isbel because his 'poor body...requires it' and he is 'driven on by the flesh' (I.iii.26–7) tells us something about Helena. And the Countess's reflections on youthful love, spoken in soliloquy, emphasise the importunities of the blood:

> Even so it was with me when I was young;
> If ever we are nature's, these are ours; this thorn
> Doth to our rose of youth rightly belong;
> Our blood to us, this to our blood is born:
>   (I.iii.123–6)

No wonder that Helena's disappointment at parting with Bertram without the physical consummation of marriage battles with her modesty for expression, and are we not free to think she wants more than a kiss?

> *Hel.* I am not worthy of the wealth I owe,
>   Nor dare I say 'tis mine – and yet it is;
>   But, like a timorous thief, most fain would steal
>   What law doth vouch mine own.
> *Ber.*   What would you have?
> *Hel.* Something, and scarce so much; nothing indeed.
>   I would not tell you what I would, my lord.

Faith, yes:
Strangers and foes do sunder and not kiss.
(II.v.79–86)

The consummation of the marriage, of course, becomes the main focus of the subsequent intrigue. And in all of this there is a frank recognition of the importance of physical and sensual love, which goes some way towards justifying the lack of romantic sentiments in the play, particularly in its dénouement.

However, the scheming for possession and satisfaction is not the whole story, by any means. Helena's docility and modesty are stressed almost as much as her determination and stealth. If her conversation with Parolles seems unchaste we must remember that Desdemona, too, banters indecently, as we may think, with Iago. But, above all, Helena's soliloquy after having read Bertram's letter of rejection in III.ii is confusing if we have thought of her as a mankiller on the warpath. In probably the most moving speech of the play, she here reproaches herself for driving Bertram 'from the sportive court' where he was 'shot at with fair eyes' and for forcing him to expose himself to the shot of 'smoky muskets' rather than return to home and safety. She resolves to absent herself and seek 'all the miseries which nature owes' so that he may be recalled from exile. There is no hint in this soliloquy of any selfish purpose for going away. And in her farewell letter to the Countess, Helena declares that she is prepared to die to release Bertram from bondage and peril:

He is too good and fair for death and me;
Whom I myself embrace to set him free.
(III.iv.16–17)

That the Countess apparently does not think her capable of so much self-sacrifice (III.iv.36–8) merely reassures us that the outcome will not be tragic. And we may for the moment suppose that Saint Jaques is in the opposite direction from Florence and that Helena means what she says about leaving the road clear for Bertram's return.

While Helena's healing of the King is patently part of a plan with an ulterior aim, her meeting with the Widow and Diana as it occurs in Shakespeare's play seems purely accidental, and the bed-trick may consequently be understood as an improvisation prompted by the possibility of using Bertram's unfaithfulness for a legitimate purpose. Of course, Shakespeare must have had his eye on the bed-trick all along, since it is the mainstay of his borrowed story, but that does not necessarily imply that he attributed its early planning to Helena. We may suppose her innocent of premeditated deceit in so far as this trick is concerned.

Nevertheless, there she is in Florence. And if this means that since leaving Rossillion she has been plotting the recapture of Bertram, she was fooling herself as well as us in the highminded soliloquy in III.ii. Shakespeare not only fails to warn us but, as it seems, deliberately misleads us. One may wonder what he is up to. Was he undecided about Helena's true character and trying to cover up his non-commitment by making her behaviour appear ambiguous? Or was he trying to get it both ways by making Helena herself ambiguous, modest and yielding yet predatory and obstinate? Or did he wish to suggest that contrary impulses struggled within her? Perhaps he simply meant to spring a surprise by introducing an entirely unexpected development, as he did later in *Measure for Measure*.

There is a curious little incident in II.i when Helena first seems to give up trying to convince the King of her ability to cure him and then resumes her solicitations. She first declares:

> I will no more enforce mine office on you,
> Humbly entreating from your royal thoughts
> A modest one to bear me back again.
>
> (125–7)

The King expresses his gratitude and again declines her help, whereupon Helena renews her persuasions: 'What I can do can do no hurt to try', etc. (133ff). Joan Rees is no doubt right in commenting that 'we are willing then to accept that Helena is not the kind of person easily to acknowledge defeat' and that this helps to prepare us for her attempt 'to accomplish the *impossibilia* that Bertram sets her'.[5] But what may be pointed out also is that the episode with the King prefigures in little the change in declared intentions which we see in Helena's journey to Florence. The difficulty remains that Shakespeare is usually more explicit in alerting us to such changes. It is hard to get rid of the sense of a major unconformity, however dual the nature of Helena may be,[6] and an unconformity, moreover, which seems to have been consciously created.

In spite of, or even to some extent because of, this unconformity
in the presentation of Helena, there is no difficulty in seeing her as
a realistic character in terms of fictional realism. The Helena of the
second half of the play is basically the same as the Helena of the
first half who schemes to win Bertram by curing the King and more
or less tricks him into marriage. She has promptings of modesty, as
when she is on the point of giving up her persuasion of the King
and when having just won Bertram as a prize she offers to release
him from obligation to marry her. But she is definitely no patient
Griselda. What disturbs the realistic portrait, therefore, is the
central soliloquy where, as Bertram's married wife, she declares her
intention of removing herself entirely and giving up her claims on
him. Indeed it is the realism which exposes the unconformity.

There have been attempts to explain Helena in other than realistic terms. Muriel Bradbrook contends that Shakespeare 'was trying
to write a moral play' and failed because he could not fit it to 'the
human problem of unrequited love'.[7] William B. Toole goes further,
seeing *All's Well* as a genuine morality play on a theological theme,
in which Helena represents both God's love and human love and
her actions even 'parallel in a rather striking way the actions of
Christ'.[8] W. W. Lawrence, followed by E. M. W. Tillyard, has
emphasised the folklore origin of the main material for *All's Well*,
which in Tillyard's view conflicts with the realism of the main characters.[9] There is no need, however, to invoke either allegory or
fairy-tale, or to see Helena as a being in a different sphere from that
of Bertram. *All's Well* is essentially a play about very human and
personal desires and frustrations. Helena and Bertram are real
enough and sufficiently down-to-earth for a serious tale of unrequited love if we overlook certain missing links in their presentation and are willing to accept the kind of improbabilities which
fiction has always shared with fairy-tale. (All of which, of course,
does not prevent it from borrowing structural features from the
morality play tradition.)

Bertram has had many severe critics and probably more numerous defenders, the latter perhaps in most cases as keen to defend
Shakespeare as to vindicate a character who calls for little admiration. Peter Ure expresses the contempt which one naturally feels for
an intolerable snob and a faithless seducer (and though social attitudes have changed there is no reason to think that Shakespeare's
audiences felt very differently from us in this case). Ure speaks of
Bertram's callous behaviour, which is evident throughout but in the

last act acquires 'such a reality of stubbornly consistent shabbiness and lack of bounty' that Ure is worried about the coherence of the play.[10] Others, however, have found in the pronouncements of various persons in the comedy, and above all in the devotion of Helena, so much that points to admirable qualities and latent virtues in Bertram, and in his circumstances so much that extenuates his dishonourable actions and speeches, that his reactions become understandable and forgivable.[11] Indeed, if we accept the evidence both of the story as such and the commentators in it we should be inclined towards charity. Shakespeare does not allow us to forget that Bertram is young and inexperienced and easily duped. He has inherited a noble title quite recently, and he may be a snob, but why, after all, should he be forced to marry his mother's lady-in-waiting whom he has no particular affection for, just because she has thrown her eyes on him? Before Helena laid claim to him he had loved and been rebuffed by another girl, Lafew's daughter Maudlin, though this is only revealed in an embarrassingly unlooked-for confession towards the end. What this young Count hankers for on leaving home, for the first time as we may suppose, is only to go to the wars, not to get married. And he is obviously fitted for the role of soldier. Altogether, there is nothing particularly odious about his behaviour except his treatment of Diana.

What is basically upsetting is that Bertram and Helena, and particularly Helena, lose their inner life and become mechanical figures from III.iii on, that is from exactly the midpoint of the play. The second half of *All's Well* resembles the second half of *Measure for Measure* in that instead of character in action we get intrigue. Critics have complained that Helena becomes 'opaque'.[12] She has few appearances and little to speak. She continues to direct the central action, but that action is itself suspended for a long time to give place to the exposure of Parolles, and then retarded by scenes of arrival at Rossillion and the arrangement of a match between Bertram and Maudlin. In Peter Ure's words, 'the Helena who is the key to the narrative and, technically speaking, still the absolutely unchallenged mover of the plot, has become even more neutral and subordinate than Bertram was in the first Acts'.[13] Evans complains that since 'we cannot witness Helena's crucial meeting with Bertram' (that is, the bed-scene), the play 'lacks exploitation of its climactic moment'. Instead we have three scenes totalling 600 lines 'which develop and exploit the practice on Parolles'. In fact, 'the principal scene of his unmasking, taking 376 lines, is the longest in the play and is set at the normal peak of the comedy'.[14] Smallwood, however, suggests a line of defence: 'Shakespeare intends', he feels sure, 'that the portrait of [Helena] established during the first three acts should remain untarnished by the necessary plot manipulation of act iv.' He admits that 'one of the crucial questions of the play is whether [Shakespeare] has succeeded in this rather daring bit of dramatic legerdemain', but, with his eye on the potentials of the theatre, Smallwood finds that the comedy achieves all that we can fairly expect of it.[15] For my own part I cannot help feeling that there is a major structural fault in the difference of mode between the two halves of the play, and that the subsidence occurs, as I indicated, at the exact midpoint of the textual record.

Parolles is not the only minor character who gets a disproportionate amount of attention in the second half. There are also the two French lords, who were probably never expected to be brought into prominence and who consequently cause a little confusion here and there when they are. They are first seen talking to the King in I.ii. They take leave for the Florentine war in II.i, when they try to tempt Bertram to join them, and they are in audience with the Duke of Florence in III.i. They could probably be identical with the two French 'Gentlemen' who bring a message from Bertram to Rossillion in III. ii, though their re-entry on the stage here follows very close upon their interview with the Duke. But not till after midway in the play do we learn that they are brothers (III.vi.104), and not till the great scene of the debunking of Parolles did the need apparently occur to give them a name: Dumaine (IV.iii.171). In speech prefixes in the Folio they are at first identified as '1.Lo.G.' and '2.Lo.E.', whatever the letters G and E are meant to signify.[16] Then in III.vi they become 'Cap. E.' and 'Cap. G.', in that order, and at the end of the scene the muddle really begins. Cap. E. has proposed a plan to hoodwink Parolles and is about to move off to put it in execution (103), but it is Cap. G. who exits to do so (105), while Cap. E. is left to accompany Bertram to his rendezvous with Diana (106–13). Next, in IV.i, Cap. E., who has now become '1.Lord E.' is after all found conducting operations against Parolles, but when the two lords meet again in IV.iii, once more as 'Cap. G.' and 'Cap. E.' it is 'Cap. E.' who is able to inform his brother that Bertram 'hath perverted a young gentlewoman here in Florence' (13–14). By now the reader's head will be turning, but all this confusion may simply have resulted from an initial careless speech attribution, and it is easily set right by a simple regularisation of the prefixes. It does perhaps show that the enlargement of the two Frenchmen's roles in connection with the Parolles hoax was improvised.[17]

As it happens there are textual indications that the Dumaine brothers were somewhat carelessly employed in the Florence scenes largely for the fun of the Parolles plot. In III.vi, Cap. E. quite point-lessly repeats Cap. G.'s exclamation, 'O, for the love of laughter, let him fetch his drum' (32–3, compare 39–41). But it is more interest-ing to notice that a passage of about thirty lines seems to have been added to the main exposure scene (IV.iii). As has been observed, Cap. E. in the beginning of this scene is able to inform his brother of Bertram's assignation with 'a young gentlewoman here in Florence'. Shortly afterwards it is Cap. G. who is in the know and finds E. 'not altogether of [Bertram's] council'. He has information that Helena is dead, that this is confirmed by her own letters and the report of 'the rector' of Saint Jaques, and that Bertram has full intelligence of all this (45–60). Where Cap. G. may have picked up this news we are not told. But, more important, there has been no preparation for it and it is both intrinsically improbable and awk-wardly included in the scene. The only suggestion Helena has made that she is seeking death is at the end of the letter she leaves behind for the Countess (see p. 79 above). But the Countess does not take it too seriously, and nor need we. The passage in which G.'s information concerning Helena's death occurs is preceded by Cap. E.'s question whether Bertram will return to France now that a peace has been concluded (39–40) and it is followed by the entry of a messenger to report that 'his lordship will next morning for France' (74–5), i.e. it is embraced by a sufficiently close repetition to alert us to the possibility of an insertion. The passage twice has the brothers addressing one another formally as 'sir' (43, 45), which occurs nowhere else. And it suddenly suggests a much longer lapse of time than we have probably sensed in the preceding action when G. reports that Bertram's wife 'some two months since fled from his house' (45–6).[18] There can be little doubt that the passage (41–71) was added after the scene was first written.

It is not altogether clear why Helena's reported death should be felt to be necessary. There is nothing corresponding to it in Boccaccio. But Shakespeare used a similar device in *Much Ado*, where the rumour of Hero's death was meant to bring about a change of heart in Claudio. And although Bertram is cynical about his loss at first (he flippantly enumerates having 'buried a wife' and 'mourn'd for her' among the 'sixteen businesses' he has dispatched in one night – IV.iii.82–5) he does, in the final scene, speak of Helena as 'she whom... Since I have lost, have lov'd' (53–4). Above all, however, the supposed demise of Helena enabled Shakespeare to amusingly complicate the plot in preparation for the spectacular dénouement. Thus the incriminating ring which was once the King's is produced when, on the assumption of Helena's death, it is proposed that Bertram marry Lafew's daughter. It may actually have been at this point in his story that Shakespeare bethought him of the usefulness of supposing Helena dead and put the report of her death into the conversation of the French lords in the scene we have discussed.

The Clown in *All's Well* bears a strong family likeness to Feste in *Twelfth Night*. Olivia thinks the Fool 'dry' and 'dishonest' and orders him out as soon as we see him in her presence (*TN*, I.v.36–9). The Countess of Rossillion calls the Clown a 'knave' and says she has heard complaints of him, and also orders him out as soon as we see him (I.iii.7–8). Malvolio and Lafew similarly express impatience with the fools of their respective plays. The latter are, in fact, both professional jesters and both legacies to their mistresses from the deceased Counts of the two households, who once took pleasure in them (*TN*, II.iv. 11–12, *AWW*, IV.v. 61–2). Lavatch in *All's Well* (his name is given only on his last appearance in V.ii), like Feste, apparently 'runs where he will' (IV.v.64); like Feste he sings, though not as prettily nor as often as Feste (I.iii.58–76); like Feste he is sad (Lafew calls him 'unhappy', IV.v.60).

Like Feste, Lavatch was perhaps not introduced into his play till it was provisionally finished. He twice interrupts the Countess's conversations, once with her Steward and once with Lafew. In the first case (I.iii) he appears inconveniently, and the Countess three times tells him to be gone before he obeys. The Steward has obviously wanted to tell the Countess something about Helena, and the scene begins with her words: 'I will now hear. What say you of this gentlewoman?' Actually the Steward's first remarks are not about Helena but about his own 'deservings', until the interruption occurs, and the Countess is then engaged with the Clown from line 12 to line 93. She then again addresses the Steward: 'Well, now', and he at last has a chance to reply to her first question: 'I know, madam, you love your gentlewoman entirely'. There is, then, a kind of repetition when the subject of the original conversation, the 'gentlewoman', is resumed. In the second case (IV.v), when Lafew is interrupted in a serious proposal to the Countess on behalf of his daughter, he has to begin again after the Clown's exit: 'And I was about to tell you, since I heard of the good lady's death', etc. (65ff).

Like Feste, Lavatch has no important function in the plot, but is used as a messenger on several occasions. He is once sent to the court with a letter from the Countess to Helena and told to bring back an answer (II.ii.57–8), but in Paris we learn of neither message nor answer to explain his mission to us. He amuses us no doubt with his quips and sallies, though 'Q' found him 'a poor thin fellow',[19] but his best claim to our appreciation lies in his highlighting of one of the central themes of the play, that of sexual desire, and in his contribution to the satire on courtly manners. As I have pointed out, his need to marry because his 'poor body... requires it' (I.iii.25–6), helps to direct our attention to the physical aspect of Helena's love. And, incidentally, his rejection of Isbel after having seen the court (III.ii.12–16) points a common finger at Bertram's rejection of Helena.[20] Most amusing, however, is his aping of courtly inanity of speech as he repeatedly ejaculates his 'O Lord, sir!' in answer to the Countess's questions and propositions (II.ii), especially when this is followed in the next scene by a demonstration of Parolles's parrot-like capping of every utterance of Lafew with a 'So I say'.[21]

Lavatch defends his place in the play, but could be omitted without difficulty or great loss. The fact that he is not present in the concluding scene, or at least has nothing to speak there, confirms the suspicion that he may be a late arrival, possibly added because the play lacked a fool and to provide a role for a particular actor. It has been suggested that his presence is 'a factor pointing to revision' and that his part 'must have been written into the original play for Armin... who only joined the company in 1599', i.e. after the first version of the play was supposedly completed.[22] There may be some plausibility in this suggestion as far as the provision for Armin's talents is concerned. It would probably place the completion of *All's Well* close in time to that of *Twelfth Night*, where the role of Feste may have been introduced on similar grounds.

The last part of the play, from IV.v. on, takes us back to Rossillion and brings all the characters of any importance together for the final showdown. Even the two French lords reappear in the concluding scene, though they fade, like Lavatch, into anonymity and complete silence (unless one of them is the 'Gent.' who replies 'I shall, my liege' when sent by the King to fetch in Bertram).

The unravelling of the central plot is preceded by a series of entanglements and surprises which raise the ending to a pitch of comic excitement at the expense of any hope we may have had of a return to the interest in character development which we found in the beginning of the comedy. The first surprise is that Lafew's family suddenly increases. In II.iii we heard of a son, who is threatened by Parolles (231–7), but there is no further reference to either the son or the menace. Now in IV.v we hear of a daughter, whom the King threatens to match with Bertram (67–73). In the last scene Bertram reveals that he was once in love with her, but again both the daughter and the proposed marriage are cancelled out of existence, this time by new events. It is the King's recognition of the ring which he presented to Helena, now unaccountably in Bertram's possession, which precipitates the dramatic reversal of the young Count's prospects (74–127). We have heard of Bertram's ring which he gave to Diana and which was a family heirloom, but nothing of Helena's ring, and certainly not that she had it from the King, which is strange considering the importance of this object. The fact that it entered into the play at a late stage seems to be testified by the need for a retrospective account of the unrecorded presentation. The King recalls:

This ring was mine, and when I gave it Helen
I bade her, if her fortunes ever stood
Necessitied to help, that by this token
I would relieve her.   (83–6)

          She call'd the saints to surety
That she would never put it from her finger
Unless she gave it to yourself in bed,
Where you have never come, or sent it us
Upon her great disaster.   (108–12)

Had we heard these words spoken on the original occasion or learnt of Helena's placing this hallowed ring on Bertram's finger during the night of love it might have added to the suspense of the exposure-scene.[23] As it is, Lafew's daughter and the King's ring provide a little intermezzo of their own, and neither the daughter nor the ring is strictly necessary to the furtherance of the main action. A suspicion of murder is momentarily raised against

Bertram, but then new matter is brought in with the arrival of Diana and her claim to have Bertram's promise of marriage. Her letter to the King refers to 'his many protestations to marry me when his wife was dead' (139–40). Actually, the nearest we come to these protestations in Bertram's own words are his assurances to Diana, in Florence, that he will 'for ever/ Do [her] all rights of service' and, on giving her his ring, 'My house, mine honour, yea, my life be thine,/ And I'll be bid by thee' (IV.ii.36–7, 52–3). This may be thought strong enough, but it is all Bertram says by way of commitment. And though Diana shortly afterwards tells us in soliloquy that 'He had sworn to marry me/ When his wife's dead' (71–2), there is no strong dramatic preparation for the breach-of-promise scandal which erupts in the final scene. Actually the promise of marriage and the appearance of Diana at Rossillion were Shakespeare's own idea. There is nothing corresponding to this complication in his source. It undoubtedly livens up the exposure scene but it pushes Helena into the wings.

In any case, Shakespeare gives considerable space to Diana's claim. She produces Bertram's ring as evidence of her truth and calls Parolles to corroborate her allegations.[24] This second ring, of course, has figured in the conditions which Bertram set down for his acceptance of Helena ('When thou canst get the ring upon my finger, which never shall come off ' – III.ii.56–7) and is an important item in the plot. We have been amply prepared to see it exhibited. Strictly speaking it should have been on Helena's hand, not Diana's. And strictly speaking, too, Helena should have been able to show Bertram, in the words of his letter, 'a child begotten of thy body that I am father to' (III.ii.57–8), instead of merely asserting a pregnancy which does not immediately convince him (V.iii.309), but these are minor adjustments made necessary by the plot manipulations.[25]

When all is said and done, what is most surprising in the final scene is not the unprepared-for incidents or the small inconsistencies, but the late arrival of the heroine after a long absence from the stage and the instant conversion of Bertram into a penitent lover. Helena enters a mere thirty lines from the end and has only three short speeches before the play is over. Bertram has even less to say in this closing exchange, after he has actually been silent for some time, and the few words he speaks seem inadequate to the occasion. There is precedence in Shakespeare for quick conversions at the end of a play, but the parallel that comes most immediately to mind, that of Proteus in *The Two Gentlemen of Verona*, hardly encourages much belief in Bertram. Considering the last scene as a whole, G. K. Hunter asks 'why, when reconciliation is aimed at, Bertram is made so unpleasant. If personal reconciliation is really the end of this scene, we can only say that Shakespeare has been extraordinarily clumsy.'[26] Bradbrook denies that all ends well and thinks the play a failure: Helena's 'devotion, tinged for the first time with bitterness, requires another mode of expression than the last dozen lines allow'.[27] 'Q' declares that 'The whole of the concluding Scene is clearly bad playwright's work, being at once spun-out and scimped.'[28]

Though, as 'Q' says, it may be 'a general characteristic of the Elizabethan Theatre to huddle its endings',[29] the case of *All's Well* is surely extreme. It may be suspected that more was once written than we now see, that either omissions were made to reduce the length for one or more particular occasions and that somehow only the maimed text survived, or that parts of the concluding dialogue were accidentally lost. Helena addresses her very last words to the Countess, who is given no reply, though she may seem to deserve a final speech. This could be a clue to lost matter. But such speculations are of little use. It is better, perhaps, to find reasons which may justify the abrupt ending, and among them perhaps the deliberate avoidance of sentimentality is the most telling. It is not the Countess's tearful expressions but the comically-expressed tears of Lafew and his benign mockery of Parolles that round off the proceedings before the King's summing-up. And it is best perhaps that we are not invited to dwell on a reconciliation that necessarily needs time to take full effect. Hunter finds that 'Shakespeare was not primarily interested in personal reconciliation', but seems rather 'to aim at emphasizing the virtue of forgiveness' and 'the major victory at the end of the play is not the achievement of a husband but the ransom of wickedness by the overflowing power of mercy'. He concludes that 'the elaboration of dénouement', though unsuccessful, 'may well be deliberate'.[30] And Bradbrook concedes that if we can disregard Helena's personal happiness as 'simply irrelevant' and consequently accept the ending as 'neither hypocritical nor cynical', the play may be found to be firmly structured around a central idea, that 'virtue is the true nobility'.[31]

The most eloquent defence of the conclusion, however, comes from Barbara Everett, who declares that 'nothing could be further from the truth than the supposition that Shakespeare is hastily huddling his drama to an end'. Her main point is that the play is, and is meant to be, open-ended, that it turns towards new beginnings as well as subsuming the past, and that 'When Helena and Bertram come together at the end of [their play], it is possible to feel (though not everyone does) a good deal of hope in the future.'[32]

It would be nice to let Barbara Everett have the last word in this matter, but it has to be remarked that if the brief resolution does give us 'a good deal of hope in the future' it is only because the seriousness with which the two protagonists have been treated at first has been irretrievably abandoned. There is a kind of reaching for it in their last speeches, in Helena's bitterness, noted by Bradbrook, and Bertram's hesitation to believe, but they have now become puppets, and it is no use protracting their dialogue.[33]

The 'old' Cambridge editors of *All's Well* strongly urged the idea of a comprehensive revision around 1603 of a play written prior to 1599.[34] There can be no denying that stylistic 'stratification', as 'Q' and Dover Wilson contend, occurs in many places and that these stylistic unconformities point to a process of assimilation from different manuscripts. Parrott speaks of

> the crying discrepancies of style in *All's Well* that point to Shakespeare's revision in Jacobean times of his earlier comedy. For one thing there is a far greater proportion of rhyme than we should expect in a play dating *c*. 1603. On the other hand, much of the blank verse is in Shakespeare's grave later manner.[35]

Odd rhyming couplets here and there fail to merge organically with the surrounding blank verse. The longer rhyming passages are for the most part of a gnomic or moralising character [36] and might well have belonged originally to a play more in the morality tradition than the extant comedy. Tillyard has examined these rhymed passages and suggested reasons for accepting them as parts of an integral process of composition, but his defence is strained. When, for instance, he points to an analogous use of rhyme in *1 Henry VI*, 'where Talbot and his son perish in couplets',[37] he does not consider that *1 Henry VI* itself probably incorporates passages from an earlier work.[38]

There was obviously more quarrying of older material in the first two acts of *All's Well* than in the rest of the play.[39] But it is hard to use the incidence of rhyme and, for that matter, of immature phrasing to explain substantive unconformities. It has to be realised that jumps and breaks in quality do not necessarily mean breaks in conception.[40] At most it may be said that Helena's great renunciation speech in blank verse at the midpoint of the play, which seems to conflict with her intention of seeking her husband, in quality far surpasses any of the rhymed passages and almost certainly must have originated in the final shaping of the play.[41] Which perhaps suggests that the 'final' shaping as we have it was only a stage in a process of revision which could have gone further. Although *All's Well* ends well enough, it might have ended better.

6

The Divided World of Vienna

As we approach what is surely the unpleasantest of Shakespeare's comedies, we can happily disengage ourselves from much of the discussion and controversy it has engendered. *Measure for Measure* is a play where it is easy to confuse moral and dramatic aspects, and they are not both, or both equally, our present concern. If we ask, 'Was it right of Isabella to value her chastity above the life of her brother?', or 'Was the bed-trick devised by the Duke a defensible expedient in the circumstances?', we are probably asking moral questions with theological and jurisprudential implications, which the play provokes but refuses to answer. We may also be thinking that the heroine should necessarily be seen as admirable, morally speaking. But we need not assume that either Isabella or her secret protector, the Duke, should be entirely admirable. It is more important that they should be credible in terms of the story. There has been a general tendency in the past to idealise Shakespeare's comedy heroines indiscriminately, but it would be an exaggeration to call either Rosaline (of *Love's Labour's Lost*) or Hero or Helena or Isabella a paragon of sense and goodness.[1]

The kind of question we have been asking all along in this study and which we must now direct to *Measure for Measure* is whether our unprejudiced expectations are satisfactorily fulfilled, specifically in this case by, for instance, Isabella's refusal of Angelo's offered bargain. And does the bed-trick comply with the strategic and modal requirements of the play as a whole? Above all, perhaps, are the extraordinary developments after the turning-point in the middle of the comedy sufficiently prepared for?

We will return to these major problems of plot and character. But first it may be useful to see that *Measure for Measure*, if its exceptionally abundant small inconsistencies, obscurities and lacunae may be relied on as evidence, was written hastily, at least in parts, and transmitted to posterity without much revision except for such things as stage directions and speech prefixes.[2] There are numerous factual anomalies, particularly relating to time, and one is a potential cause of real confusion: Isabella at the end of her first interview with Angelo is appointed to return on the morrow 'at any time 'fore noon' to hear the deputy's answer to her plea (II.ii.156–61), and it must be assumed that Claudio will be reprieved till then. But it seems clear from the context that she returns to the deputy after a short interval on the same day and that the original command that Claudio be executed on the following morning (II.i.33–4) is unrevoked. For only after the second interview do first the disguised Duke and then Isabella visit Claudio in his cell, and Isabella had said she would communicate with him 'soon at night' (I.iv.88–9). Admittedly Isabella's second interview with Angelo, when it occurs, does give the impression of being dated according to her appointment with him for the morrow, and we may wedge in an extra day before she goes to see her brother if we wish, but this only creates new difficulties. After the second interview, too, Angelo makes a further assignation with Isabella (II.iv.166), which would compound the confusion if we paid attention to it.[3] We are at liberty to accept a little juggling with time-concepts, and certainly Isabella's dealings with Angelo and the moral struggles of both seem to require a larger time-space than the events allow; but only if we see Claudio's doom as fixed and irrevocable (we are continually reminded that his sentence is for the following day) do we get a sense of panic-producing deadlock, as well as a clear time-scheme: one day for Isabella's appeals, the Duke's intervention, and the bed-trick (comprising the longest part of the play, I.ii–IV.i), another for news of Angelo's treachery and for plots to deceive him as to Claudio's execution (a short section, IV.ii–iv), and a third day for the Duke's return and the final unmaskings (IV.v–V). That the Duke's absence from Vienna as registered by Lucio and others, as well as the comic plot, seem to go by a different calendar than the main plot is a feature of time-treatment at different levels of action which we have to get used to in Shakespeare's plays.[4]

Apart from this timing problem concerning the interviews with Angelo, information is chaotic with regard to the hour of the day fixed for Claudio's execution (at 9 or 4 or 8 o'clock) and the expected day of the Duke's return (in four days or two or one).[5] And other small mysteries abound. In Act IV we find the Duke tirelessly dispatching letters by various messengers, or saying he has sent them, mostly to Angelo and Escalus, and some of them, for

unexplained reasons, are apparently meant to bewilder the recipi-
ents as to his intentions and state of mind (IV.ii.198–202, IV.iv.1–3).
A friar has two different names,[6] and other named characters are
introduced without any explicit purpose.[7] Something may have
been lost which would have explained the mysterious summons of
Flavius and the no less mysterious appearance of Varrius (Romans,
to judge by their names) in the very short fifth scene of Act IV, and
this may have had to do with the apparently conflicting instructions to Angelo and Escalus for a rendezvous with the returning
Duke both 'at the consecrated fount/A league below the city'
(IV.iii.97–8) and 'at the gates' of the city (IV.iii. 131, IV.iv.4). But
there is no clue as to what, if anything, is missing.

Something was almost certainly lost in the scene at Mariana's
house. While Mariana and Isabella are off-stage, or in the background, coming to an understanding about the practice against
Angelo, the Duke has a soliloquy of six lines on the calumny to
which greatness is exposed. This soliloquy is far too short to give
the women a credible chance to talk, and moreover it is thematically quite inappropriate. It was obviously, as is generally agreed,
transferred by Ralph Crane or some other scribe or editor from an
earlier context at the end of one of the Duke's conversations with
Lucio, where it thematically belongs and where a portion of the
complete soliloquy still remains (III.ii.179–82). The most likely
explanation is that the manuscript sheets containing the Duke's
original musings in the Mariana scene had somehow gone astray
and that the transfer of the six lines was a stop-gap remedy.[8]

There are a number of unusually long scenes, for the most part
loosely jointed, with exits and new entrances breaking up the dialogue and continuity of events, and in some of these scenes there is
a disarray which points distinctly to alterations and patching.
S. Musgrove has singled out three where the fragmentary construction is particularly visible.[9] He moves on to very thin ice in trying
to reconstitute the original order and contexts of the components he
identifies, but the symptoms of disturbance and rearrangement are
there for all to see.

To begin with, there is the scene of Claudio's arrest, I.ii. It com-
mences with a conversation between Lucio and two Gentlemen,
touching first on the subject of war (which proves to be of no
importance even as a background to the plot), then turning to vene-
real diseases, at which point Mistress Overdone appropriately
appears to report that Claudio has been arrested and to tell why.

There is also mention of a 'proclamation' which apparently has some connection with the arrest. Lucio and the Gentlemen exit 'to learn the truth of it', leaving Mistress Overdone to commiserate with herself on her loss of custom. Almost immediately the Clown, as he is called in the Folio, enters with news of the arrest once more and details of the proclamation. He practically repeats Mistress Overdone's words, and what makes this repetition impossible is that Mistress Overdone now professes ignorance both of the offence and the proclamation, having only a few minutes previously been able to specify the former, including the names of Claudio and Julietta, and heard the Gentlemen talking of the latter. She now once more complains of her misfortune, when the Clown (who is addressed by her as 'Thomas tapster'[10] but will later give his name as Pompey Bum) announces the arrival of the Provost leading Claudio to prison and of 'Madam Juliet'; whereupon he exits with Mistress Overdone, while according to the Folio stage direction Lucio and the Gentlemen return in the company of the Provost, Claudio, Juliet and the Officers.[11] Thus we are twice told about Claudio's arrest in almost the same words and about a proclamation, and the Bawd twice fears for her business, there are two different groups of characters who expect the arrival of the prisoner and initially exit before he actually appears, and there is a flat contradiction in Mistress Overdone's knowledge of the arrest and her subsequent ignorance of it. Clearly one of the passages containing the report of the arrest should be omitted. And since the first part of the composite scene provides a vivid introduction both of Lucio – who will become prominent in the second half of the comedy – and of Mistress Overdone, while the following incident introduces only the less important Pompey, with very little characterisation of his mistress, one might be inclined to retain the former passage and jettison the latter. On the other hand, if we chose to replace the whole beginning of the scene, down to the withdrawal of Lucio and the Gentlemen, by Pompey's account of the arrest, we would achieve considerable abbreviation, we would save the speaking parts of the two Gentlemen (who are not heard of again after this scene) and we would avoid bringing up the subject of war against the King of Hungary, which may be felt to be misleading. Jowett and Taylor maintain that 'the entire passage with Lucio and the anonymous two gentlemen... is an addition designed to replace F's opening dialogue between Pompey and Overdone' and that it shows 'many characteristics suggesting the hand of... Thomas Middleton'.

Crane, they conclude, 'transcribed both this and the short passage it was designed to replace'.[12] This explanation perhaps makes it less difficult to decide which passage to prefer. But it is not inconceivable that, as in other cases we have seen, Shakespeare wrote alternative passages and wished to preserve both for different occasions. Or the whole scene, as it was available in the copy for the Folio, may simply have awaited final editing.

Then there is the courtroom scene, II.i, beginning with a very serious conversation between the two judges, Angelo and Escalus, and proceeding to the interrogation of that repository of malapropisms Constable Elbow and his irrepressible prisoner Pompey, with the hapless Froth making a third respondent. The examination is too long and tedious for Angelo, who departs in the middle of it. Shortly afterwards Escalus dismisses Froth, only to begin questioning the prisoners in proper form. He demands information concerning Pompey's occupation and employer which has already been provided while Angelo was present (61–6, 82). Finally, after both constable and prisoners have been dismissed, there is a short exchange between Escalus and a third judge, whose presence in the courtroom we have had no means of inferring from the dialogue. Whether or not Musgrove (p. 70) is right in thinking that two separate examinations have been combined in this scene, it certainly looks as if the interrogation starts afresh soon after Angelo's departure. There is an interesting verbal clue in the systematic switch which occurs a little after the middle of the scene from 'your honour' (fourteen times) to 'your worship' (eight times) used by Elbow and company in addressing the judges. It would be a fair guess that Shakespeare composed the scene at several sittings and forgot some of his details between one stint and the next.

The third scene which shows a piecemeal construction is the most important of all, the great prison-scene at the centre of the play. In the Folio it fills all of Act III, though modern editions, following Pope and Capell, sensibly mark a new scene for the Duke's encounters with Elbow, Pompey and Lucio. Even if we adopt this division, however, there is some rough jointing in what forms pretty exactly the first half of Act III. It contains the two superlatively poetic and moving conversations between Claudio and the Duke and Claudio and Isabella, both in perfectly controlled blank verse. But separating them is a short passage of eleven or twelve lines of irregular verse and prose, including a number of alexandrines (44–55). This passage dispatches a lot of business: the

Duke bidding farewell to Claudio, Isabella arriving to see her brother, and the Duke drawing the Provost aside – 'Provost, a word with you' – with a request to conceal him where he may eavesdrop on the siblings. Then as Isabella prepares to leave after her passionate denunciation of her brother's weakness, the Duke again steps forward and everything changes to prose. He asks Isabella to wait while he speaks briefly to Claudio, he bids Claudio a second farewell, then once more he requests, 'Provost, a word with you', only to send the Provost away almost ignominiously ('That, now you are come, you will be gone') before he takes Isabella in hand to praise her beauty of mind and body and initiate her into his plan for a rescue operation. Once more a lot of business is crowded into a little space. What may have happened here is that Shakespeare first wrote the two blank verse conversations with Claudio, the Duke's and Isabella's, and only then hit on the idea of the bed-trick and decided to let the Duke overhear the meeting of brother and sister. He consequently inserted the irregular passage which separates the two conversations with Claudio; and, having also settled for a change of style as a matter of contrast and perhaps for ease of composition, continued the scene in prose after Isabella's violent outburst. The Duke's awkward request to the Provost merely to be gone and the repetition of his 'Provost, a word with you', may have served as a rough stitching for the new passages.

A sense of creative impatience is suggested by the sudden transition from verse to prose at this emotional climax of the play,[13] where the speakers – Isabella, the Duke, Claudio and the Provost – are characters who would customarily speak in verse. In fact, Isabella and Claudio speak prose only in this one scene, but prose from now on becomes the dominant medium, though with scatterings of verse passages, just as there are frequent occurrences of prose lines in the verse dialogues of the first part. This transition from verse to prose is one feature of a comprehensive change which constitutes the main critical problem of *Measure for Measure*. Rossiter finds it 'evident that the texture of the writing – the tenseness of image and evocative quality – undergoes an abrupt change when the Duke begins talking prose in III.i.; and that this change applies more or less to all the *serious* matter thereafter'.[14]

There is an almost complete difference in structural kind between the two halves of the play. The first half is built on a conflict of character and principles, and our expectations depend on our idea of the individuals involved in the conflict. The action develops to a large extent in terms of persuasion and argument and, in addition to confronting each other, the principals of the mounting tragedy are tested for their fortitude and their humanity. Reactions are revelations, and the outcome is in the balance. Shakespeare makes the most of the uncertainty as to Angelo's firmness. Both Escalus and the Provost are made to intercede unavailingly for Claudius, but it is strongly suggested that Isabella's youthful, womanly charm may soften him and, during two long interviews, emotions and intellect engage in a tense duel until the beautiful novice breaks down the iron deputy's defences in a way that horrifies her. The questions now become, will Isabella accept Angelo's condition, and will Claudio respect Isabella's refusal of that condition? Eventually, is there any way out of the impasse they are led into?

The second half is entirely dependent on the mechanics of manipulation and deception. From the moment the Duke takes things in hand in III.i, every development is planned and we feel confident that things will work out according to programme. There is only one unexpected event of any importance, Angelo's betrayal of his promise to pardon Claudio, which is necessary for the remaining intrigue.[15] This intrigue is directed by the aims of restitution, revenge and reconciliation, by which every strand of action and all the characters of any significance are disposed at the end in a tidy pattern. Again Shakespeare makes the most of his opportunities, now of a different kind than in the first half, by protracting and complicating the dénouement and by adding the exposure and discomfiture of Lucio as a comic emphasis. We may still be asking questions, but we are no longer much concerned with psychological explanations.

The plot of the second half changes in focus as well as in kind. In part one of the play the action centres on Angelo, Isabella and Claudio, in part two on the Duke and to a remarkable extent on Lucio, while Mariana comes into the plot as almost a new principal. Claudio fades into near-insignificance and remains merely a cause, while Isabella is silenced 84 lines from the end and has no word to speak even when reunited with Claudio, or proposed to (twice!) by the head of state, though there are ample opportunities, of course, for dumb show. All this cannot avoid affecting our impression of the characters, and we may consider the main ones in turn.

Angelo has a spotless reputation and is presented as a worthy deputy. He is praised for his virtues both by Escalus and the Duke, the latter claiming to know him thoroughly (I.i.22–31). It is soon revealed, however, that the Duke distrusts him for unspecified reasons, though in a general way because of his preciseness and coldness, and that he suspects him of being a 'seemer' (I.iii.50–4). Nevertheless, when Angelo's internal restraints break down and he is shown nakedly as susceptible to temptation and capable of hot desire, we may yet feel that in his warped way he remains sincere and honest with himself and us – and even with Isabella. There is a confidence-inspiring motion in his behaviour when at his first meeting with Isabella he asks the Provost to stay after first ordering him to leave (II.ii.16–26), as if he fears already that Isabella may make him change his mind and that he needs a steadying influence. The betrayal of Claudio, however, and particularly the Mariana affair, reveal a baseness in his character which we have not had reason to expect.[16] There has been no hint of any broken liaison before the turning-point of the plot, nor has Angelo expressed any sense of guilt beyond the self-recriminations of his soliloquy at the end of his first interview with Isabella.

Isabella is introduced as a person of high and firm convictions, about to enter a strict monastic order. She is a sister in a double sense but feels the obligations of religious sisterhood more strongly than those of consanguinity. Significantly she uses the plural pronoun in her pitiless utterance 'More than our brother is our chastity' (II.iv. 184), as if already submerging her own personality in the anonymity of her order.[17] She pleads with Angelo with the fervour of Christian faith, begging for mercy and charity:

> Why, all the souls that were, were forfeit once,
> And He that might the vantage best have took
> Found out the remedy. How would you be
> If He, which is the top of judgement, should
> But judge you as you are? O, think on that,
> And mercy then will breathe within your lips,
> Like man new made.
>
> (II.ii.73–9)[18]

Having achieved nothing with Angelo even after her second appeal, she goes to report to Claudio in prison, and at first we may feel that her words are still saturated with theological meaning:

> There is a devilish mercy in the judge,
> If you'll implore it, that will free your life,

But fetter you till death.
(III.i.64–6)

Almost immediately, however, she dismisses all ideas of sin and damnation and speaks only of honour and shame. 'In this transvaluation of values,' says Lever, 'chastity is yoked not to charity but to "honour". Standards have slipped down from a spiritual plane to the level of a brittle social code where nobility is the true virtue and chastity is an aspect of physical self-regard.'[19] She even echoes the epicureanism expressed by the Duke in his conversation with Claudio before her arrival. This is Isabella:

O, I do fear thee, Claudio, and I quake
Lest thou a feverish life shouldst entertain,
And six or seven winters more respect
Than a perpetual honour. Dar'st thou die?
The sense of death is most in apprehension;
And the poor beetle that we tread upon
In corporal sufferance finds a pang as great
As when a giant dies.
(III.i.73–80)

We may have been disposed to find Isabella lacking in Christian charity when, after Angelo has threatened to draw out her brother's death 'to ling'ring sufferance' (II.iv.165–6), she can still declare, 'More than our brother is our chastity'. But what should we feel when, completely ignoring this threat of torture and telling Claudio that 'The sense of death is most in apprehension', she refuses to save him on grounds not of religious conviction but of mere honour? True, some have defended her intransigence as an example of Christian steadfastness,[20] but even then they have found it hard to excuse the brutality of her repudiation. And more often critics have found her distraught and terrified, by nervous tension after what she has gone through, by physical panic at the thought of sexual violation, or by the shaking discovery of sexual inhibitions and repressed desires in herself.[21] We may have various grounds for being unsurprised by her refusal of Angelo's bargain, even if we question its moral validity. But it may certainly be maintained that, after the anguished confrontations between Isabella and Angelo, the prison-scene drops Isabella to a level of human frailty which makes her far less attractive, though perhaps more interesting, than the high-minded novice of Acts I–II. This does not make the prison-scene less powerful and harrowing, however. And we are still incompletely prepared for the transformation which takes place when the erstwhile novice, whom we have just seen so unyielding, without a moment's hesitation falls in with the Duke's (to all religious and moral sense outrageous) proposal that she should pretend surrender to Angelo.[22] And not only that, she is willing to abet the Duke in arranging a copulation which, in spite of what jurists may argue, can hardly seem very different to the audience from that which Claudio was deservedly apprehended for.[23] It is as if her novitiate is entirely forgotten, and in fact she is not treated, spoken of, or addressed as a 'sister' after first meeting the Duke except when, in recapitulating her story to the now-unmasked Duke in the last act, she recalls that she was 'in probation of a sisterhood' (V.i.75).[24]

Isabella's eager compliance with the disguised Duke's suggestion ('The image of it gives me content already, and I trust it will grow to a most prosperous perfection', III.i.260–1) is completely at variance with what we have learnt about her in the first half of the play, though perhaps her promptness to welcome the idea of the bed-trick may be read chiefly as a sign of personal relief. 'Shakespeare's fault', says Rossiter, 'lies in giving Isabella no transitions. She ought to require some over-persuading before she permits Mariana to do rather more than Julietta had done by way of risking her soul.'[25] As for her response to the Duke's offer of marriage at the end, our interpretation of her silence must depend on our reference to one or the other of the contradictory characters which she presents to our view in the two different halves of the play. Attempts have been made to sophisticate the Duke's plot into a moral education. By being kept ignorant of her brother's survival, observing Mariana's generous love, and being persuaded to forgiveness in spite of what she thinks has happened to Claudio, Isabella is taught not only to set charity above justice but to trust her own womanliness.[26] This is a comfortable explanation, and there is no need to refute it. But we are never told whether Isabella learns to set charity above chastity, which after all was her main problem. What we do see is something which is theatrically very effective: her demand for 'Justice! Justice! Justice!' (V.i.26) after her insistent clamour for mercy in the early scenes and followed by her sudden surrender to the call for mercy at the end.

On the plot level, Claudio and Juliet are the individuals whom the play is all 'about', and at least Claudio promises at first to become a central character as he is haled off to prison and there awaits his sentence. He provides the Duke with an occasion for the play's most memorable speech of moral philosophy, and there is nothing more intense in *Measure for Measure* than Claudio's one conversation with Isabella. But the second half entirely loses interest in Claudio as a person. He comes on momentarily to hear his death-warrant but, for all we can tell, seems entirely indifferent (IV.ii.61–6). Then he appears again for the last few minutes as a mute. As for Juliet, she remains a shadowy figure throughout, and it may be doubted whether she has more than two brief appearances on the stage, in only one of which, in II.iii, she has a small speaking part.[27] We are repeatedly reminded that she is 'very near her hour' (II.ii.16), but nothing is heard of either birth or continued pregnancy at the end, nor is there any more talk of the dowry problem which prevented Claudio's and Juliet's formal marriage.

The Duke has been found by many critics to be perhaps the most puzzling character of the play, and there have been widely different views of his role, ranging from that of a deeply flawed and somewhat mischievous manipulator of other people's lives to that of divine Providence and an image of Christ.[28] I would think we should not place too much emphasis on the Duke's psychology or on his symbolical significance, however. Certainly from the point of view of our present enquiry he is primarily a schemer and manager, necessary for the furthering of the action.[29] His disguise disqualifies him from complete humanity in the first place. It is probably meant to be impenetrable, though it has been suggested that Lucio sees through him.[30] And it is his friar's hood more than his personality which lends him authority, to the extent that he has been accepted as Mariana's confessor, though his professed opinions, as expounded to Claudio, are in conflict with his religious disguise and may be held to represent his own secular thoughts. These thoughts are sceptical and atheistic, and it is the Duke's epicureanism which provides the nearest approach to a philosophical background to the play, since the fervent Christian faith from which Isabella draws her strength in her interviews with Angelo is not sustained. Duke Vincentio even invokes the classic atomic theory:

> Thy best of rest is sleep;
> And that thou oft provok'st, yet grossly fear'st

Thy death, which is no more. Thou art not thyself;
For thou exists on many a thousand grains
That issue out of dust.
                                        (III.i.17–21)

'The Duke's description of the human condition eliminates its spiritual aspect and is essentially materialist and pagan,' says Lever.[31] The Duke promises Isabella such worldly rewards as 'revenges' and 'honour' (IV.iii.135–6) and with this she appears to be satisfied. Keeping up the pretence of her brother's death, he also comforts her with a brief repetition of his extinction theory:

That life is better life, past fearing death,
Than that which lives to fear.
                                        (V.i.395–6)[32]

His motive for keeping Isabella in the dark about Claudio should probably not be enquired into too closely. It may have been partly intended to make her forgiveness of Claudio a real act of self-conquest, as has been suggested, but chiefly the deceit was technically necessary for the spectacular resolution of the last scene: first the death-sentence on Angelo seen as a demonstration of 'measure for measure', a death for a death, then the reprieve of both Claudio and Angelo.

What remains the most definite inconsistency in the Duke's speeches and behaviour is his final wooing of Isabella, worded a bit oddly twice over,[33] after he has several times assured us that he is not attracted to women and eschews love. To Friar Thomas, who has evidently thought him engaged in an amorous adventure, he declares:

No. Holy father, throw away that thought;
Believe not that the dribbling dart of love
Can pierce a complete bosom.
                                        (I.iii.1–3)

This might have been spoken by Angelo and is perhaps as credible. But he also protests to Lucio, 'I have never heard the absent Duke much detected for women; he was not inclined that way' (III.ii.118–19). The talk here is of whoring, but (unless one chooses to credit Lucio's response, 'O sir, you are deceived') the impression remains that the Duke is sexually unimpressionable, which makes his proposal to Isabella just another of the final surprises.

Lucio may be best regarded as a character in the 'humours' category, and the list 'of all the Actors' appended to the Folio play describes him as 'a fantastique'. In the first two acts he has a plot function as Claudio's messenger to Isabella and as Isabella's prompter in her appeal to Angelo, but, as Stevenson says, 'he survives in the second half as one who delights in almost unmotivated slander'.[34] There may be something missing in his part since at III.ii.198–9 Escalus gives an order to have Lucio brought before him on the information of Mistress Overdone: Lucio has a child by Kate Keep-down and has promised her marriage. This information seems to be the main point of the little Overdone episode, but the order of arrest is evidently not effected and, when Escalus meets Lucio again in the final scene, the former politely addresses him as 'Signior Lucio' (V.i.259). It is left to the Duke to inflict the appropriate punishment on the libertine.

We have seen that the passage in I.ii where Lucio converses with two Gentlemen and receives news of Claudio's arrest is incompatible with the following passage where Mistress Overdone is the recipient of the news. One may wonder, as I have suggested, whether the Lucio passage was an afterthought and meant to replace the original dialogue between Overdone and Pompey. It is interesting, in any case, to observe that in two other places Lucio causes inconsistencies by appearing when he is not expected. At the end of Act I he takes leave of Isabella after advising her to plead to Angelo for her brother, but in II.ii he nevertheless accompanies her to the Deputy. And, in the long, loosely-jointed third scene of Act IV, *he* turns up in or near the prison, instead of the expected Provost, whom he is unaccountably made to ask for, bidding the Duke and Isabella 'Good even' when it is obviously morning.[35] It is also remarkable that Lucio to a large extent absorbs our attention (especially in the theatre) in the second half of the play and that the broadly comic Lucio sub-plot, if we may call it so, of calumny and exposure, dominates the ending at the expense of all the principals save the Duke. One senses an enlargement of Lucio's part, possibly for the benefit of Robert Armin if he played it.[36] And at the same time there may have been a shift from the matter of his sexual offence, which could have been intended as a low parallel to Claudio's, to the matter of his poisonous slander.

Do we feel cheated of a more dignified conclusion? Some critics have proposed *Measure for Measure* as one of Shakespeare's most successful comedies,[37] but more have found it disappointing in its loss halfway of both emotional tension and moral seriousness, and in its descent to mechanical solutions and farcical wit entirely dependent on substitution and disguise. The trouble was that Shakespeare pointed it towards tragedy as soon as he decided that Isabella was not, as in Whetstone, to yield to her evil tempter but to remain indomitable and impregnable. If he still wanted a comedy he must devise some such hocus-pocus as that which we witness.[38] He may have felt that the bed-trick worked well enough in *All's Well*. And it is evident at once that *Measure for Measure* is another trickery play, using the same main expedient for a happy ending as its predecessor. Like *All's Well*, it begins with a searching study of character, then disintegrates on the level of tragic conflict and is reintegrated on that of comic intrigue, though there are still dark undertones. Shakespeare evidently had a rooted idea about pretended death as a catalyst for moral renewal. In *Romeo and Juliet* the pretence tragically fails but in *Much Ado* it has an effect, although delayed, and in *All's Well* it works according to plan. It will be used again in *Cymbeline* and *The Winter's Tale*. The long-sustained pretence of the death of Claudio has been seen as a means of bringing Isabella to a radically new sense of human values. But if this was intended, it is not made sufficiently explicit to counteract the moral triviality of the latter part of the play.

Possibly Shakespeare underestimated the loss which his change of key entailed, though he must have realised that an Isabella would not lend herself as well as a Helena to the kind of legerdemain which the resolution required. But considering *All's Well* and *Measure for Measure* together, one may certainly wonder whether Shakespeare was experimenting in a new form of comedy. The use of prose in unexpected places [39] could be for ease of quick composition. But the remarkable mixture of verse and prose, chiefly in scenes which bring 'high' and 'low' characters together,[40] could also indicate an experimental approach to verbal implementation which mirrors the wedding of unusually distinct tragic and comic elements of drama. It rather looks as if Shakespeare kept the resolution of his plot undetermined until he had created a seemingly hopeless situation and then sprang his surprise. In which case he would have expected his audience willingly to forgo the moral and psychological dimensions which might have continued through the second half of the play and to treat that half simply as a good story in the manner of a folk-tale or Italian *novella*. The generic difference between the two halves would have been part of a deliberate plan. The success, however, is highly debatable, and Shakespeare himself can hardly have been satisfied with the experiment; at least, he did not repeat it. *Measure for Measure* was the last of his ostensibly realistic comedies.

The state of the extant text with its many irregularities and anomalies may suggest that a more finished product might have been forthcoming given the opportunity; theoretically, indeed, may have been completed and lost. The obvious unconformities we have considered, such as the repeated news of Claudio's arrest and the contradictory timings of Isabella's second interview with Angelo, belong mainly to the first half of the play and may simply be the result of incomplete revision. The numerous smaller inconsistencies, on the other hand, such as the conflicting time indications for the execution and the Duke's return, as well as the missing matter in several places, are mostly clustered in the second half, and it is these especially which suggest hasty composition. These could easily have been ironed out. But there still remains a gap between ethical levels and between initial complication and dénouement which seems unbridgeable unless by theatrical magic.[41]

7

Fortune against Life-Force: The Pagan World of *Pericles*

The difficulty of dealing with *Pericles* in a study of this kind hardly needs pointing out. Its structure, which is very much that of a travelogue, admits of incessant arrivals and departures which break up the plot, its shifting focus on different places and persons leaves little room for development of character, and its use of narrative, dumb shows and occasionally highly stylised dialogue gives an impression of technical randomness which defies ordinary standards of consistency. There is also a remarkable unevenness both as to phrasing and versification in the various parts of the play.[1] Add to these internal qualities the uncertainty as to how much of the matter is Shakespeare's, where his contributions begin and end and who else was behind the writing, and one may with good reason despair of any attempt to scrutinise the text systematically for unity and coherence. *Pericles* has attractions of its own for the theatre and perhaps particularly invites operatic treatment,[2] but it is not a drama governed by the flexible order and submitting to the methodic restraints that we usually find in Shakespeare.

Nevertheless, we cannot altogether ignore the accepted fact that Shakespeare had a hand in the play or the inference that he had a certain responsibility for its total effect, even if he actually wrote only some of the scenes and adopted the rest without too many qualms. It is generally held that Shakespeare's share was mainly the last three acts, from the great storm-scene on, whilst the first two, with the possible exception of one or two passages, were by another hand.[3] Gary Taylor and MacDonald Jackson believe that 'no textual theory can make it credible that Shakespeare wrote the bulk of the first nine scenes, and that a variety of evidence points to George Wilkins as his probable collaborator'.[4] In this they differ from the minority of critics, notably Philip Edwards, who are inclined to think that the whole play was of Shakespeare's original authorship.[5] But, like Edwards, they consider the extant text the result of memorial transmission and hence marked by numerous corruptions of the kind commonly found in reported texts. Since Taylor and Jackson also regard Wilkins's narrative version of the Pericles story published in 1608, *The Painfull Adventures of Pericles Prince of Tyre*, as a report of the lost original play by one of its co-authors, they credit this prose romance with a textual authority supplementary, if not quite equal, to that of the 1609 Quarto attributed to Shakespeare.[6]

I am not entirely convinced that reporting from memory produced the play as printed, at least as far as Shakespeare's accepted share is concerned. Nor do I think it likely that Shakespeare and Wilkins (or some other collaborator) divided the composition of the play between them by mutual agreement, since there seems to be too great a discrepancy of talents for a direct association of this kind. It rather looks as if Shakespeare undertook either to rewrite parts of an already existing play (which may well have come into his hands in a reported state),[7] or to complete a play left unfinished by a less gifted writer.[8] There is probably no way of deciding which of these alternative possibilities is the more credible, nor indeed is there any need for my present purpose to reject the theory of memorial transmission of the whole play. But it seems clear that Shakespeare must have found in the primitive effort that came under his eyes the suggestion of an overall thematic unity which he could develop. And the scenes of his own composition may be expected to exhibit both a heightened control and a moderate adjustment to the data provided by their preceding or surrounding parts.

Neville Davies has revealed a structural pattern in *Pericles* which would seem to indicate a conscious, tight organisation of scenes and incidents.[9] He finds a symmetry of paired thematic elements on either side of the central scene in which Pericles rises to the height of his fortune at the court of Simonides before disasters overtake him. The demonstration of this symmetry is interesting enough to modify our experience of the play as we might consider it spatially, but it does little to change it as an experience of consecutive moments in time. *Pericles* presents itself very frankly as a romance exhibiting the usual meandering features of this genre, and if it has a firm pattern beneath the sequential freedom it only means that the poet was quite aware what he was doing in choosing that freedom. Whether or not he took over a play to finish it or initiated his own he chose the romance form and brought his art to bear on it.

To R. S. White, *Pericles* is 'perhaps the one wholly successful dramatised version in English of this essentially episodic and narrative form'.[10] Many critics in fact accept the loosely-articulated structure of *Pericles* as a valid form of theatrical artistry and point to its manifest advantages.[11] Wilson Knight speaks of the 'story-value' which Shakespeare creates by his 'poetic magic',

> relying more deeply than ever before on this magic itself and alone rather than on a realistic coherence, the poet enjoys a new and indeed extreme relaxation, the very opposite of plot-compactness. For poetry is now expected to make, rather than to bind and harmonize, his story.[12]

Story-value and poetry, however, are hardly sufficient by themselves to recommend *Pericles* as a genuine drama, and the defenders of its dramatic validity usually assert an ideal and thematic unity besides. Edwards thinks that 'Our sense of a lifetime's experience is enhanced by the very discontinuity of the action'; and, moreover, in building 'an arch of time which spans many years ... the play suggests the passage not only of individual lifetimes but also of human life itself'. Edwards finds 'the real continuity in the development of relationships', chiefly that of father and daughter.[13] Knight sees 'Pericles' story ... forming itself into a significant design .... We are watching something like a parable of human fortune, with strong moral import at every turn.' And the resurrection of Thaisa by Cerimon brings us to 'a dramatic disclosure metaphysical rather than moral, indeed visionary rather than metaphysical, as we watch life blossom and glow from the very jaws of death'. Shakespeare, says Knight, gives a 'fresh, and explicitly transcendental, meaning' to the structural elements in *Pericles*. It 'might be called a Shakespearian morality play'.[14]

Knight's emphasis on the religious aspect of the play is repeated and developed by F. D. Hoeniger in his Arden Introduction. 'Clearly,' says Hoeniger, 'the course of Pericles' life is shaped mainly by Providence and only secondarily by his human contacts and his own actions. There is, moreover, ample justification for regarding certain human characters in the play, notably Cerimon, as tools of the divine purpose.' The view of life which informs the play is not, in Hoeniger's opinion, 'unlike the traditional Christian view of the sufferings man must undergo before he can penetrate to a full vision of God's goodness and purpose for him'. Hoeniger consequently finds that 'the structure of *Pericles* closely parallels that of certain miracle or saint's plays'.[15] Not all critics, however, are equally convinced of the religious meaning of *Pericles*. Edwards takes a questioning attitude: 'it must be said that in the play taken as a whole divine guidance and direction seem fitful and inconstant'; and finally 'the play tends to affirm both the certainty that the supernatural is active on earth, and also the complete mystery of its ways'.[16] Kenneth Muir demurs more determinedly: 'The restoration of wife and child seem[sic] to be due to the blind working of fate, rather than to the inscrutable workings of Providence.'[17]

We must clearly take a fresh look at the role of the supernatural in *Pericles*.

We should first notice that in the main sources of Shakespeare's story the lives of the human actors are almost completely directed by superhuman powers. In *Confessio Amantis* there is a curious fusion, or confusion, of Christian and pagan divinities. God and fortune (both written with small initials) have about equal shares, jointly or separately, in Pericles' sorrows and joys, fortune being mostly responsible for the woes and god for the recoveries. Occasionally god is distinguished as the supreme arbiter ('god allmight', 'the hie god') and there is one mention of 'goddes purveance', or God's providence. It is god, not Diana, who directs Pericles to Ephesus.[18] But it is fortune who is credited both with the initial disasters and the ultimate happiness that befall the hero and his family.

Laurence Twine's *The Patterne of Painefull Adventures* is exceedingly pious.[19] Twine misses no opportunity to refer to God's benevolent succour of virtue in distress. With the exception of one instance, fortune can hardly be said to be personified in Twine's narrative and on the few occasions when it is mentioned it is subject to God's providence. There is nevertheless a clearly-voiced philosophy of mutability to account for the pattern of catastrophes which oppresses the hero, and even the title of the tale emphasises 'the uncertaintie of this world, and the fickle state of mans life'. Twine does not mention Neptune, Diana's temple is inhabited by 'holy Nunnes', and in one place it even becomes a Church. Apollonius (Pericles) is 'commaunded by an Angel in the night to go to Ephesus'. The edifying narrative closes on a note of homiletic fervour as Twine records the death of Lucina (Thaisa), who

followed her deare lord into the everlasting kingdome that never
shall have end, which so farre exceedeth the kingdome, which
forthwith she left unto her yoong sonne Altistrates to inherite, as
heavenly joyes surmount the earthly, and the bright sunne sur-
passeth the smallest starre.[20]

It is a remarkable fact that *Pericles* abandons all this Christian
piety and resolutely turns to the classical deities. And this can
hardly be for precautionary reasons, to avoid charges of profanity,
for gods and goddesses are brought into the action in both the narrative presentations and the dialogue parts of the play in ways
which assert their participation in the affairs of men and dramatise
their respective influences. But *Pericles* not only rejects the
god/fortune dichotomy of *Confessio Amantis*, but practically
reverses Twine's concept of fortune as a more or less passive mech-
anism regularly foiled by the goodness of God and leaves men to
fend for themselves against both Fortune and 'the gods'. In the first
scene and from the third scene of Act II to the end, 'the gods' are
ceaselessly invoked and sworn by.[21] They are sometimes named
individually, and one has the impression that the classical pantheon
is more fully represented in *Pericles* than in any other play in which
Shakespeare had a hand with the exception of *Cymbeline*. Jove, Juno
(or Lucina), Diana (or Cynthia), Neptune, Apollo, Cupid, Hymen,
Thetis and Priapus are all at least mentioned. Heaven (or 'the
heavens') and above all Fortune are frequently called upon and
there are occasional invocations of the 'powers'. As all these seem
to be identifiable with the gods in their manifestations, however,
there is not much need to discriminate. 'Heaven' may perhaps seem
a bit ambiguous, especially since the term is often used in other
plays as an inoffensive synonym for God, but the three occurrences
in *Pericles* of 'God' in the singular are plainly without special
significance.[22]

In two instances we hear of 'the good gods'[23] but the epithet has
an optative rather than indicative function, and I cannot agree with
Wilson Knight that the gods are 'conceived as kindly' and that they
'counter the chance-like concept of "fortune"'.[24] (An exception must
be made for Diana, whom we shall return to.) In the very first scene
Pericles is deceived by the gods 'that made me man, and sway in
love' (as the text has it), inflaming his desire for Antiochus' daughter–mistress (20–2), and he has a revealing comment which reflects
on the deities as well as on Antiochus:

Kings are earth's gods; in vice their law's their will;
And if Jove stray, who dares say Jove doth ill?
                                        (104–5)

Cleon reproaches heaven for the desolation which has fallen upon
Tharsus (I.iv.16, 33), and Pericles, shipwrecked and washed ashore
at Pentapolis, entreats the stars not to pursue him with further 'ire'
(II.i.1–11). At the report of Thaisa's death in the storm at sea he
breaks into bitter complaint:

                    O you gods!
Why do you make us love your goodly gifts,
And snatch them straight away? We here below
Recall not what we give, and therein may
Use honour with you.
                              (III.i.22–6)

The gods, virtually headed by Fortune, are arbitrary and unpredictable. There is repeated emphasis on their moods and their way-
wardness. Thus when Pericles escapes drowning, Gower, the
presumably objective observer, remarks that Fortune *'tir'd with
doing bad,*/Threw him ashore, to give him glad' (II.Chor., 38–9; my
italics). And when, on the voyage from Pentapolis, another tempest
is raised, it is because 'fortune's mood/Varies again' (III.Chor.,
46–7). Among the gods it is Neptune who is most persistently
angry and seems to torment men for his sport. Almost at all times
the sea is both dangerous and cruel, and Pericles, as his name practically implies, is constantly in peril.

The gods can be both incensed and propitiated. And being
moody they sometimes relent. In fact some of the episodes may
seem to support a belief in their ultimate kindness. There is first
Pericles' armour being retrieved from the sea, so as to enable him to
compete in the tournament for the hand of Thaisa; there is Marina
being saved by pirates from being murdered by Leonine; and there
is Pericles fortuitously arriving at Mytilene and Marina being
brought aboard to revive him. Above all there is the resurrection of
Thaisa by Cerimon. In the case of the armour, however, Pericles
thanks Fortune alone for this unexpected clemency

Thanks, Fortune, yet, that after all thy crosses
Thou giv'st me somewhat to repair myself;
                              (II.i.120–1)

The pirates do save Marina from death but they carry her to a worse – or potentially worse – fate. Even Neptune has merciful moments, and we are undoubtedly meant to feel that his annual feast is an occasion for magnanimity. While his triumphs are celebrated, the seas are calm and he allows Pericles to find an anchorage in Mytilene. But it is nowhere suggested that Neptune is responsible for bringing together father and daughter. And as for Marina's appearance on shipboard, Pericles again attributes his happiness to Fortune: 'her fortunes brought the maid aboard us' (V.iii.11). Nor does the actual resurrection-scene in Ephesus compel a providential explanation. Seeing the coffin which contains Thaisa, Cerimon remarks, ''Tis a good constraint of fortune/It [the sea] belches upon us' (III.ii.55–6). It is by studying physic, not metaphysics, that Cerimon has gained knowledge 'to speak of the disturbances that/Nature works, and of her cures' (31–8), and it is by the operation of Nature that Thaisa, herself described on her first appearance as one 'whom Nature gat/For men to see, and seeing wonder at' (II.ii.6–7), is restored to life, for, as Cerimon says,

Death may usurp on nature many hours
And yet the fire of life kindle again.
                    (III.ii.84–5)

As it kindles, Cerimon remarks, 'Nature awakes a warm breath out of her' (95). It is true that Cerimon sees an immortality attending his own 'virtue and cunning', 'making a man a god' (27–31), and that his gentlemen friends exclaim, 'The heavens, through you, increase our wonder,/And set up your fame forever' (98–9), but it is only at the end of the closing scene that Cerimon's performance is explicitly called a miracle and he himself is proclaimed an instrument of the gods.

It may be felt that this interpretation does not take account of the role of Diana as an active force for good in the play. She is throughout a benevolent goddess[25] and the protector first of Thaisa, who becomes her votaress, then, too, of Marina, who cherishes her and calls upon her for help. She intervenes as a *dea ex machina* in the final crisis to direct Pericles to her temple at Ephesus. But until the moment of her manifestation she is not actually seen to be doing much, and her intervention effects nothing that could not have happened by further chance. To Pericles she appears in a dream, which is a way of attenuating her reality, however real she may look on

the stage. Marina never sees or hears her. As the embodiment of
one specific virtue she is very much a pagan goddess and belongs
in the company of Juno and Neptune. In fact, in the collocation in
Pericles of Neptune and Diana there is a strong reminder of their
roles as opponents in Lyly's fanciful *Gallathea*. In the collective
activities of the gods in Shakespeare's play these two are seen to
represent merely opposite tendencies to destroy and preserve.

It is the ending of *Pericles*, however, which suggests that there
may have been a providential purpose all along. Pericles, reunited
with Thaisa, wonders

> who to thank
> Besides the gods, for this great miracle.

Thaisa replies:

> Lord Cerimon, my lord; this man,
> Through whom the gods have shown their power; that can
> From first to last resolve you.

And Pericles rejoins:

> Reverend sir,
> The gods can have no mortal officer
> More like a god than you.
> (57–63)

Pericles has already given thanks to 'the holy gods' in the great
recognition scene (V.i.198). There may be a suspicion that the gods
have simply 'tir'd with doing bad' in his exclamation, 'You gods,
your present kindness/Makes my past miseries sports' (V.iii.40–1).
But now, finally, the gods mete out reward and punishment strictly
according to desert. Gower's Epilogue is explicit:

> In Antiochus and his daughter you have heard
> Of monstrous lust the due and just reward.
> In Pericles, his queen and daughter, seen,
> Although assail'd with fortune fierce and keen,
> Virtue preserv'd from fell destruction's blast,
> Led on by heaven, and crown'd with joy at last.
> (1–6)

That 'led on by heaven' certainly looks like a declaration of faith in divine providence, and critics tend to apply it as such to the whole play. It is comforting, no doubt, to see wickedness punished and virtue rewarded, but we have seen the wicked flourish and the good people suffer for so long that we may well wonder what the gods have been up to. And, before the end, their evident moodiness has given us no great cause for confidence in their concern for justice.

It has been suggested that the protagonists, throughout their peregrinations and misfortunes, have been put on trial for their faith and virtue, and that Pericles may be an image of Job.[26] Like Job he is tormented through no fault of his own and without any purpose apparent to himself. But I see nothing very extraordinary in Pericles as a hero (apart from his endowments in dancing and music and his prowess in arms, all attested at the court of Simonides) or anything very exemplary in his conduct and his fate. At every opportunity he both preaches and practises obedience to the whims of the gods, to the extent that he may seem contemptibly servile, and he ends as a broken man incapable even of speech until Marina restores him. He has learnt nothing to modify his acceptance of fortune, and indeed there has been nothing to learn. There has certainly been no sense of a trial, and the moody Neptune would not in any case have been the right god to impose one.

With Marina it may seem a little different, but we surely feel that it is her own strength of character that wins through without supernatural intervention. It is her chastity and firmness which save her from the perils of the brothel and preserve her virtue, a virtue which is primarily earthly and moral though by implication spiritual too.[27] Her human fortitude is reinforced, no doubt, by her faith in Diana, but even Gower as presenter does not suggest that the goddess is either testing or actively helping her. When she retains an unquestioning faith in the gods and redeems her father, there is something Christ-like about her, but if we pursue such Christian implications where would this put the moody gods who ostensibly preside over human destinies in the play?

The trial idea will not stand scrutiny. Nor do we have a parable of patience, as Hoeniger maintains.[28] Pericles has patience, but it is worn out. Marina's strength is not in patience but in resistance and endurance. And if we are made to feel that everything comes out right in the end by a kind of inner necessity it is not because a Providence has been at work but rather because there is a life-force allied to Nature herself which eventually, after countless ups and downs, works against the thwartness of things towards the destruction of evil and the triumph of good, both in the councils of the gods, whatever and whoever they may be, and more obviously in the sphere of human action and suffering. I suggest that this intimation of a life-force is what informs and even inspires the whole play up to the final scene, without serious inconsistencies in the various parts.

The ending, which suggests that the gods have all the time been leading towards a happy conclusion, does of course create a slight inconsistency, but the inconsistency does not extend backwards into the play as far as Bertrand Evans will have it.[29] Nor do we need to extract a general philosophy from the expressions of joy and thankfulness which fall from the royal lips at the close. I am personally inclined to see these phrases as an example of the pious remarks which may have been thought suitable for an ending, as they were probably found appropriate at the end of an earlier play in which Fortune flouts both Providence and free will, *Romeo and Juliet*.[30] Gower's summing-up in the Epilogue could then be put down to the kind of obligatory edification to be expected of a presenter. Altogether there is a fairly consistent picture of what may be regarded, if we wish, as the symbolical role of mythical gods in the world of man, and of the responsibility of man (meaning man, woman and child) for his own actions and his own destiny. Nor is there much to suggest that Shakespeare was at variance with his hypothetical predecessor in the authorship of the play as far as the use of the supernatural is concerned.

Other things, too, help to tie the parts of different authorial provenance together. Bertrand Evans thinks '*Pericles* is the only play of Shakespeare's from which the entire first act could be removed without damage to the rest'.[31] But the wooing of the princess of Antioch in the first act has an intimate thematic relationship with that of the princess of Pentapolis in the second (and with the reversal of the incest motif – 'Thou that beget'st him that did thee beget' – in the last act). Both ladies, of Antioch and Pentapolis, are paragons of beauty, richly endowed by Nature as we are told in both cases, but one is impure, the other pure, and together they illustrate a truth always dear to Shakespeare, the difference between appearance and reality. Pericles also behaves differently in the two wooings, and may be seen to learn a lesson. In Antioch he is driven by inflamed desire, or lust, while in Pentapolis his modesty prevents him at first from even admitting his wish to possess Thaisa. There is a certain resemblance in all this to the two experiences in love of Romeo, and in Thaisa's candidness we may discover again some of the innocent frankness of Juliet.

Underlying Pericles' quest for a bride in both cases, and thereby providing some of the plot-motivation, there is perhaps his need of an heir to the throne of Tyre. This, it may be supposed, sends him on his wooing expedition to Antioch and lends importance to his marriage in Pentapolis, to the birth of a daughter and to his care for her upbringing. The theme, it is true, is never made very explicit, but it is suggested here and there: by Pericles' solicitude for the good of his subjects (I.ii.25–34, 118–19) and particularly his declaration to Helicanus:

> I went to Antioch,
> Whereas thou know'st, against the face of death
> I sought the purchase of a glorious beauty,
> From whence an issue I might propagate,
> Are arms to princes and bring joys to subjects. [sic]
> (I.ii.70–4)

Further, by the anxiety of the lords of Tyre owing to the long absence of their Prince, and their attempt to crown Helicanus in his stead (II.iv.26–39, III.Chorus 26–8); and finally by the instalment of Marina and her husband on the throne of Tyre, while Pericles and Thaisa will reign in Pentapolis (V.iii.80–2). If we catch sight of this submerged theme it will serve as another unifying link through the wayward adventures of the hero.

The main theme which unifies the romance, however, is that of father and daughter (or in one case mother and daughter). It is echoed throughout the play and manifested in a variety of moral and emotional relationships, from the incestuous loathsomeness of Antiochus and his offspring, through the affectionate decorum of Simonides and Thaisa and the murderous jealousy of Dionyza on behalf of her daughter Philoten, to the sublimity of fulfilled parental and filial love in Pericles and Marina.

There is one strange inconsistency, however, which becomes apparent in what is clearly Shakespeare's share of the play. In the Chorus introducing Act IV and the first scene of that act, it is Dionyza alone who resents Marina's skills and graces and who plots to murder her. Gower tells us

> That Cleon's wife with envy rare
> A present murderer does prepare
> For good Marina, that her daughter
> Might stand peerless by this slaughter.
>   (IV.Chor.37–40)

She is 'cursed Dionyza' in Gower's presentation. In the third scene of the same act Cleon is horror-struck to learn of the supposed murder and violently reproaches his wife:

> Thou art like the harpy,
> Which, to betray, dost with thine angel's face,
> Seize with thine eagle's talons.
>   (46–8)

Dionyza thinks Cleon will take her advice in the end, and we see in the dumb show of scene iv that he falls in with her pretence and assists in deceiving Pericles. Nevertheless Gower as Chorus still speaks only of 'wicked Dionyza' (IV.iv.33) even after the dumb show, and it is therefore quite surprising that Cleon, not Dionyza, should be represented in the last act as the chief culprit. Thus Marina reports to Pericles that

> cruel Cleon, with his wicked wife,
> Did seek to murder me;
>   (V.i.171–2)

Pericles then tells Helicanus that Marina

> is not dead at Tharsus, as she should have been,
> By savage Cleon;
>   (214–15)

Pericles first purposes to set out for Tharsus 'there to strike/The inhospitable Cleon' (250–1), but he is deflected to Ephesus, where, at the shrine of Diana, he announces that Marina

> at Tharsus
> Was nurs'd with Cleon, who at fourteen years
> He sought to murder.
>   (V.iii.7–9)

And in Gower's Epilogue which closes the play we are told concerning 'wicked Cleon and his wife' that

> when fame
> Had spread his cursed deed to th'honour'd name
> Of Pericles, to rage the city turn,
> That him and his they in his palace burn....

In *Titus Andronicus* there is a similar tendency to blame Saturnine
for the atrocities committed by Tamora.[32] But there is a closer parallel between *Pericles* and *Lear*, especially if we recall the scene in the
latter play in which Albany storms at Goneril for her cruelty to
Gloucester and the King. One is reminded, too, perhaps, of the role
of King Cymbeline in the play which supposedly followed *Pericles*.
But why should Albany and Cymbeline be disculpated and ultimately rewarded with our love and respect while Cleon is reviled
and punished?

One explanation may be found in the sources of the *Pericles* story.
In Gower's *Confessio Amantis* it is Dionyse alone who instigates the
death of Marina (who is there called Thaise) but there is no expression of horror on the part of Strangulio (Cleon) or reproof of
Dionyse and, since Strangulio joins with his wife in deceiving
Pericles, there is nothing very surprising in both being made the
objects of Pericles' revenge. So we are told at the end:

> Slain is the mordrer and the mordrice
> Through very trouth of rightwisnesse.[33]

In this matter, however, *Pericles* is closer to Twine's *The Patterne of
Painefull Adventures* than to Gower, and Twine includes both
Strangulio's horror and reproof of his wife and the casting at first of
the sole blame on Dionisiades after the attempted murder.[34] It may
well be the summary justice inflicted on their rulers by the people
of Tharsus as recounted by Twine that inspired the play's account
of the exercise of justice by the people.[35] It may be added that, on
the whole, George Wilkins's *Painfull Adventures* (1608) independently follows Twine in these particulars.

It is possible that Shakespeare, if he had the final redaction of the
play, was just not sufficiently attentive to realise that he was contradicting himself. But his singling out of Cleon for blame has no real
warrant in the sources, and the excuse of carelessness is not very

satisfactory. Another explanation may perhaps be offered which at least has a certain logicality. Since the father-and-daughter theme is such a persistent structural element of the play, it might well be expected to exert an influence towards uniform patterning and hence to bring the stepfather rather than the stepmother into the foreground of the murder case. In this way Cleon as well as Antiochus is set up as a foil to Pericles. As Shakespeare tells the tale, both are destroyed by fire along with their wicked partners, to satisfy the gods. It is interesting to notice that Cleon and his wife are presented on their first appearance as both pitiable and compassionate and that Shakespeare twice makes Cleon invoke the curse of heaven on himself and his family should they prove ungrateful to Pericles or remiss in fulfilling their obligations to him (I.iv.101–4, III.iii.20–5). It is as if we are being paradoxically prepared for the operation of the curse.

An inconsistency in *Pericles* which has received more attention from critics than that of Cleon's guilt (which has been surprisingly little remarked upon) is that of Lysimachus' lechery. The Governor of Mytilene, it will be remembered, on entering the brothel apparently as a well-known customer, asks the price of 'a dozen of virginities' and demands of the Bawd, 'How now, wholesome iniquity, have you that a man may deal withal, and defy the surgeon?' (IV.vi.19–25). Even after some talk with Marina he still wants his pleasure with her: 'Come, bring me to some private place; come, come' (89–90). Then, as the dialogue turns from prose to verse,[36] he suddenly changes and asserts, or pretends, that he came 'with no ill intent'

> I did not think
> Thou couldst have spoke so well; ne'er dreamt thou couldst.
> Had I brought hither a corrupted mind,
> Thy speech had alter'd it....
> For me, be you thoughten
> That I came with no ill intent; for to me
> The very doors and windows savour vilely.
>
> (101–10)

It is hard to understand that Marina's few words of reproach and self-defence as recorded in the play should have elicited the Governor's praise of her eloquence – 'I did not think/Thou couldst have spoke so well'. It is even harder to believe in the Governor's profession of innocence after what we have seen and heard. Lysimachus is not simply converted but metamorphosed into a different person, a man with an uncorrupted mind, incapable of bawdry. Surprisingly enough, the inconsistency is introduced in the play and is non-existent in the sources. In *Confessio Amantis* the Governor does not even appear in the brothel but falls in love with Thaise after she has been reunited with her father and he entertains them both on shore. In Twine, the Governor does indeed go to the brothel to be the first of Tharsia's customers, but he engages in no prurient talk with the Bawd, attempts no persuasion of Tharsia but is quickly persuaded by her, and above all makes no profession of innocent intentions.[37]

Excuses have been found both for Lysimachus and Shakespeare. Lysimachus, says Kenneth Muir,

> has to be fundamentally decent to enable him to marry Marina; but he has to be something of a rake to enable him to be a prospective client in the brothel. Most of Shakespeare's audience would not have worried about this; and they would cheerfully assume that he had been converted...by Marina's purity. But Shakespeare himself seems to have had a twinge of uneasiness on the matter and he throws in a hint at the end of the brothel-scene that Lysimachus, like the Duke Vincentio in *Measure for Measure* or a modern social scientist, was making a study of the red-light district for reputable motives.[38]

I think the uneasiness is understandable but that the solution of turning Lysimachus into a sort of social scientist, whether it was Shakespeare's own or he inherited it from an earlier author (as the problematic state of the verse and the curious diction might suggest) was unfortunate, to say the least. It would no doubt have been better to make Lysimachus' conversion more convincing. As it happens, this is what Wilkins does in his *Painfull Adventures*. The prose romance presents no discrepancy at this point. The Governor comes to the brothel for his pleasure, takes Marina's tears 'to be some new cunning' and threatens to punish her 'further lingering'. Marina is then made to speak with real eloquence and persuasiveness in an exhortation of some length which has the effect of moving the Governor to confession and repentance: 'I hither came with thoughtes intemperate, foule and deformed, the which your paines so well have laved, that they are now white.'[39]

Taylor and Jackson propose that Wilkins's version reflects what was originally in the play. And to explain the amputated impression of the conversation between Marina and Lysimachus and the latter's odd denial of coming with any 'ill intent', as the play produces the scene, Taylor suggests that the Master of the Revels interfered and required a revision. 'During the Jacobean period', he points out, this dignitary 'was particularly sensitive to allusions to the promiscuity of courtiers', and with regard to the brothel episode '*P.A.*'s account is extremely objectionable, politically; Q's is entirely innocuous'.[40] This seems a plausible enough explanation and may at least be set beside the author's wish to whitewash Lysimachus in order to groom him for his role as a bridegroom.

We may still agree with Philip Edwards that 'the *idea* of the whoremonger becoming a bridegroom is surely not offensive' and that Marina's 'acceptance of Lysimachus' love is a measure of the alteration of his nature which she has brought about'.[41] Shakespeare has a number of undeserving husbands who are rewarded with good wives after a perfunctory conversion: Proteus, Claudio, Angelo and Bertram all belong to this brotherhood. What chiefly reconciles us to the marriage of Marina and Lysimachus, however, is that it is devoid of romance, or rather of any attempt to highlight it in romantic fashion. We may feel disappointment in the anti-climactic fading-out of Marina in the concluding scenes after she has been prominent in a series of tense episodes in which she is threatened with death and dishonour and, in one of the most moving episodes in Shakespeare, restores her father to life and happiness; and after she has begun to reveal a live personality herself. She is not asked about her feelings for Lysimachus, to whom she is given in marriage, and in the final scene, when she meets her mother for the first time in her life, she has only one little speech.[42] However much the traditional formula of romance may lead us to expect a focus on young heroines and affairs of love, *Pericles* eschews this formula.[43] The story is concerned to restore order and justice, not to dwell on romantic sentiments. It is symptomatic that the betrothal of Pericles and Thaisa in Pentapolis is conveyed in a humorous rather than romantic scene, with Simonides pretending to be furious with his daughter's choice and the as-yet-undeclared suitor abjectly excusing himself (II.v.24–92); and that their reunion in Ephesus is a pale thing compared to the highly-charged recognition scene of father and daughter. This latter scene stands out with such imaginative empathy as almost to constitute a major unconformity. As for Marina and Lysimachus it may be felt that their succession to the throne of Tyre is thematically more important than their connubial bliss.

Pericles is a play with major and minor flaws.[44] Among the more noticeable ones are the contradictory impressions we receive of such secondary characters as Cleon and Lysimachus and the somewhat uncertain focus which, in some of the tensest scenes, brings Marina into prominence, only to ignore her more or less in the ending. There is an extreme unevenness in style which can only be explained as a sign of divided authorship or the revision of very juvenile work. But *Pericles* has more unity than is often allowed, and there is no obvious division of labour apparent in the development of basic ideas of theme and plot. No doubt there is an inconsistency in the introduction of references to Providential intervention towards the end, but on the whole it is Fortune in various shapes which determines the course of events, and Nature or what a much later playwright would have called the Life Force which determines their outcome. The father-and-daughter motif runs through the whole play and the theme of quest is central to all the adventures of the almost tragic hero. These things remain at the centre of Shakespeare's deepests concerns as a dramatist from now on, and *Pericles* provides an illuminating entry into the world of Shakespeare's romances.

8

Romance and Realism in *Cymbeline*

Praise has been lavished on the virtuosity with which, in *Cymbeline*, Shakespeare brings all the dispersed and disguised characters together in the final act and produces a chain of revelations which leads up to general joy and harmony.[1] But it may be questioned whether a simpler plot structure and fewer surprises for the silly king might not have made the play as a whole, and the conclusion in particular, more satisfying dramatically. The main unconformities of *Cymbeline* (probably with one exception, as we shall see – Posthumus' vision of ghosts and gods) are not due to changes of plan but to complications of plot.

There are at least four plot-strands: the banishment of Posthumus, Iachimo's wager, Belarius' abduction of the princes, and the conflict with Rome. The presence and activities of a wicked stepmother and her son may perhaps be said to constitute a fifth.

Shakespeare's first idea may well have been the one he seems to have derived from an anonymous play, *The Rare Triumphes of Love and Fortune*, which was printed in 1589.[2] He may also have gone direct to Heliodorus' romance *Aethiopica* for ideas and materials, as Carol Gesner argues persuasively.[3] But *The Rare Triumphes* is his most easily recognisable source. This play deals with the banishment of a gentleman of unknown parentage who has won the love of the king's daughter (named Fidelia), and the consequent separation of the lovers leading to a dangerous quest before they are reunited. The king's son plays an active part in opposing his sister, and there is an old champion of the king who lives in exile in a remote cave and who provides a refuge for the lovers. All these ingredients are easily recognisable in *Cymbeline*. In addition, Jupiter steps in at the end of the old play to decide the quarrel between Venus (Love) and the goddess Fortune, who have been manipulating the ups and downs of the protagonists. In *Cymbeline*, too,

124

Jupiter puts in an appearance and pretends to set everything right. Shakespeare had found interesting themes in the unwilling separation of spouses when he wrote *The Comedy of Errors* many years earlier, and *Pericles* presumably just before *Cymbeline*. He would return to the theme in *The Winter's Tale*. The separation of Posthumus and Imogen certainly seems the most substantial part of Shakespeare's plot complex and it remains the central concern of the play, in spite of Posthumus' long absence from the stage which puts the weight of the action on Imogen alone.[4]

Love and Fortune in the old play actually conduct a wager to see which is the stronger, and it may not be too fanciful to suppose that this wager partly suggested the addition of the Iachimo intrigue to the Cymbeline story. The wager between Posthumus and Iachimo on Imogen's chastity, however, is based on Boccaccio's *novella* of Bernardo, Ambrogiuolo and the former's wife, told in the *Decameron*, and on a slightly different German version of the same tale Englished in 1518 (and later editions) as *Frederyke of Jennen*.[5] In both versions a group of merchants meeting in Paris dispute about the constancy of women, and one of them, upholding the impregnable virtue of his wife, accepts a bet on her faithfulness, whereupon his challenger gains access to her, hides in a chest in her closet, and deceives her husband, much as in Shakespeare's play. The duped and embittered husband gives orders to have his wife killed, but his servant disobeys and saves her life. From then on until the final reunion, the sources and the play give different accounts, Shakespeare bringing in the Belarius material as his unique contribution. But the essential elements are the same in all versions, and it will be easily seen that Shakespeare's inclusion of the wager and its consequences makes for an exciting complication of the original plot. There is much, of course, that reminds one of *Othello* in this story of deceit and fury, and a little that reminds one of *Much Ado*. In fact the defamation of virtuous mistresses and wives seems to have become a favourite theme of other playwrights besides Shakespeare during the five or six years after the appearance of *Othello*: witness Beaumont and Fletcher's *The Woman Hater* and *Philaster*. In Shakespeare's elaboration of Iachimo's attempted seduction of Imogen we may also see a test of virtue not unlike that which Marina is exposed to in *Pericles*.

If we try to follow Shakespeare's train of thought as he built up his play, we may further suppose that he wished to provide a kind of historical setting by identifying his king with the British Cymbeline, who ruled, according to Holinshed, about the time of Christ. Whatever religious assumptions entered into the play would not be Christian, however, but entirely pagan, which, apart from other considerations, could be an advantage as avoiding conflict with the 1606 profanity act. Shakespeare's Kings Cymbeline and Lear are related both by historical remoteness and by their repudiation of their daughters, and both are related in turn to Pericles, who loses his daughter, providing another example of recurrent themes. The choice of Cymbeline as the King of the new play also brought in Cymbeline's two sons, and Shakespeare's thematic bias evidently suggested that they, too, might be lost and found, so producing the kidnapped princes. Finally, the addition of the familiar fairy-tale figure of the wicked stepmother and her unsavoury offspring[6] would turn the whole composite plot into a brew of remarkable thickness.

Looking at the action in linear development, we find three main parts. Acts I and II deal with the banishment of Posthumus and the wager between Posthumus and Iachimo, containing scenes located in Cymbeline's palace plus two scenes at Posthumus' residence in Rome. Acts III–IV are mostly located in Wales (returning to the palace in two scenes and to Rome in one) and deal with Imogen's journey and the affairs of Belarius. Act V presents the battle between British and Roman forces, the revelations of identity, and the conclusion of peace. Imogen's story remains at the centre of interest throughout but, especially in the second part, this becomes a string of adventures and a question of her survival rather than of her reunion with Posthumus. The middle part of the play, in fact, tends to drag as we move through episodes involving in turn Pisanio, Belarius with his supposed sons, then Cloten and finally Lucius, none of which advances the action significantly. Belarius addresses the audience under cover of a long extra-dramatic and naively undramatic soliloquy to explain his own and his young companions' secret history (III.iii.79–107).[7] In fact the Belarius matter encroaches on the main plot and may easily be felt as an unnecessary complication. It may even raise false expectations of a sibling romance between Imogen and one or both of the disguised princes. Nor is the recognition of Belarius and the princes in the dénouement closely linked with any other part of the plot, particularly since we have never seen Cymbeline grieving over the loss of his sons or so much as heard him speak of them (though they are

mentioned once or twice by other characters). So we are hardly prepared for his joy at their return. Cymbeline is not much of a father,
anyway, bad or good, and it may seem surprising that this unim-
portant character should give his name to the play and have the last
word in it. It is the stepmother who is clearly behind Imogen's
adversities, just as she is behind Cymbeline's breach with Rome.[8]
And in fact the Queen and Cloten are too important in the opening
part of the plot, or are made to seem too important, to be got rid of
before the conclusion as summarily as they are. Even in romance,
villains are usually defeated more climactically.

If we consider how the other plot-elements are fitted together, we
may first wish to admire the way in which the banishment and the
wager elements have been interlocked so as to make the former an
occasion for the latter and so as to aggravate the physical separation of the lovers by an emotional divorce. But the conflict with
imperial Rome creates a problem. The Roman business comes in
only intermittently at first, in Acts II–III,[9] but from the moment
when Lucius enters with captains at IV.ii.333 there is a war-situa-
tion. Cymbeline is there from the beginning to meet it, but the mili-
tary transactions have nothing at all to do with the separated lovers
except for bringing them together on the battlefield (in this respect
Cymbeline differs markedly from *Troilus and Cressida*). The same
setting in ancient Britain serves both the banishment part of the
love-plot and the whole war-plot well enough.[10] It is otherwise,
however, with the wager-story, which, though fully integrated with
the banishment of Posthumus, suits awkwardly with the evocation
of the Rome of the Cæsars. Iachimo is very much a creature of the
Italian Renaissance and surprising as a member of Lucius' army.
His first appearance in Britain and his subsequent description of
Imogen's bedroom (II.iv. 66–91) turn Cymbeline's palace into a cin-
quecento palazzo. As Nosworthy remarks 'the curious imbroglio
of . . . the dawn of the Christian era and the Renaissance is too much
at odds with the action to be convincing'.[11]

This discrepancy is mainly one of anachronism. But there is more
serious unconformity in the collision of the irresponsible spirit of
romance, which informs most of the play, with the realism which
pervades the Roman material, both ancient and Renaissance. The
court of Cymbeline forms an appropriate background for the
romantic intrigue of true lovers torn apart by a decree of banishment and the virgin wife running into improbable adventures in
wild woods and mountains in her quest for her beloved. To the

same romantic world belong the exiled warrior and the kidnapped princes, while the miraculous revelations at the end are the height of romantic wish-fulfilment. But the gaging of ducats and diamonds, the attempted seduction, and the duping of the husband are presented with a solidity of characterisation and a realistic turn of dialogue which we may recognise from both tragedies and comedies which preceded the romances, *Much Ado*, for instance, or even *Othello*.

The characters, consequently, tend to oscillate between romance and realism. Nosworthy finds that 'there is, at times, a destructive reality about the main personages of the play'.[12] Expressing a similar discomfort, Joan Rees observes that, due, as she thinks, to 'the proliferation of story-lines', 'when moments of strong passion emerge from the mêlée, they astound us with their sudden force'.[13]

It is instructive to compare *Cymbeline* with Beaumont and Fletcher's contemporaneous romance *Philaster*, which exhibits a striking resemblance in some of its main story-elements.[14] *Philaster* is firmly and simply plotted compared to Shakespeare's play and never tempts us to confuse its fiction with the real world or its characters with people breathing ordinary air. *Cymbeline* has a much greater specific gravity and is immeasurably more powerful in its portrayal of emotions, but the cost is a certain loss of coherence between levels of theatrical experience, and a general instability of characterisation. Imogen and Posthumus, who are drawn more realistically in the Iachimo scenes than elsewhere, lose their credibility in the last act. And there both Posthumus and Iachimo, after a long absence from our sight, are shown to have undergone a change of heart which, especially in Posthumus' case, might have deserved more of an explanation than we are accorded.[15]

The kind of inconstancy which results from the pull between romance and realism is perhaps most obviously noticeable in the conduct of the Queen and Cloten. The former is a folklore embodiment of scheming malice and witchcraft but also the voice of proud resistance to foreign dominion.[16] Her deathbed confession as reported at the end does nothing to help her credibility. In Granville-Barker's judgement, 'never is she co-ordinated into a human being'.[17] The braggart Cloten, comically realistic on one level, becomes heroically patriotic and even modest as to his own attainments as he confronts the Roman envoy: 'We have yet many among us can gripe as hard as Cassibelan: I do not say I am one: but I have a hand' (III.i.41–2). Shakespeare, in fact, seems to have got himself in a dilemma both in *Lear* and *Cymbeline* by having the wrong people on the patriotic side of an international conflict. Albany as well as Cymbeline's Queen and Cloten are given noble motives to defy invading forces. Foakes, who has an interesting analysis of Cloten, sums him up thus: 'alone with his followers he appears a quarrelsome fool, but he can speak verse of distinction when thinking of Imogen, and he challenges the Romans in good plain sensible English'.[18] It must be added, however, that in Foakes's view 'there is no need for a stable and consistent portrayal and development of characters; they may be liberated from consistency, since they too are part of a dramatic world where anything can happen, however strange, yet true.'[19] We may bear this warning in mind and yet feel that romance requires a certain firmness of outline.

The romantic mood is also jeopardised by a strong bent towards tragedy which some critics have found disturbing. Nosworthy complains that 'the bulk of the play is over-tragic in tone and conception'.[20] It is mainly, of course, Iachimo's turpitude which causes the tragic gloom. Had the lovers been able to go on hoping for a reunion despite their trials, the feel of the play might have been more buoyant. As it is, Imogen, in despair when she thinks Posthumus dead, and having already rejected suicide in a surprising access of Christian scruple (III.iv.77–9), goes into Roman service, and Posthumus in despair seeks to die. Their surprise and delight when everything is cleared up are actually all the more intense and dramatic for having been thought impossible, but the clouds break almost too late to dispel the funereal atmosphere.

We come now to the roles of the ghosts and Jupiter who appear so spectacularly in the final scene. There has been considerable controversy over the authenticity of the supernatural episode and the doubts are understandable. Posthumus has had little or no thought of his lost family before this scene, and Jupiter, though he and the gods have been mentioned and invoked quite frequently, has never been felt to represent an active influence, as the gods are in *Pericles*. Parrott refuses to accept 'the choral chant of the ghosts' as written by Shakespeare's hand – 'It is incredible that Shakespeare at his weariest and weakest could have written such pitiful stuff' – but he thinks Shakespeare must have 'planned, or at least accepted, the vision of Jove on the eagle'.[21] In Evans's opinion the whole vision is strictly superfluous since Jupiter contributes nothing to the dénouement and it has already been made plain 'that *Cymbeline* could now end happily without the services of a controlling force'. 'But,' says Evans,

> a chance ending, for artistic if not philosophical reasons, was manifestly intolerable to Shakespeare: always, everywhere, he must have a divinity – either within or without man – that shapes the ends of action. Hence in V.iv Jupiter advises us of what we could not have guessed during the first four and a half acts – that the world of *Cymbeline* has been under control all the while;

Evans concludes that 'Jupiter is an artistic fraud – but perhaps the shrewdest in the plays'.[22]

Others have felt that the resolution of all the incompatibilities contained in the action could only have been brought about by divine intervention, so that Jupiter has a genuinely significant role to play.[23] To Wilson Knight the vision of Jupiter 'occurs in a work saturated with religious suggestion' and 'is exactly in tone with the play's theological impressionism'. He sees *Cymbeline* as 'a vast parable' of the destiny of Britain, and Jupiter as the protector of the nation, who manifests his continued care by his prophetic theophany, while Posthumus, through whom the prophetic message is conveyed, is 'a symbol of British manhood'. Knight refuses to see the allegedly poor quality of the poetry as an argument against Shakespeare's authorship of the vision: 'Such purely aesthetic judgements are surely irresponsible'. On the contrary, comparing the poetry of the visionary passage to that of analogous scenes in other plays he finds its deviance from Shakespeare's usual manner exactly right for a passage of supernatural and transcendental content.

When Knight calls this play 'a work saturated with religious suggestion' his statement is correct in so far as the frequent invocation of 'the gods' and the occasional prayers to the heavenly powers are concerned. It is especially Imogen and Posthumus who call on the gods, and the indications are that they are singled out in this way to emphasise their piety and goodness. Pisanio has some significant appeals to 'the gods' or 'the heavens', while Belarius and his adopted sons characteristically address themselves to 'heaven'.[24] In the last act, when events have turned in his favour, Cymbeline too becomes remarkably pious (his first recognition of 'the gods' is at V.v.l). But Iachimo speaks of 'the gods' only as an ironic echo to

Posthumus (I.v.83) or as part of his hypocritical attempt to deceive Imogen (I.vii. 91, 177); and Cloten and the Queen do not use the word at all, though Cloten once swears by Jupiter, once by the devil, and once prays to Fortune.[25] A great number of individual deities are actually named in the play, especially by Iachimo, whose identity as a Renaissance courtier is particularised by his familiar references to classical mythology. In fact it seems that what Knight's religious saturation amounts to is partly a way of differentiating the characters as good or bad, partly a means of adding 'local' colour to a play ostensibly set in ancient Roman times. Although there are appeals to 'the gods' there is nowhere any sense that supernatural powers direct the course of events for bliss or woe,[26] not, that is to say, until the last act, when (and I here entirely agree with Evans) it has already been made quite plain 'that *Cymbeline* could now end happily without the services of a controlling force'. Interestingly enough, there is no pious exclamation of any kind in the main body of the great climactic scene at the centre of the play in which Pisanio shows Imogen Posthumus' letter ordering him to kill her. The name of Jupiter (or Jove) occurs eleven times in the play apart from the theophany (beginning as late as II.iii.124), but Diana runs up with five mentions, Juno has three, and there are numerous others.[27] The agents of evil, the Queen and Cloten, are taken off virtually by their own wickedness with no need of supernatural intervention (it is clearly suggested that the Queen takes her own life in despair on Cloten's disappearance), while Iachimo is brought to repentance by being defeated in battle, as he thinks by a British peasant.

Whatever the religious implications of the parade of classical deities, they are certainly not Christian. And the Christian spirit of forgiveness which triumphs in the ending is hardly prompted by Jupiter. In this connection we should not disregard the absolute religious nihilism of the famous dirge sung over the supposed corpse of Imogen, and its insistent refrain saying that golden lads and girls, chimneysweepers and lovers, the great and the learned, all must 'come to dust'.

Even if we should agree with Knight that Jupiter is necessary to bring about the happy resolution, we may ask why the spirits of Posthumus' family should be included. And why the future prosperity of Britain should be magically connected with the person of Posthumus, who has played no heroic role before his appearance in the battle and only assumes independent importance in the last act.[28] Now, as it happens, there are a number of textual clues which suggest, not necessarily that Posthumus' dream is not of Shakespeare's authorship, but that the whole vision was a late insertion, prompted perhaps by the author's memory of Jupiter in *Love and Fortune* (where the god has a definite function) and motivated by a wish to satisfy the taste of the Blackfriars audience for shows of ghosts and gods, even by a felt obligation to use the theatre's hoisting machinery. In addition there may have been the wish to augment the conventional piety of the closing scene, already established by the closing speeches of Cymbeline and the Soothsayer.[29]

Posthumus' speech on waking from his dream is highly suspect. We need not, perhaps, be surprised by the fact that it is partly in rhyming couplets, though rhymes are infrequent in *Cymbeline* except at scene-ends and though Posthumus comments sarcastically on one occasion on being tempted to rhyme (V.iii.55–63). After all, his waking speech follows close upon Jupiter's rhymed verse. But that speech makes reference to only half his vision, and that the least important. Posthumus speaks of having seen his parents and brothers but, incredibly enough, makes no mention of Jupiter; in fact, he does not recall the vision of Jupiter till 300 lines later (at v.428–9). Instead, finding what he here calls a 'book' on his breast (it is a 'tablet' in line 109 and a 'label' in line 431), he asks, 'What fairies haunt this ground?' (133). He obviously has no inkling of how it got there and can only think of a commonplace explanation.[30] What is perhaps even more strange, Posthumus seems not to have heard or understood his spectral father's revelation of Iachimo's villainy or Jupiter's promise that his trials are at an end and that he will be reunited with Imogen. He makes no allusion to these surely sensational communications, and his one wish when the gaolers re-enter to fetch him is simply to die. He is patently ignorant of what he should have learnt in his dream when the actual revelations do occur.

The message of the 'book' is read out by Posthumus, but shrugged off for the nonce as incomprehensible. It is repeated word for word and expounded by the Soothsayer when Posthumus recalls his vision, and it seems strange that it should receive attention twice over, seeing that the Soothsayer has himself had a vision which is also expounded. Thus there are explanations in quick succession of two prophecies, both featuring a vision of Jove's eagle and promising a prosperous future to Britain. But one prophecy, that of Posthumus' book or tablet, is explained after all the specific events it foretells have already come to pass, while the Soothsayer's is interpreted with great dramatic relevance in the penultimate speech of the play in the context of Britain's peace with Rome: it is a vision of Roman greatness transferred to Britain. A duplication of visions and prophecies hardly seems necessary and Posthumus' seems the more redundant. If his vision was an addition to the original script, it follows that the explanation of it was also added in consequence.[31]

In fact there is an indication of the kind which I have often found in Shakespeare's plays to suggest strongly that Posthumus' dream and the enclosing soliloquies together with his passages of dialogue with the gaolers were not in the play as originally completed. When Posthumus is first captured by British soldiers the Second Captain orders, 'bring him to th' king' (94). But Cymbeline in dumb-show 'delivers him over to a Gaoler'. Then follows the episode we have been discussing, at the end of which Posthumus is apparently to be taken away to be hanged. However, a messenger enters with the command, 'Knock off his manacles, bring your prisoner to the king' (193–4). So we are back where we started before the gaolers and the dream. No reason is given why Posthumus is first dismissed by Cymbeline, why he is to be hanged, or why Cymbeline recalls him. His dismissal at first can only have been to allow for the insertion of the hundred lines containing the vision. The repetition of the order to bring him to the King shows what happened in the course of writing and revision.

This still does not explain the lack of connection between the dream and Posthumus' soliloquy on waking from it which I commented on above, but we must suppose that there were several stages of revision and addition and that something may have got muddled in the process of editing. The unusual length of the play [32] gives rise to speculations as to material which may have grown from a shorter version or, conversely, passages that might eventually have been deleted had the author overseen the printing. We will not pursue such speculations, but it seems fair to emphasise that the dream-vision is not the only episode that some critics have found superfluous,[33] that there is an unusual amount of soliloquising for expository purposes in this play, and that the final scene has passages of recapitulation which seem unnecessarily longwinded.[34]

Love and Fortune, Heliodorus, Boccaccio and Holinshed, with an addition of folklore and reminiscences of *Much Ado* and *Othello*, make a mixed dish to provide the raw materials for a self-contained dramatic structure. Shakespeare must have been aware that he was experimenting precariously with difficult combinations, but we cannot tell whether he was satisfied with the result. What we can tell is that in comparison with his own practice and achievements both earlier and later, not omitting *Pericles*, *Cymbeline* suffers to an unusual degree from a lack of coherence both in plot and mood. The love-conflict and the war-conflict mesh not at all until the last act, and even there they are only superficially wedded. The Belarius component is loosely grafted on to Imogen's story, and Posthumus' vision of his ghostly relatives and of Jupiter is an intrusion of superfluous supernaturalism which contradicts the theme of the play's most famous lyric. The historical setting is divided. In the depiction both of the principal and the subsidiary characters, realism yields to romance and vice versa, and tragic feelings are perhaps stirred too exclusively and too long for a play which aims at a happy conclusion.

Few would call *Cymbeline* a great play, and some remember it only by the moving dirge sung over the body of 'Fidele'. It is the boldly and vividly portrayed character of Imogen/Fidele which chiefly holds us through the incredible vicissitudes of her fortunes, and which rescues the spirit of romantic comedy when threatened with too much oppression. In the somewhat heterogeneous blend of themes one may sense a kind of musical medley, and it is interesting to note that *Cymbeline*, like *Pericles*, has inspired operatic treatment.[35]

9

Like an Old Tale

The title of *The Winter's Tale* is echoed in the dialogue. A sad winter's tale 'of sprites and goblins' is what Prince Mamillius proposes to tell his mother (II.i.25–6), and we certainly become acquainted with sprites and goblins of the mind soon enough as we enter into the action. Towards the end there are wonderful happenings. Three times in the course of the last two scenes characters in the play remark that the events they witness are 'like an old tale' (V.ii.28, 62; iii.117) – in fact, as the 'Sec. Gent.' opines, 'so like an old tale that the verity of it is in strong suspicion' (ii.28–9). This, of course, is in the first place a way of disarming the disbelief of characters and spectators alike and affirming the 'verity' of the seemingly incredible events within the terms of the story. But it is also a way of fixing those terms and so creating the right kind of receptive mood in the audience.[1] It has often been said that there is a conscious theatricality about the romances, and perhaps more so about *The Winter's Tale* than about the other comedies in this group, as if the author is almost flaunting his privilege to make and break with sovereign licence.[2] And indeed the number and the nature of the surprises which we encounter in *The Winter's Tale* can best be made acceptable on the supposition that they were fully intentional.

This is particularly true of the greatest surprise of all: the 'resurrection' of Hermione after she has been thought dead for sixteen years. The resurrection scene forms the unquestionable climax of the play, and much of its effect is due to its unexpectedness.[3] Whether it was so planned from the beginning or the result of second thoughts needs to be discussed.

No one denies that Shakespeare has been at pains to assure us that Hermione truly dies in the third act, when her son is reported dead. Paulina swears to it and challenges Leontes to 'go and see' (III.ii.203–4). Leontes in turn asks to be brought 'To the dead bodies of my queen and son' and vows to 'visit/The chapel where they lie' daily as long as he lives (234–43). That he actually does see the body of Hermione and 'says many/A prayer upon her grave' is confirmed in the concluding scene, though he now has to concede 'for I saw her,/*As I thought*, dead' (V.iii.139–41, my italics). It is also generally found significant that Antigonus, before landing in Bohemia, has a vision of Hermione's spirit and receives a message from her, sufficient proof both to him and to us that 'she hath suffer'd death' (III.iii.16–42). Finally she is repeatedly spoken of as being dead, and as late as the penultimate scene we are told of Perdita's reaction to Leontes' 'relation of the queen's death' (V.ii.83–4).[4] Bertrand Evans thinks Shakespeare provided a few clues at the last moment to prepare us for the real state of things, but these clues are nowhere decisive.[5] The question is, would Shakespeare have insisted so methodically on Hermione's death if he had planned all along to restore her to life without resort to supernatural explanations?

In Greene's prose romance *Pandosto*, the main source for Shakespeare's story, there is no such restoration. Hermione dies and remains dead. The focus at the end is very much on Pandosto's (the king's) lust-troubled reunion with his daughter. Shakespeare's first impulse would presumably have been to follow Greene in this as in other parts of the tale. When Simon Forman saw *The Winter's Tale* at the Globe in 1611 he wrote a summary of the plot which agrees in all essential respects with the play as we know it except that there is no mention of the statue scene or of Hermione's resurrection. I take this to be strong evidence that the scene was not then in the play. Muir has thrown doubts on Forman's reliability,[6] but, as David Bergeron puts it, 'How anyone could witness the statue's coming to life and not report it almost defies explanation'.[7] I can only conclude that Shakespeare revised his play at some time after the performance witnessed by the astrologer. The idea of the statue scene, probably suggested by the account of Pygmalion in Ovid's *Metamorphoses*, must have caught his fancy.[8] He had previously in two plays (*The Comedy of Errors* and *Pericles*) dealt with the quasi-miraculous reunion of husband and wife after long separation, and of both with their offspring, and in the present instance there was the additional highlight on forgiveness at the end to require the inclusion of the wronged wife. The romantic ending, too, would benefit from the cumulated happiness which Hermione's presence provided. Above all, perhaps, the artist–author may have been motivated by a feeling for balance independent of the mechanics of the plot: the rejection of Hermione is so much a dominant theme of the first half of the play that it needs to be balanced in the second half by a counter-movement, her vindication and return to love.[9] All in all, Shakespeare had plenty of reasons to change his ending.

The result of the change is that we are presented with a great deal of false information concerning Hermione's demise which Shakespeare seems to have left unrevised; and we have to come to terms with it. It is possible for us, of course, to join those critics who, believing that everything was planned as we have it, find the misinformation a brilliant way of ensuring that we will be suitably and delightfully dumbfounded; or those who deny the absoluteness or the unambiguousness of the statements about Hermione's death and so find no contradictions. Nevill Coghill sees *The Winter's Tale* as 'a play about a crisis in the life of Leontes, not of Hermione' and emphasises the importance to Leontes of finding the woman whom 'he had thought . . . dead by his own hand . . . unexpectedly alive':

> That is the miracle, it seems to me, for which Shakespeare so carefully prepared. It had to be a miracle not only for Leontes, but for the audience. His first dramaturgical job, then, was to ensure that the audience, like Leontes, should *believe her dead*. For this reason her death is repeatedly reasserted during the play by a number of characters, and accepted by all as a fact. Shakespeare's next care was to give credentials to the statue. The audience must accept it *as a statue*, not as a woman . . . . [10]

The deception, then, in Coghill's opinion, is a necessary piece of dramatic strategy. Barbara Mowat defends it on slightly different grounds. She points out that 'Hermione's resurrection is only one of many surprises in this play' and mentions a number of major incidents for which we are unprepared. 'More significantly,' she says, 'we are more than once actually misled about the play's action', and again she cites examples. The deception concerning Hermione's death, therefore, ' is only an exaggerated form of milder deceptions practiced on the audience throughout the play, just as the sense of wonder accompanying her revival is an enlarging of the many moments of surprise or delight that the play provides.'[11] In the world of romance surprise itself is a major asset.

It is indeed hard to conceive of any reasonably sensitive theatre-goer not being thrilled and delighted by the animation scene, and we may be disposed to forgive the cheating which has arguably enhanced our delight in it. Shakespeare may have discovered that the deception would work that way and so simply retained the untruths after they became untruths. But this would be a matter of serendipity on his part, not of premeditation. It does not devalue the product, but it tells us something about his working methods.

In the meantime, before he altered the dénouement, he had developed Perdita, as his story required. The oracular message brought from the shrine of Apollo points forward to one decisive event, the finding of Leontes' lost heir, and this event is what the play would originally and perhaps exclusively – certainly chiefly – have been heading for. The Oracle is our guide to the principal plot-business of the play. Even in the statue-scene we are made to remember the importance of Perdita.[12] It is she who wants to see the effigy of her mother. And when Hermione is brought to life and explains why she has secluded herself so long she gives the only reason which agrees with the prophetic utterance concerning Leontes' heir:

> for thou shalt hear that I,
> Knowing by Paulina that the Oracle
> Gave hope thou wast in being, have preserv'd
> Myself to see the issue.
>
> (V.iii.125–8)

Why otherwise should she want to hide for so many years from Leontes, who repented of his jealousy as soon as she fainted before him? Surely not to punish him all that time, punishing herself perhaps even more?

The love of Perdita and Florizel is not central in Shakespeare's conception of the tale as is that of the corresponding persons in *Pandosto*. We do not see it either awakening or growing. Perdita herself is only in focus in Act IV, like Marina in *Pericles*. But there she becomes hardly less impressive a character in her own right than does Marina. And the reunion of father and daughter in *The Winter's Tale* is prepared for not only by the words of the Oracle but by our acquaintance with Perdita at sixteen. No wonder, then, if we have great expectations of a moving scene.

The alteration which in all likelihood reversed the ending of the play as far as Hermione is concerned may well have affected the presentation of Perdita's story as well, not so as to change the occurrences but so as to make its conclusion less climactic. The way in which Simon Forman describes the scene in which Perdita is recognised by her father strongly suggests, in my opinion, that the episode was originally staged:

And the kinge of bohemiā his sonn maried that wentch & howe they fled into Cicillia to Leontes. and the sheppard hauing showed the letter of the nobleman by whom Leontes sent a [she?] was that child and the Jewells found about her. she was knowen to be Leontes daughter and was then 16 yers old.[13]

It is especially the detail of the shepherd showing the letter which has the look of being reported from visual observation. Whether or not there ever was such a scene for the principals to enact, however, what we actually have is a narrative rendering of the great disentanglement and of the joy of the reunited relatives and friends. It is not a narrative in the sense of being merely told by a presenter; in fact, it is conveyed in a lively dialogue between several gentlemen, one of whom has witnessed the whole meeting between the kings and their children. Critics have urged conflicting views concerning the merits of this gentleman's description and his style of speech. Some have found them deplorable, while to others the moving brilliance of the scene is such that it surpasses anything that could have been done in actual performance. In answer to Quiller-Couch's condemnation, Coghill maintains that 'in practice this scene is among the most gripping and memorable of the entire play'. 'There is no doubt', says J. H. P. Pafford, 'that the incident must be recounted. If staged it would lengthen excessively an already long play, it would be tedious because much would have to be said which was well known to the audience, and it would weaken the final scene.'[14] At all events it cannot be denied that the episode as we have it in narrative surrenders its climactic function to the statue-scene at the end of the play. Shakespeare apparently decided to reserve his main emotional impact for the reunion of Leontes and Hermione, thus reversing the relative prominence of the father-and-daughter and husband-and-wife reunions which he chose in *Pericles*. Two distinct scenes of equal prominence, we may suppose, would have been too much. He did try once, in *Cymbeline*, building all the discoveries and recognitions into one final scene, but it would not be surprising if the resultant complication discouraged a repetition of the same pattern.

If anything is needed to complete the evidence for revision in the last act we may perhaps find it in the irregularities attending the role of Autolycus. This character has no place in *Pandosto* but probably had his origin in the *Metamorphoses*, where a person of that name appears as a thief and liar.[15] One strange thing about Shakespeare's Autolycus is the recurrent failure of people in the play to recognise him. It is repeatedly remarked that he has been Florizel's servant. He seems to be wearing a false beard in the sheep-shearing scene and in the subsequent meeting with Florizel and Perdita (see IV. iv. 713–14), which no doubt sufficiently explains by theatrical convention why the Prince fails to know him. But why when he takes off his 'pedlar's excrement' is he not recognised by the Clown, whom he already fooled before he disguised himself?[16] He is wearing unaccustomed clothes, it is true, having exchanged his own pedlar's get-up for Florizel's rustic garb (IV.iv.636). But thereby hangs a tale, too, for in Florizel's discarded rustic dress he speaks first as if he is a soldier (IV.iv.724) and then, pointing to his apparel, assumes the role of a courtier: 'Seest thou not the air of the court in these enfoldings?' (730–1).[17]

Autolycus' behaviour in the meeting with the Shepherd and his son, following upon the reported scene of reunion and rejoicing, is surprising. He has suddenly become deflated, and his new humility can hardly be explained solely by the social promotion of the rustics. One suspects the loss or omission of a scene in which Autolycus is exposed as the rascal he truly is, perhaps by being at last recognised by Florizel as the servant who was once 'whipped out of the court' (IV.iii.87). There seems to be adequate preparation for such an exposure, and it would help to justify Autolycus' inclusion among the Bohemians who sail for Sicilia. As it is, there is nothing else to necessitate his presence in Sicilia. Even his bringing the Shepherd and the Clown aboard the Prince's ship in order to make them tell their story to Florizel rather than to the King is to no purpose, since Polixenes meets them in Sicilia before they have disburdened themselves of their news (V.i.188–92) and they might as well have gone to the King straight away as they intended. Autolycus' excuse for this breakdown of communication is so ludicrous that it can only have been invented to cover a rift in the story. He explains in soliloquy that since the prince was

> at that time overfond of the shepherd's daughter (so he then took her to be), who began to be much sea-sick, and himself little better, extremity of weather continuing, this mystery remained undiscovered.   (V.ii.117–21)

Altogether, Autolycus' contribution to the plot proves negligible, but there are clear indications that he was once to have been more functional and that the petering-out of his role came about as the result of basic changes in the dénouement. If at one time a general recognition scene was actually written to be staged it is at least natural to suppose that Autolycus had a small but meaningful part in it.[18] Autolycus was no doubt wanted in the play chiefly as an extra-dramatic entertainer whose songs would be a special attraction, but it would be characteristic of Shakespeare to try to put him to further employment.

One of the surprises in *The Winter's Tale* which has been most widely discussed is the sudden exhibition of jealousy in Leontes. Since the whole action of the play has its inception in this jealousy it is no matter of indifference how it is introduced. The trouble is that we find no explicit indications in the text that Leontes suspects his wife and friend of misbehaviour until he breaks into his vehement aside:

> Too hot, too hot!
> To mingle friendship far, is mingling bloods.
> I have *tremor cordis* on me; my heart dances....
> (I.ii.108ff)[19]

And if we compare Shakespeare's treatment of Leontes with the circumstantial account of the king's growing greensickness in *Pandosto* it looks as if Shakespeare deliberately aimed at a shock-effect. It is possible, of course, for an actor to mime an emotion which is not expressed in words, or which is disguised in words, and there seems to have been a general tendency in modern productions of *The Winter's Tale* to show that Leontes is jealous from the moment when he appears on the stage, the assumption perhaps being that that is what Shakespeare intended.[20] Directors choosing this solution somewhat resemble Iago suggesting to Othello that there has been a long period of unfaithfulness. The audiences have not always been convinced as easily as Othello, however,[21] and in any case the positing of a growth of jealousy in Leontes prior to the opening of the action can only be a way of remedying what is felt as a dramatic hiatus. It is more natural, perhaps, to look for clues in the text which may suggest, in spite of the seeming innocence of the words, that there are murky currents below the surface. In fact, several critics who have subjected the dialogue to close scrutiny have maintained that Leontes' outburst of passion when it comes is adequately prepared for within the scene itself.[22] Again, however, a comparison with Greene's story confirms the impression that Leontes' derangement is not only objectively unfounded but dramatically unexpected, as if the King almost from one moment to the next changes from being a trusting husband and hospitable friend into a brainsick tyrant. If we need an explanation of the suddenness it may possibly be found either in psychological theory or in metaphysics. David Holbrook chooses the former when he asserts that 'the stability of any human being's make-up, or of any relationship, can be wrecked by an inward psychic earthquake, with surprising suddenness, and *at any time*'.[23] Wilson Knight, on the other hand, thinks the case of Leontes demonstrates the power of evil, which is inherent in human nature and needs no rational motivation to break out and overpower the subject:

> His evil is self-born and unmotivated. Commentators have searched in vain for 'motives' to explain the soul-states and actions of Hamlet, Iago and Macbeth, without realizing that the poet is concerned not with trivialities, but with evil itself, whose cause remains as dark as theology.... In Leontes we have a study of evil yet more coherent, realistic and compact; a study of almost demonic possession.[24]

We are left ultimately with the fact that in the universe of romance we must not question too closely the motivations of the beings which inhabit it and that abrupt changes of behaviour must be accepted on faith. This, it must at once be added, does not exclude the presence of a fair degree of realism, and, of all the characters in *The Winter's Tale*, Leontes is the one who comes closest to being studied in depth. He worries over his suspicions, which understandably solidify when he learns of Polixenes' flight (ll.i.36ff).[25] He is an unpredictable and somewhat irresponsible character, but Shakespeare apparently did not want to load him with excessive weakness by including his incestuous attempt on his (as yet unrecognised) daughter to which Greene gives so much space: there is only a relic of this incident in Leontes' momentary desire for Perdita, which is immediately reproved by Paulina (V.i.222–7). Barbara Mowat finds Leontes a selfish and cowardly character, and seems to think him poorly portrayed, but to Wilson Knight 'Leontes is more complex than Othello as a study of jealousy and more realistically convincing than Macbeth as a study of evil possession.'[26]

Another character who is portrayed with a high degree of realism is Paulina, and it is interesting to see that in her case, as in that of Leontes, there is at one point a sudden emotional transformation as if the author makes a jump in his story. Having brought the news of Hermione's death to Leontes, she reviles him in violent terms. But when Leontes expresses contrition and an anonymous Lord reproaches her for her boldness of speech, all in only four lines, she begins her very next speech by saying she is sorry and by comforting the man she has just cursed (III.ii.207–24). We may again refer this seeming inconsistency to the pattern of surprises in the play.[27] An actual inconsistency, though a minor one, which relates to Paulina, is the statement by Leontes at V.iii.136–8 that she had agreed to take a husband by his consent as he to take a wife by hers. Actually we hear of no such mutual agreement in the earlier scene, where only Leontes swears to be ruled by Paulina if he ever marries again (V.i.69–82).[28]

The happy ending to all estrangements in *The Winter's Tale* is presented with a certain ironical detachment: it is like that of 'an old tale'. There is not much here of the conventional piety which we find in the ending of *Pericles* and *Cymbeline*; in fact it is only the statue of Hermione placed, as we learn, in a chapel (V.iii.86), which gives us a momentary sense of a divine presence, that of Hermione herself. As we witness the animation of the statue we may feel that a miracle is being enacted;[29] but we are soon to be disabused of this illusion, helped by the prominence of the down-to-earth Paulina as stage-manager. It is by human agency alone that Hermione is both preserved and restored, and we are to be in no doubt of this. The only miraculous thing is the way she has been kept hidden so long.

Hermione calls on the gods to bless her daughter (121–3), but neither in the ending nor in the play as a whole are the gods often invoked or made unequivocally responsible for what happens. Apollo may be said to be the presiding deity but his part is practically limited to the judgements and the prophecy spoken by his Oracle and he is only once or twice mentioned by name outside the scenes having to do with the mission to Delphos and the trial of Hermione, i.e. II.i and III.i–ii. [30] On two occasions there is a recognition of his intervention in the action, but in neither case is there an objective confirmation of his agency. The first occasion is when Mamillius is reported dead and the conscience-stricken Leontes, who has just denied the truth of the Oracle, cries out, 'Apollo's angry, and the heavens themselves/Do strike at my injustice' (III.ii.146–7). He entreats Apollo to pardon 'My great profaneness 'gainst thy Oracle!' (153–4). This must be accorded due importance but need not be overemphasised as more than an expression of personal anguish. It may be noted that the servant who reports Mamillius' death explains, rationally enough in terms of drama, albeit incredibly in realistic terms, that the prince 'is gone', as he says, 'with mere conceit and fear/Of the queen's speed' (144–5). The other occasion when Apollo is thought to have intervened is the scene on the coast of Bohemia when Antigonus wrongly thinks that Perdita is 'the issue of King Polixenes' and imagines Apollo wants the baby to be laid 'Either for life or death, upon the earth/Of its right father' (III.iii.42–6). What is incontrovertible here is that Antigonus helps to fulfil a prophecy, but so do many people in Shakespeare's plays, without the direction of deities. And if Apollo is responsible we may be permitted to think, remembering the fates of Antigonus and the mariners, that he exacts a gruesome toll of innocent human lives to achieve his purpose.

There is no need to attach importance to Leontes' perfunctory and parenthetical remark at the very end of the play that Florizel 'is troth-plight' to Perdita 'heavens directing' (V.iii.150), and anyway 'heavens' is a vague enough term. It is certainly remarkable that Apollo is not mentioned specifically in the dénouement.[31] It confirms the impression that this time the human *personae* are to be held entirely responsible for their own actions. In *The Tempest* we move into a metadramatic situation where the gods are mere figments of the mind.

Summing up, there is only one area of actual technical unconformity that matters in *The Winter's Tale*,[32] that which comprises Hermione's reported death and her rediscovery. I have argued that the contradiction between Hermione dead and Hermione living came about as the result of a major change in the original ending of the play, one which also involved the treatment of Perdita's reception in Sicilia and the exposure of Autolycus; but once the change was made the contradiction was no doubt exploitable, and I find no difficulty in agreeing with those critics who find it dramatically effective.[33] Certainly the 'old tale' aspect of the play invites a tolerant acceptance of the lies it tells.

10
Prospero's Project

Shakespeare is exactly as secretive about his purposes in *The Tempest* as is the dramaturge and stage-manager at the centre of this metadrama. Prospero stands above and beyond the other characters in the play, who have no way of knowing what is in his mind, and only rarely and briefly does he confide in the audience.[1] Nor does his maker in the guise of any other *persona* offer the least explanation of what is going on. The result is a play full of inexplicitness and ambiguities[2] and critics have divided themselves into opposite camps in viewing it as a plain story or an allegory. Even as a plain story it is far from unequivocal. And as an allegory (or a masque, as some suggest) it presents a great diversity of possible meanings ranging from the personal to the universal, from the political to the metaphysical.[3] We cannot even be sure of its geographical location, whether in the West Indies or the Mediterranean or just anywhere. It is particularly difficult to determine whether Shakespeare intended this impenetrability all along or whether it was partly fortuitous. Barbara Mowat assimilates the romances to what she calls 'open form drama', which is characterised by 'thematic discontinuities, character dislocations, separations of speech from action, of emotional expression from character and from the "facts"'. 'It is impossible', she says, 'to identify what was the cause and what the fortunate effect in the design and construction of these plays.'[4] This seems a fair statement of the difficulty which confronts us in attempting to analyse the constitution of *The Tempest*. It is all too tempting to suspect unconformities in the texture which belong genuinely either to the design of the characters or to the overall view of life which the play may be seen to embody. We shall have to proceed with caution, recognising apparent inconsistencies for what they are, but not necessarily ascribing them to merely contingent causes.

Raymond Powell thinks there were inherent contradictions in Shakespeare's chosen material. Shakespeare 'seems to have wanted to shape his subject-matter into something like allegory, while at the same time subverting that tendency by developing and exploring his material in an altogether freer and less constricted way'. And his problem was 'compounded by his use of the romance form', which meant, among other things, introducing ideal or stereotype representatives of goodness and wickedness while concurrently individualising them in more realistic terms.[5] Joan Rees takes a related view when she sees the narrative conditions of the romances, those by which the story-teller is justified in manipulating the logicality of events (or 'cheating') for the sake of an ideal structure, as conflicting with 'life with its unbiddable emotions, its unexpected blanks, its unwanted and uncongenial demands'. In *The Tempest* there might have been a perfect romance-ending but for the intrusion of these anarchic forces, and their disruptive influence leaves the play 'open-ended'.[6] Rees does not see this as entirely damaging, but a more positive assessment is offered by Barbara Mowat. Describing the romances as 'experimental blends of narrative and dramatic modes', she finds that their peculiar structure 'helps us to experience – rather than merely to become intellectually aware of – the wonder and complexity of story, of drama, and of life'.[7]

Clearly, the use of a narrative mode without an objective narrator had both advantages and disadvantages. On the one hand, our curiosity is sustained and the dramatic tension is kept up by the secrecy of the presiding sage, himself involved in the events he contrives.[8] On the other hand, a guide to an understanding of his purposes may be felt to be much-needed and is worryingly wanting.

Prospero's very character is in doubt.[9] Comments in word and deed by other persons, often our best pointers to the character of an observed individual, are sometimes strongly derogatory. Ferdinand in soliloquy calls his taskmaster 'crabbed' and harsh (III.i.8–9). Ariel frets at the continual servitude which Prospero imposes on him, and Caliban asserts (truthfully or not) that Prospero's spirits all hate him (III.ii.92).[10] Even Miranda thinks her father speaks too 'ungently' to Ferdinand (I.ii.447); and by deceiving Prospero while she thinks him 'hard at study' (III.i.19–21) she implies his unreasonableness. Against this must be set Miranda's very explicit defence of her parent after his show of 'ungentleness':

My father's of a better nature, sir,
Than he appears by speech: this is unwonted

Which now came from him.

(I.ii.499–501)[11]

Ferdinand, too comes to revise his opinion of the man who will now be his father-in-law:

So rare a wonder'd father and a wise
Makes this place Paradise.

(IV.i.123–4)

Prospero's behaviour provides an equally divided picture. His account of his past life as Duke of Milan gives the impression of a peaceable recluse, and on first coming to the island he seems to have been benevolence itself, not only freeing Ariel from Sycorax's curse but cherishing and educating Caliban as if he were his own child. Now, however, he is temperamental and irascible. His ungentleness to Ferdinand on the latter's first appearance may be understood as a pretence, though he has some justification for seeing the prince as a 'spy' and a 'traitor' by association with his usurping father.[12] But Prospero's impatience with Ariel is patently genuine, and his harshness to Caliban is barbed with loathing. In all three cases he describes, almost with relish, the torments he will subject his captives to if they do not obey him.

To Ariel –

If thou more murmur'st, I will rend an oak,
And peg thee in his knotty entrails, till
Thou hast howl'd away twelve winters.

(I.ii.294–6)

To Caliban –

If thou neglect'st, or dost unwillingly
What I command, I'll rack thee with old cramps,
Fill all thy bones with aches, make thee roar,
That beasts shall tremble at thy din.

(I.ii.370–3)

To Ferdinand

I'll manacle thy neck and feet together:

> Sea-water shalt thou drink; thy food shall be
> The fresh-brook mussels, wither'd roots, and husks
> Wherein the acorn cradled.
>
> (I.ii.464–7)

The sufferings he actually visits on the court party (shipwreck, loss, hunger, fright) are vividly presented, and those he inflicts on Caliban and his fellow conspirators are as fierce as even Prospero can invent, short of flaying them alive. He declares at the beginning of his 'project' that his care for Miranda is his only motive – 'I have done nothing but in care of thee,/Of thee, my dear one' (I.ii.16–17) – and he represents Miranda to Ferdinand as 'a third of mine own life,/ Or that for which I live' (IV.i.3–4). There is no need to doubt his deep love of his daughter, or, for that matter, his affection for Ariel (V.i.49). And his ability to forgive his enemies at the end speaks eloquently in his favour. But is loving care of anyone the main motive for his behaviour?

Prospero's library was once large enough for his ambition. Now the island is too small. Now he wants power, and he has acquired the means of obtaining it, both in the world of spirits and – with the aid of the spirits he commands – in the world of man. There is a topical political dimension to the play, which is highlighted in an article by Curt Breight on 'The Tempest and the Discourse of Treason'.[13] As Breight points out, 'the discourse of treason is *central* to a thirty-year period of English culture beginning in the early 1580s', and *The Tempest* strongly reflects both the political anxiety of the age and the cruelty with which it pursued the suspected enemies of the regime. It was on the background of the Bond of Association of 1584 that Shakespeare's Ferdinand could be thought a party to spying and treason.[14] And the torture which Prospero devises for his would-be assassins –

> Go charge my goblins that they grind their joints
> With dry convulsions; shorten up their sinews
> With aged cramps; and more pinch-spotted make them
> Than pard or cat o' mountain.
>
> (IV.i.258–11)[15]

– is not a whit more horrible than what was actually practised in England under James I.

Are we perhaps to assume that the character of Prospero undergoes a change, that he changes suddenly and violently and for the worse after Caliban's attempted rape of his daughter? Before that event he might well have seen his island as something approaching Gonzalo's utopian dream, at least as a pleasant retreat for a studious scholar. But he has had a rude awakening to the reality of evil, and seeing it in sexual terms makes it appear as a potentiality for evil in Nature itself. The shock which he experienced twelve years earlier, when he was deposed and marooned, is now revived to new bitterness. And with it comes a craving for revenge. If this is a correct interpretation Prospero undergoes another change when, in a passage which has often been seen as crucially significant, he is persuaded by Ariel to forgo his vengeance:

> [*Ari.*]   Your charm so strongly works 'em,
> That if you now beheld them, your affections
> Would become tender.
> *Pros.*   Dost thou think so, spirit?
> *Ari.*   Mine would, sir, were I human.
> *Pros.*   And mine shall.
> Hast thou, which art but air, a touch, a feeling
> Of their afflictions, and shall not myself,
> One of their kind, that relish all as sharply
> Passion as they, be kindlier mov'd than thou art?
> Though with their high wrongs I am struck to th' quick,
> Yet with my nobler reason 'gainst my fury
> Do I take part; the rarer action is
> In virtue than in vengeance
>   (V.i.17–28)

It would make Prospero more interesting if he is seen to change twice than if he is experienced as a character without development. But neither his change to thoughts of vengeance nor his change to forgiveness is made explicit, because both have to do with his grand 'project', which is never clearly revealed.

The word 'project' is not often used by Shakespeare, and only once in any one play apart from *The Tempest*. Prospero's 'project' is mentioned twice in different speeches, first by Ariel (II.i.294) and then by Prospero himself (V.i.1), and it is echoed in the Epilogue. Ariel also refers to Caliban's conspiracy as a 'project' (IV.i.175). Apparently the word is meant to be significant. But the only part of Prospero's plans which is disclosed to the audience is the bringing together of Ferdinand and Miranda. 'It goes on, I see,/ As my soul prompts it', remarks the wily father as he observes the entrancement of the young couple (I.ii.422–3). Apart from this, the references, as Powell says, 'are cryptic in the extreme':

> Prospero refers explicitly neither to revenge nor to forgiveness; his most urgently expressed need is to have his enemies in his power, and to what this will form the prelude is left unstated. A third possibility is that Prospero himself does not know what he is going to do and that he makes up his mind only at the end of the play. But the evidence fails to point unequivocally to this interpretation any more than it does to the other two.[16]

The magician's concern for his daughter, expressed early on ('I have done nothing but in care of thee') and the success of the first part of his scheme touching the lovers, may seem to indicate that the happiness of Miranda remains his central object – after all, it is her nubility which has radically altered his situation on the island. She is, as he tells Ferdinand, 'that for which I live'.[17] But his plans for his daughter are realised without the need for further measures other than returning somehow to Milan, and it definitely seems to be his own 'zenith' and his own 'fortunes' that Prospero has in mind in his explanation to Miranda of why he raised the 'seastorm':

> by my prescience
> I find my zenith doth depend upon
> A most auspicious star, whose influence
> If now I court not, but omit, my fortunes
> Will ever after droop.   (I.ii.180–4)

'Here cease more questions', he then admonishes her.

As for revenge or forgiveness, there can be little doubt of the impression created by the first four acts if we see them in isolation from the fifth: Prospero is bent on punishing the enemies whom he now holds in his power (the word 'enemies' is sounded repeatedly). And it may not be irrelevant to notice, by way of analogy, that Caliban's 'project' is undisguisedly one of revenge.[18] If Prospero engineered the attempt by Antonio and Sebastian to murder Alonso, this could be seen as part of his main purpose, and the intention would surely have been to expose and punish the plotted regicide in the end rather than merely hush it up.[19] Even the kind of punishment Prospero contemplates may be hinted at in the conditional doom pronounced by Ariel:

> Ling'ring perdition – worse than any death
> Can be at once – shall step by step attend
> You and your ways;
>
> (III.iii.77–9)

'Ling'ring perdition' suggests nothing more clearly than that the court party should in their turn be marooned on the island, which in spite of Gonzalo's raptures could be rendered considerably less hospitable to them than it has been to Prospero.[20]

As a condition of pardon Prospero, through Ariel, demands 'heart-sorrow/And a clear life ensuing' (III.iii.81–2). But the immediate response of the villainous court trio hardly indicates a will to repentance. Alonso briefly recognises his 'trespass' (99). But in fact Alonso in his despair merely stumbles away to join his son who, he is now convinced, 'i' th'ooze is bedded' (100). And the two prime villains, who at the beginning of the scene were plotting a new attempt to kill the King, think themselves beset by fiends, whom they now rush off to fight (102–3). One is all the more surprised to hear Gonzalo remark at the end of the Harpy scene that the three evildoers are made desperate by their awakened guilt:

> their great guilt,
> Like poison given to work a great time after,
> Now 'gins to bite the spirits.
>
> (III.iii.104–6)

Even at the end of the play, when Prospero's enemies know themselves to be at his mercy, only Alonso seems somewhat contrite. But all he brings himself to say by way of apology is: 'Thy dukedom I resign, and do entreat/ Thou pardon me my wrongs (V.i.118–9).[21] Sebastian's muttered comment on Prospero's lenience, 'The devil speaks in him' (129), expresses simply fear and contempt, and Antonio remains stubbornly silent. There is not much visible evidence of the 'inward pinches' of which Prospero speaks:

> Thou art pinch'd for 't now, Sebastian. Flesh and blood,
> You, brother mine, that entertain'd ambition,

Expell'd remorse and nature; whom, with Sebastian, –
Whose inward pinches therefore are most strong, –
Would here have kill'd your King;

$(74-8)^{22}$

The 'inward pinches' suggest twinges of conscience. But Sebastian and Antonio show no sign of a guilty conscience. And the merriment of the wicked brothers at the sight of Caliban and his bedraggled companions betokens no chastened mood in them. It is as if Shakespeare tried to follow up two lines of thought simultaneously, one leading to conversion, the other to punishment. But in spite of suggestions of penitence, we are chiefly struck by the unregenerate behaviour of two of the villains. It can hardly be argued, therefore, that the possibility of redemption by repentance which Ariel offers on Prospero's behalf in the Harpy scene prepares at that point in the play for a happy ending bringing merited forgiveness. It is more reasonable to suppose that retributive justice rather than forgiveness was uppermost in Shakespeare's, as in Prospero's, mind until quite late in the play.

Logically 'ling'ring perdition' should follow upon the lack of 'heart-sorrow'. Prospero's condition for forgiveness is not changed. But it is dropped. It is Prospero's mind which is changed and Ariel who persuades him to relent.[23] Ariel's persuasion is hardly a mere echo of Prospero's own thoughts, and Prospero clearly experiences a short but real psychomachia as he implicitly rejects his former stipulations and explicitly annuls the penalties attached to their non-observance. He accepts that he cannot force full repentance. But neither does he overcome his sense of injury sufficiently to offer unstinted forgiveness. Alonso is acquitted, but with no great warmth ('Behold, sir King,/ The wronged Duke of Milan', 106–7). As for Antonio, Prospero's first feeling on seeing him in the final reckoning is one of undeniable blood-kinship ('Flesh and blood,/ You, brother mine'), but only a little later his revulsion gets the better of him and his forgiveness sounds grudging, to say the least:

For you, most wicked sir, whom to call brother
Would even infect my mouth, I do forgive
Thy rankest fault, – all of them; and require
My dukedom of thee, which perforce, I know,
Thou must restore.

(130–4)

The recognition and subsequent denial of brotherhood seems to point to two different degrees of clemency. Bonamy Dobrée finds Prospero's forgiveness of his enemies Senecan rather than Christian.[24] Something remains to the end to make it dubious, as if the will to revenge has left an unremovable residue of bitterness. This impression may have been initially caused by something as objective and almost technical as Shakespeare's wish to provide a measure of poetic justice – the villains must not be too easily white-washed. But it remains true that many critics have sensed a disillusionment in the last act, as if Prospero not only gives up his magic but compromises on his aims.

To what extent this spells failure for Prospero is an interesting problem. W. C. Curry thinks Prospero in his last actions transcends his former imperfect self, which depends for its improvement on white magic, or theurgy, and renounces his conjuring as he approaches a state of union with the gods.[25] Cosmo Corfield, on the other hand, argues that Prospero's magic is tainted from the start with impure goetic impulses, that this is made evident in the 'Ye elves' speech (V.i.33–57), and that this is why he comes to see it as 'rough magic' and has to renounce it without achieving his aim of ennobling humanity. 'Prospero's crisis', he says, 'is an admission... of hopeless involvement with the world', and his 'crisis speech ['Our revels now are ended...' –IV.i.148–63] accepts his vision of perfectibility for what it is – Pisgah sight'. Even then Prospero fails to reintegrate with his fellow humans, as is indicated by his death-wish ('Every third thought shall be my grave', 311). 'The final sense we have of his magical failure is that of infinite humiliation.'[26]

Curry's and Corfield's views are extreme as well as diametrically opposed and I see no reason to subscribe to either. But there are intermediate views. Robert Egan, in an article antecedent to Corfield's, also finds Prospero presumptuous and shortsighted but maintains that he learns a real lesson: that he cannot usurp 'the divine prerogative of vengeance', that 'as an artist, he must limit his ends to the revelation of truth and self-knowledge; as a man, he can presume no further', and that 'Only through unconditional forgiveness and acceptance of human nature... can art be capable of comprehending and dealing with the realities, good and evil, of the world.'[27] In fact, Prospero's flawed forgiveness can be seen most positively as a symptom of Shakespeare's restoration of his sage to the world of real people, which is composed of all kinds of men, but where human nature is essentially limited and fallible. This view of humanity is consonant with a Christian philosophy of life. And it may be worth noticing that in the shipwreck scene at the beginning of the romance Gonzalo calls his companions to join the King and Prince at prayers (53), Prospero in the second scene attributes his and Miranda's salvation from the sea to 'Providence divine' (159) (he calls Miranda 'a cherubin...that did 'preserve me', her smile was 'infused with a fortitude from heaven') while in the final scene Ferdinand ascribes his winning of Miranda to 'immortal Providence' (189). (The Epilogue, of course, directly alludes to the Lord's Prayer in its closing lines, but it may not be entirely justifiable to see it as part of the play proper.)[28]

We may trace Christian references throughout the play if we wish, usually disguised as invocations of 'heaven' or 'the heavens'. Miranda in I.ii three times invokes 'the heavens' (once curiously repeating her compassionate exclamation 'O the heavens', lines 59, 116). Prospero, Alonso and Gonzalo invoke the heavens twice each in different places. There may be simply a deliberate avoidance of profanity in this usage, as in the awkward phrase 'The wills above be done' (spoken by the pious Gonzalo at I.i.66).[29] But the general philosophical atmosphere of the play is also inimical to overt Christian reminders. They clash with the dominant pagan universe of spirits and with the role of Prospero as a conjurer of spirits. In the final reconciliation scene, Gonzalo calls upon 'the gods', not Providence, to 'drop a blessed crown' on the affianced couple:

For it is you that have chalk'd forth the way
Which brought us hither.

(201–4)

We need not be too solemn about Gonzalo's reliance on 'Fate' and 'destiny' as we listen to his benevolent cursing of the boatswain in the shipwreck scene, confident that the unceremonious mariner will live to be safely hanged on dry land (I.i.30–1). But we can hardly overlook the serious philosophical message of Ariel's harangue to the 'three men of sin' in the Harpy episode where he denounces them in the names of Destiny, Fate and 'the powers':

You are three men of sin, whom Destiny, –
That hath to instrument this lower world
And what is in't, – the never-surfeited sea

Hath caus'd to belch up you;

. . . .

          I and my fellows
Are ministers of Fate.

. . . .

The powers, delaying, not forgetting, have
Incens'd the seas and shores . . . .

                        (III.iii.53–74)

These are pagan ideas. Actually, as Walter Clyde Curry has demonstrated, it is possible to place Providence itself in the context of a pagan mythology, as the power which presides over 'the higher kingdom', while 'the subordinate kingdom', or what Ariel calls 'this lower world', is administered by Destiny, or Fate.[30]
Nor must we forget Prospero's early statement of his faith in Fortune and the stars:

By accident most strange, bountiful Fortune,
(Now my dear lady) hath mine enemies
Brought to this shore; and by my prescience
I find my zenith doth depend upon
A most auspicious star, whose influence
If now I court not, but omit, my fortunes
Will ever after droop.

                        (I.ii.178–84)

This astrological science has no place in a Christian scheme of things. In fact Curry emphasises Shakespeare's complete dependence, in *The Tempest*, on a pagan system of thought as revived and developed during the Renaissance:

in *The Tempest* . . . the artist is revealed as having passed definitely under the influence of Renaissance thought. He no longer employs Christian myth as the integrating principle of tragedy; here he creates an altogether different world, which is dominated by classical myth and integrated by a purely pagan philosophy.[31]

Even the Epilogue is assimilated in Curry's interpretation to pagan mystery. It represents the final stage of Prospero's aspiration to transcend his baser nature and merge with the gods.[32] Robert West also thinks that magic in *The Tempest* 'suggests Neo-Platonism and

Cabalism rather than scholasticism for the pattern of its demonology, but', he goes on, 'it builds on their practices and experiences, leaving their rationalizations latent'. West maintains that Shakespeare was not intellectually confused in his use of the supernatural, 'but merely preserved the proper mysteriousness of his subject'.[33] Still, as West is chiefly concerned to demonstrate, Prospero's 'spirit magic' is of a highly censurable kind. And there can be no doubt that it firmly suppresses any intimations we may have or receive of Providential control in a Christian sense. (I here disregard the idea that Prospero himself may be seen to represent Providence, which seems altogether unacceptable in view of his imperfections.)

When Prospero renounces his magic he not merely dismisses his spirits but pronounces them 'insubstantial', the stuff of dreams only. That he comprises in this vision 'the great globe itself' and 'all which it inherit' is an extension of his demystifying mystification which has its own function in the philosophical pattern of the play. But the rejection of the spirits comes first. And to pronounce them unreal and hence harmless was perhaps an easier way out than to deny their usefulness for good purposes. Prospero suffers a change of faith. Did Shakespeare feel, too, that he had overstepped the bounds of legitimate occultism and decide to abandon it with the best excuse he could invent before Prospero's farewell to the enchanted island? If so, neither Prospero nor Shakespeare had the heart to deconstruct that wonderfully engaging spirit Ariel, who is simply set free at the last to flit among bees and cowslips.

As it is, we are left in the conclusion with a group of humans whose only stay is in Providence and prayer. We are also left with Ariel and with vivid impressions of a pagan world of spirits which will not entirely dissolve into nothingness. But the main contradiction is not between Providence and magic, but between belief in a real universe ruled by God or gods and inhabited by spirits, on the one hand, and, on the other, the complete scepticism of the 'Our revels now are ended' speech. The *theatrum mundi* idea as here introduced implies that all is illusion, a 'baseless fabric'. And in human life nothing points beyond extinction, being 'rounded with a sleep'. When Prospero says, 'Every third thought shall be my grave' (311) he says nothing about what comes after the grave. Hamlet was bewildered by that puzzle, and we may be mystified by the contradictory beliefs embedded in *The Tempest*. Perhaps Shakespeare foresaw this problem when, in answer to Alonso's bemused remark, 'there is in this business more than nature/ Was ever conduct of', he makes Prospero reply, 'Do not infest your mind with beating on/ The strangeness of this business' (V.i.243–7). Prospero promises an explanation 'at pick'd leisure/ Which shall be shortly single', and the sleight-of-hand involved probably leaves us satisfied that Alonso will get it, though we do not.

A little more needs to be said about the goddesses who appear in the betrothal masque. Since we are explicitly told that these actors are mere spirits who melt into air, we are not asked to think of them in the same way as Diana in *Pericles* or Jupiter in *Cymbeline*. In fact there are no theophanies in *The Tempest*. But, moreover, it seems most likely that the goddesses were interpolated into the pageant, which originally included simply Ariel, masked as Ceres, performing a dance with a group of nymphs impersonating reapers. This would match the dance of naiads with which Ferdinand is entertained in I.ii and to accompany which Ariel, dressed as 'a nymph o' th' sea' (301), sings his 'Come unto these yellow sands,/ And then take hands';[34] as well as the dance of 'strange shapes' led by Ariel as a Harpy in III.iii. Frank Kermode accepts the whole masque as 'an integral part of the play',[35] but I am more convinced by the arguments for textual alteration in this scene presented by Dover Wilson and Irwin Smith.[36] It certainly looks as if Ariel originally was to have brought in the reapers at once: Prospero's command 'bring the rabble' (37) is hardly applicable to goddesses. Ariel is to 'incite them to quick motion' (39) and he promises that

> Before you can say, 'come', and 'go,'
> And breathe twice, and cry, 'so, so,'
> Each one, tripping on his toe,
> Will be here with mop and mow.
>   (44–7)

Again hardly suggestive of goddesses. It would be in keeping with a dance of reapers if Ariel impersonated Ceres, as he says he did a little later.[37] I would suggest that the interlude first began with Ceres speaking the words now attributed to Iris: 'You nymphs, call'd Naiads, of the windring brooks', etc.[38] We would thus have Ariel calling in the nymphs as he does in the yellow-sands scene.

The unconformities in the composition of the masque are not the only textual irregularities in *The Tempest*. The latter half of the long second scene of Act I contains a number of details which are

inconsistent with information in the rest of the play and point to
discontinuous inspiration. We are told twice that Ariel is to be
released after two days (298, 424), whereas both before and after
this information he has only three hours to wait (I.ii.240,
V.i.4,186, 223). The Duke of Milan's (i.e. Antonio's) son is mentioned uniquely in this passage (441) and appears nowhere else.
Miranda fails to connect Ferdinand with what she has heard of her
father's history even when she learns that he is Prince (or, as he
thinks, King) of Naples (437–50). There are outcrops of irregular
metre, especially in lines 298–308, suggesting what Dover Wilson
calls 'botchery'.[39] And, most interesting of all, this is the only part
of the play where Caliban is unequivocally counted as a human
being. Miranda says that Ferdinand 'Is the third man that e'er I saw
(448), the two others necessarily being her father and Caliban; and
her father a little later remarks, referring to Ferdinand, 'Thou
think'st there is no more such shapes as he,/ Having seen but him
and Caliban' (481–2).[40] In III.i, however, Miranda, speaking to
Ferdinand, asserts 'nor have I seen/ More that I may call men than
you, good friend,/ And my dear father' (50–2). In various parts of
the play other than the passage in question, Caliban is a slave, a
mooncalf, a monster, a fish, a beast, a devil, a demi-devil, a mis-
shapen knave, but never a man. There is no need in the present
context to discuss his actual nature or appearance, though this
matter has occasioned a good deal of comment. What concerns us
here is that Shakespeare at one stage definitely thought of Caliban
as human although born of a witch, whereas in other places one
cannot be sure.

Could the second half of I.ii have been written before the expository narrative which fills the first half? And did Shakespeare fail to
revise the last 200 lines or so of the scene after modifying his plans?
At least the two days remaining of Ariel's servitude and the
mention of Milan's son must have belonged to an early idea of the
play if they were intentional; perhaps the conception of Caliban as
recognisably human, too. In any case, a welding of slightly different
conceptions of a work in progress need not be in doubt.

That the whole of the second scene was worked over with an eye
for readjustments is borne out by a curious contradiction. When
Prospero first intimates that he is about to reveal his life-story to
Miranda, who knows no more, he says, than that he is 'master of a
full poor cell,/And thy no greater father', she declares, 'More to
know/Did never meddle with my thoughts' (21–2). Then only a

few lines further on she contradicts this statement: 'You have
often/ Begun to tell me what I am, but stopp'd,/ And left me to a
bootless inquisition' (33–5). Apparently she is curious to know
more after all. After the former of Miranda's declarations, Prospero
remarks, ''Tis time/ I should inform thee farther', and before the
latter he repeats, 'For thou must now know farther'. The repetition
is obviously unwanted and points to an intended omission not
observed in the publication of the play: Miranda's lack of curiosity
about her own and her father's past was only a first thought which
the author rejected.[41]

In other parts of the play there are not such evident disturbances.
It is interesting to speculate, as Irwin Smith has done, that
Prospero's great valedictory speech beginning 'Our revels now are
ended' (IV.i.148–58) was the original epilogue of the whole play,
moved to its present position to give Ariel time to change out of his
Ceres costume before 'the rabble's dance' (though, as I have indicated, I see no need for this change of costume, since Ariel was
Ceres in 'the rabble's dance' anyway). Smith points out that the
lines of Prospero's speech

> are wholly out of accord with Prospero's state of mind. They are
> not lines that Shakespeare would have put into the mouth of a
> man who has just awakened to a sense of mortal peril and the
> instant need to defend himself, nor of a man shaken by unprece-
> dented anger.
>
> Furthermore, although the passage purports to describe the
> masque just ended, it does nothing of the kind.[42]

The valediction speech would no doubt be effective as a closure to
the complete play, even, one might like to think, as a closure to a
life's work of brilliant theatrical fantasies, but in the absence of
solid evidence for a transference from an end-position to its present
place one must allow it to make its full impact in the scene where it
occurs.

There is more to be said, perhaps, for the suspicion that something is missing between the end of Act IV, where Ariel and
Prospero are the last persons on the stage, and the beginning of Act
V, where they immediately reappear.[43] Such exits and entrances of
the same persons in adjacent scenes are rare in Shakespeare, and
there seems to be no good reason why the overlap should be
wanted here. It has been held that the act-division would provide

an interval during which there might be music or other light enter-tainment.[44] But this brings us to a question of structure where the shape of the action rather than its formal divisions must be taken into account. Shakespeare obviously exerted himself in *The Tempest* to observe the neoclassical rules of unities, but it is far from certain that the Horatian five-act arrangement of the printed play was his own. As it features in the Folio, it is artificial and arbitrary. The fourth act, for instance, has only one scene and is relatively short. Take away the masque, and not much is left. The first act, on the other hand, is inordinately long and could conveniently be termi-nated at the entry of Ferdinand, making the first movement consis-tently expository, forming the *protasis*. From the entry of Ferdinand to the exit of the drunken clowns in III.ii, the second main move-ment of the play is concerned with the progress of love and the hatching of murder plots (the *epitasis*),[45] until in III.iii and IV.i Prospero takes the initiative to immobilise and chastise his enemies and unite the lovers, making this third part of the play largely a counter-movement, or *catastasis*: it contains Prospero's spells – the Harpy scene, the betrothal, and the hunting of the clowns. Finally, the fifth act as we have it is the dénouement or *catastrophe*.[46] The play in fact divides so naturally into four main parts that it is rea-sonable to suppose that this structure was the result of careful plan-ning. But the divisions are not such as would call for intervals, which would be merely distracting. If in fact a scene has been can-celled or lost between Acts IV and V, the awkwardness remains as a clue.[47]

I have omitted a number of minor inconsistencies and loose ends from my discussion of *The Tempest*.[48] Some of them contribute to the general sense of indefiniteness which pervades the play, but they are mostly of the kind that will occur in any play not based on the strictest realism. Our focus has been on Prospero's character, on the nature of his magic practices, and on the announced 'project' which he pursues. For whose sake does he raise the tempest and harry the shipwrecked courtiers – to husband Miranda or to climb to his own 'zenith'? We have to recognise both these aims, though with regard to priorities we should notice that the project gathers 'to a head' (V.i.1) only after the lovers are formally engaged. And are we to expect revenge or forgiveness? I have argued that we get forgive-ness in spite of what we are chiefly led to expect and also that Prospero changes in respect of his original intentions and under the influence of the human feelings that Ariel at the crucial point is made to express. But there is no visible repentance in the two most villainous characters, so Prospero's condition of pardon is unfulfilled, nor is his forgiveness ready to forget past crimes and injuries. It is no doubt right to see his victory as a partial failure from a moral and spiritual point of view, though an opposite interpretation is offered by some critics. It is also hard to avoid conflicting views of Prospero's magic, and it may be that Shakespeare had scruples in presenting it as entirely legitimate and hence made his sage in the end describe it as 'rough magic' and abjure it. Certainly there are contradictions in the metaphysical and supernatural preconceptions of the play. Christianity jostles with pagan demonology and both with the stars and destiny. And the nihilism of the 'We are such stuff' speech denies them all. There seems to be something finally unresolvable in all this, and this may in fact be the poet's message, if there is one, and the legacy of his works. Prospero promises explanations 'at pick'd leisure', but for the present he advises: 'Do not infest your mind with beating on/ The strangeness of this business'.

Unconformities, then, may be good for teasing us out of thought. But there are more definite and less functional unconformities. Some of the details of I.ii point to broken composition. Did Shakespeare intend his action to take two days before he settled for a strict unity of time? Did he mean Caliban to be human or a monster? And did he have any purpose in bringing in the son of the Duke of Milan? There is textual disturbance, too, to prove the masque of goddesses a late idea introduced into a scene already completed. The masque, of course, may have been meant for special performances at court, possibly in connection with the betrothal and marriage of Princess Elizabeth and the Elector Palatine.[49] This does not mean, however, that it became an indissoluble part of the play. One lesson that modern scholarship seems to have learnt is that Shakespeare's plays were not unalterable entities, and that we cannot know all versions as variously performed in various places and at various times. But the clues to insertion left around the masque of goddesses show that we are not without information.

11

Conclusion

The comedies and romances we have been considering belong in part to the period in Shakespeare's authorship when his relatively simple vision of moral issues achieved its greatest triumphs in lighthearted comedy before that vision was darkened and complicated by more deeply disturbing insights into the human condition. *As You Like It* and *Twelfth Night* are still light enough to keep us continuously amused, but *Much Ado About Nothing*, which probably preceded them, already approaches a concern with wickedness and suffering which exceeds in gravity anything we find in the comedies up to and including *The Merchant of Venice*. The dating of the plays written somewhere between 1598 and 1602 is not precisely established, but *Twelfth Night* may have been roughly contemporaneous with *Hamlet*, which opened up a tragic vein intensively exploited at the Globe for as long as eight years.[1] It was at the beginning of this tragic phase that *Troilus and Cressida*, *All's Well That Ends Well* and *Measure for Measure* appeared, a pseudo-tragedy and two comedies, the latter presenting an overall comic structure which was all but overwhelmed by tragic implications. Not till two Roman plays (*Antony and Cleopatra* and *Coriolanus*) and possibly *Timon of Athens* had exhausted his motivation for tragedy did Shakespeare discover less psychologically searching and more emblematically universal dramatic subjects which reverted to comic solutions while retaining a strong tragic awareness of weakness and corruption. The first three of the resultant romances were still set in ancient times, the last in a more contemporary period. All move among pagan gods and spirits, but *The Winter's Tale* and *The Tempest* may be said to be guided to a conclusion by a basic belief in Christian repentance and forgiveness.

The mixture of comedy and tragedy which we find in *Much Ado* works well enough in that play, where two separate issues help to keep the sinister element within bounds without preventing a skilfully contrived interaction between the different plot strands. *All's*

Well has a fairly even blend of the comic and the tragic (or the potentially tragic) throughout. But it is a different matter with *Measure for Measure*, where the tragic and the comic parts make up two halves of a broken masterpiece. It is also an extreme example of the violent yoking of realism and fable. When we come to the romances, however, the general fancifulness of the action allows for a degree of generic variety which the more realistic plays resist. There is a general pattern of recurrent misfortunes till near the end, when happiness is more or less miraculously produced. But in the case of *Cymbeline*, in particular, it may be felt that the dominant tragic pattern is held too long to prepare us for the comic conclusion.

The strength of the tragic tone in some of the problem comedies and romances may have been unplanned and unforeseen, and it is natural to suppose that the author's absorption in the delineation of his characters and his serious involvement in their fates and conflicts led to difficulties having to do with proportion and structure. *All's Well* becomes unbalanced because the portrait in depth of Helena is given up after the midpoint of the play, and though to some extent interest in Helena is replaced by interest in Bertram there is never the same seriousness again. Character in action is replaced by intrigue pure and simple. On the other hand, apart from an ambiguity regarding Helena's intentions on stealing away from Rossillion, her portrait is not actually changed to another likeness, nor is there an abrupt transition, for intrigue features in the first part before it monopolises the second. Again it is a different matter with *Measure for Measure*, where Isabella, as we have seen, becomes a new person, either because Shakespeare had headed her for tragedy and changed his mind or because he had to get her back at any cost on a chosen path to a comic solution after her problem had got out of hand. A change of mind may also be suspected in *The Winter's Tale*, where as likely as not the restoration to life of Hermione was a revision prompted by her lifelike presence in the first part of the play; and though in itself a brilliant *coup de théâtre*, it was implemented at the expense of Perdita's role and in spite of all the misinformation about Hermione's death it left scattered about the play. But in general Shakespeare was less intimately involved with the characters of his romances than with those of his earlier comedies, and this is true of Prospero as well as Pericles or Imogen. They never acquire the complete humanity of a Helena or an Isabella and therefore never escape from the dramatist's control.

Sometimes the indications are not so much that Shakespeare revised his initial plans but that he was in two minds or at least open-minded about his intentions at the outset. Thus if Prospero seems lacking in solid humanity (which of course is not necessarily in itself a fault in drama) it is partly because he remains mysterious concerning his 'project' and we cannot tell for certain whether he wishes from the first to convert and forgive his enemies or to punish them. Or in fact what Shakespeare wished him to wish. The doubtful symptoms of repentance in the shipwrecked party also contribute to a sense of something not clearly worked out. Prospero's magic is not unequivocally of a permissible kind. And among the lesser enigmas in the same play there is the human or monstrous anatomy of Caliban, which seems to be left undecided. If we turn back to the first comedy discussed in this book, *Much Ado About Nothing* it shows plentiful signs of what could be either changes of mind or vague intentions: the many ghost characters, for instance, the senseless villainy of Borachio and the complicity of Margaret, above all the protracted business of proxy wooing and the different versions of Don Pedro's behaviour as a go-between. The list could be amplified with examples from the other plays, like the question of Orsino's rank in *Twelfth Night*, to take a minor inconsistency, or the conception of Imogen in *Cymbeline* in very realistic or very romantic terms, to take a larger unconformity.

There is one important area where a general undecidedness is very noticeable, that of the supernatural and metaphysical. In the comedies imagined as set in the contemporary world there is no great problem until we come to *Measure for Measure*. Christianity both in its theological aspects and ecclesiastical functions is taken for granted. There are friars and priests, genuine or impersonated, in *Much Ado, As You Like It, Twelfth Night, Measure for Measure* and by implication in *All's Well. As You Like It* is particularly saturated with Christian allusions and ways of thinking, and its occasional introduction of classical mythology, unless forced by censorship,[2] partly belongs to the picture of courtly fashion, as in the case of the oaths pronounced by Rosalind and Celia, partly may be regarded as a concession to a taste for charades as in the case of the Hymen episode. In *Measure for Measure*, however, we begin to find contradictions. The disguised Duke impersonating a friar comforts Claudio with thoughts of death which are far from Christian. Death is sleep and annihilation, no more: 'thou exists', he says, 'on many a thousand grains/ That issue out of dust', and these will be dispersed in death. Isabella, a novice who sets her faith against the sinful lust of Angelo, echoes the Duke's epicureanism to defend her sanctity *vis-à-vis* her brother, who, however, falls back into his fear of hell. The plot of *Measure for Measure* requires a strong Christian atmosphere of sin and grace, and the materialistic philosophy of the Friar–Duke seems gratuitously introduced.

Measure for Measure is generally dated 1604. *Othello*, probably of the same year, depends like *Measure for Measure* on a Christian setting; so does *Macbeth*, produced in 1606. *King Lear*, however, which immediately preceded *Macbeth*, is consistently pagan in its reference to the gods, and after *Macbeth* Shakespeare set all his plays except *The Tempest* and *Henry VIII* in pre-Christian times. Since this change in his choice of background coincided with the passing of the Act to Restrain Abuses of Players (1606), he may simply have wished to avoid the nuisance of constantly having to pacify the Master of the Revels. But if we examine the philosophical views expressed in *The Tempest* and remember the strange contradictions in *Measure for Measure* we can hardly avoid the suspicion that Shakespeare at 40 was theologically adrift. One may wonder what conflicts of belief were going on in his mind.

It may be of interest to note that the gods in the romances are for the most part of little real importance in determining events. In most cases and places they can be assimilated to Fortune, who, or which, is a conventional personification of the unforeseeable nature of evironmental forces, the reverses and obstacles which man would have to fight against in any case, like the storms in *Pericles*; or of more propitious accidental happenings. To some extent the gods are rhetorical embellishments, or elements of local colour, a matter of pattern. It is useless to deny that the characters in these plays believe in a supernatural reality; in fact their sense of being at the mercy of unseen powers gives a dimension to their struggles without which they would seem less human. But if we look at the actions objectively it will be easily seen that failures and successes hardly need to be ascribed to the gods. Pericles and Marina draw on their own human strength and endurance. In *Cymbeline* and *The Winter's Tale* mortal love pitted against hatred and jealousy is the main propulsive principle. There seems to be an attempt in the first three of the romances to ascribe decisive turns for the better to the work of the gods who may be said to preside over these plays: Diana, Jupiter and Apollo. But Diana, as we have seen, is mostly inactive and in the climactic ending of *Pericles* strictly unnecessary, the theophany of Jupiter in *Cymbeline* is probably a late interpolation and again unnecessary, and Apollo in *The Winter's Tale* is an oracular voice, little more. The gods are useful in diffusing a feeling of awe and a sense of ceremony and in increasing our awareness of the exemplary importance and symbolical significance of the human fates which we witness. But they should not be drawn into interpretations of the metaphysical meanings of the plays.

In *The Tempest* there is considerable confusion. The ambience is clearly Christian and good fortune is several times ascribed to divine Providence, but at the centre of the current action there is Prospero's magic and his world of spirits, which is not that of the angels and demons of Christian mythology. Prospero also believes in the need to 'court' the influence of the stars, and at the end of the story Gonzalo prays to the 'gods' to look down on the lovers,

> For it is you that have chalk'd forth the way
> Which brought us hither.

Completely contradictory in relation to the spiritual beliefs and manifestations of various kinds is the very conscious denial of a transcendent reality in the best-known passage of all in *The Tempest*, the speech beginning 'Our revels now are ended' and containing the lines

> We are such stuff
> As dreams are made on; and our little life
> Is rounded with a sleep.

Altogether there is a metaphysical uncertainty in Shakespeare's late comedies and romances which produces unconformities of a special kind where conflicting views are attributable to the author rather than to his characters. There is nothing like these philosophical unconformities in the earlier plays. But throughout his career Shakespeare was fascinated by the inner resources of the individuals he portrayed – by what I have called, with a Shavian term, the Life Force – whatever their dependence on or independence of religious influences outside themselves.

The pious endings of *Pericles*, *Cymbeline* and *The Tempest*, with thanks rendered to the gods for bringing everything to a happy conclusion, are mainly conventional and ornamental, adding in each case an impressive flourish to the halting of the action and bringing us to rest after the excitement of the dénouement. But endings were not always easy to manage after the complexities of the plots. *Twelfth Night*, *All's Well*, *Measure for Measure* and *Cymbeline* had a great deal of matter to resolve at the end, and there is evidence of the difficulty this presented. Shakespeare fortunately avoided the simplest and least convincing expedient, that of overtly using a *deus ex machina*. Diana comes very close to this function in the apparition-scene of *Pericles* but is veiled in a dream. In *Cymbeline*, Posthumus makes no use of the information imparted to him by his supernatural visitors (who also appear in a dream). Prospero, of course, is a sort of *deus ex machina* all along and no more in the last act than in the first. The Duke in *Measure for Measure* has a similar role without the magic. But neither Prospero nor the Duke has knowledge or power we are not apprised of or which we are totally unprepared for – unless, indeed, we count the Duke's revelation in the middle of the play concerning Mariana and Angelo. What Shakespeare resorted to instead of supernatural revelations and marvels was unexpected happenings of a more human kind. The sudden conversions of Oliver and Duke Frederick in *As You Like It*, or of Borachio or Iachimo are not meant for scrutiny and bear no comparison with those of Claudio in *Much Ado* or Angelo in *Measure for Measure*, but they serve on the technical level. The reported confession of the dying Queen in *Cymbeline* is a transparent contrivance to provide information not otherwise available.

A much-favoured device for ending the complications in the comedies and romances is the dropping of disguises, which leads to a natural and satisfying resolution of conflicts due to mistaken identities. This sort of surprise occurs in a majority of the plays we have considered. In *The Winter's Tale* it is used in a special way which is highly effective when Hermione disguised as a statue reveals herself as a living woman. This may further be seen as a version of the pretended-death device which we also find in *Much Ado*, *All's Well* and *Measure for Measure*, and of the supposed-death device which features more or less prominently in *Twelfth Night* (Sebastian), *Pericles* (Marina and Thaisa), *Cymbeline* (Imogen) and *The Tempest* (Ferdinand). In *The Winter's Tale*, however, the 'resurrection' of Hermione clashes with information previously given out, in *All's Well* the reported death of Helena is very casually introduced and remains unexploited in the recognition scene (it merely provides a possibility for plans of Bertram's remarriage and motivates his perfunctory remorse), and in *Measure for Measure* it has always been a problem why the Duke should lie to Isabella about her brother's death even if we understand the technical need for the misinformation.

Another device which is resorted to several times is the recognition of a ring worn significantly by one of the characters. It figured amusingly in *The Merchant of Venice* and is repeated in *All's Well* and *Cymbeline*, though in the former Shakespeare seems to have bethought himself of a second ring in addition to Bertram's heirloom only when he was sorting out the strands of the dénouement, for the King's gift of a ring to Helena, now flaunted by Bertram, is not mentioned in any earlier scene. There is also a ring in *Twelfth Night*: it is sent by Olivia to Cesario/Viola on the pretence that she is returning it to its owner. But Viola scornfully throws it on the ground, where it has no purpose unless, as I suspect, Shakespeare when he wrote that episode intended that Sebastian should find it and Olivia recognise it on his finger. The ring-device as used in other plays makes the idea sufficiently plausible.

One way of solving plot-entanglements is in itself so much of the plot that it cannot be referred merely to the ending. This is the so-called bed-trick or substitute-mistress trick used in *All's Well* and *Measure for Measure*. In both plays it forms an important part of the final unravelling, and in *All's Well* it is not hard to accept it as consonant with the characters of the persons involved and with the atmosphere of the story. In *Measure for Measure*, however, Shakespeare appears to have needed a drastic solution at an early stage of composition and resorted *faute-de-mieux* to an expedient which had worked well once but would not work equally well again.

All's Well and *Measure for Measure* are two of the plays in which the ending seems huddled. The final humiliation of Bertram and his reconcilement to Helena are skimped. Angelo and Mariana are well taken care of, but one may wonder about Isabella. Lucio gets a disproportionate amount of space and time, but Claudio and Juliet are all but forgotten, and several lords whom the Duke desired to meet fail to turn up. In *Twelfth Night* there seems to have been a similar difficulty in bringing the characters together for a tidy finale. Viola's Captain is absent, but even more important characters like Toby and Maria are only present by report at the very end, when we learn that they have married in literally no time. What is mostly surprising in many of the endings, however, especially to a modern theatregoer accustomed to female stars in central female parts, is the way in which the heroines seem to fade into the background. Isabella has been mentioned. We also have very few words at the end from Viola, Marina, Perdita and Miranda; and Helena makes an extremely late final entry. Shakespeare may have wished to upstage his youngest actors a little when the time came for applause, and he must also have counted on a supplementary use of pantomime to busy the ladies, though instructions for it have not been transmitted to us (does Isabella accept the Duke in dumb show?).

Either during composition, during rehearsal or later, Shakespeare evidently engaged in a fair amount of revision of his own plays. There are clear signs of scenes and passages having been added to provisionally completed manuscripts, and in some cases we may have to do with interpolation by other hands. There is also evidence for the intended omission here and there of passages which were nevertheless preserved in print, as well as for actual omissions and transpositions which were deliberately or accidentally effected. The most usual substantive clues to both additions and intended omissions are the logically unfunctional repetitions of phrases and lines occurring before and after the passages in question as if to stitch together the frayed edges of the embracing dialogue. This is a phenomenon which is observable in all phases of Shakespeare's authorship.[3]

Some of the apparent additions have to do with a feature of the plays which we have discussed: the ornamental function of the gods of the classical pantheon. I have argued that the Hymen episode of *As You Like It* may be one such addition, and there are even clearer indications that the apparition of Jupiter in *Cymbeline* and the masque of goddesses in *The Tempest* are interpolations in scenes which, if it were not for the attractions of spectacle, might have been better without them.

Other major additions may be seen in the introduction or expansion of clown parts in *Twelfth Night*, *All's Well* and *Measure for Measure*, changes which could have a connection with the recruitment of Armin to the Chamberlain's Men and the wish to make the most of his voice and histrionic talents – unless the occurrence of similar apparent additions in *The Two Gentlemen of Verona* and *The Merchant of Venice*, in which Launce and Launcelot were probably played by Will Kempe, simply means that comic roles were often created separately and inserted into completed scenes.[4] Feste quite obviously displaced Viola in the singing entertainment at Orsino's court and he very probably replaced Fabian both in the nocturnal carousal in Olivia's house and in a number of other scenes. Lavatch, in a much smaller role, intrudes into several scenes in *All's Well* where there is little need for him. In the same play Parolles and the French lords get a surprising amount of space and attention. They may have been wanted from the start simply to fill in the sequel after the most serious part of the play was over at midpoint. But Lucio in an analogous comic role in *Measure for Measure* seems, by signs which have been noted, to have had his part considerably enlarged after it was first apportioned to him. The continuation of the prison scene of *Measure for Measure* after Isabella's impassioned interview with Claudio, that is to say about the point where the play breaks in the middle, also has indications of interpolated matter, but there has been so much trial and error in this place that it is hard to tell what came first and what was added.

Passages which were apparently intended for omission and may have been marked for deletion have been identified in the foregoing chapters in *As You Like It* (Orlando's opening complaint expressed twice over); in *Much Ado* (contradictory reports of the Prince's conspiracy with the Count); in *Measure for Measure* (repeated reports of the arrest of Claudio, and the two-part examination of Froth and Pompey); and in *The Tempest* (Miranda's contradictory statements concerning her curiosity about the past). The interesting thing about these passages from a textual point of view is that they betray themselves pretty regularly by the signs I have mentioned. It is much more difficult to determine whether passages once present have been cut and consequently lost to us, or simply lost. We might have expected a Mariana scene in which she and Isabella discuss the Duke's plan to deceive Claudio. We might have expected a longer interview between Marina and Lysimachus in *Pericles* so as to make his surrender to Marina's eloquence more convincing. These are two cases where a loss may be suspected. It is a different matter with encounters and exchanges which Shakespeare for various reasons did not provide. In *Much Ado*, for example, there are at least three instances of this kind. Don Pedro's conversation with Hero during the dance, the scene at Hero's window on which so much prior attention is focused and which is so decisive for the subsequent action, and the first meeting of Benedick and Beatrice after both have been gulled, which is anticipated both by the other characters and by us with the liveliest curiosity. In addition there are the 'ghost characters' whom we might expect to meet in scenes which were apparently not written.

The cases of unfulfilled expectations mostly have to do with adjustments of original plans, we may suppose, which usually meant overall improvements in spite of local disappointments. In *Much Ado* Shakespeare decided to leave Claudio cynical after learning of Hero's death and so did not put the Friar's prophecy of repentance into effect. We do not like this Claudio but we probably find him more credible and even perhaps more tolerable than an immediately tearful penitent would have seemed. The same play exemplifies another kind of adjustment which is not uncommon in Shakespeare, that of the time scheme: the action of *Much Ado* is contracted by four days after Leonato has firmly announced a week's interval between his daughter's engagement and her marriage. In *As You Like It* the legitimate ruler has been exiled for a long time, as we must eventually believe, though in the opening scenes it looks as if there has been a very recent coup d'état. And in *The Tempest* Ariel is to be released after a few hours, though at first there is talk of two days. The changes in these cases seem to have been deliberate, but there must have been a degree of carelessness in the failure to revise completely so as to eliminate inconsistencies. In other cases there was probably carelessness or forgetfulness pure and simple, as in the sudden information about the lapse of an incredible three months in the last act of *Twelfth Night*, or the many confusions about hours and days in *Measure for Measure*. By all accounts Shakespeare never felt the need to prepare his papers for publication in print before it was too late.

We must not forget the element of expediency which naturally dictated many changes away from directions already pointed out or of qualities already defined in the plays. Once Shakespeare decided to use the bed-trick in *Measure for Measure* it was expedient to introduce a changed Isabella who would willingly enter into the Duke's rather lubricious conspiracy for the taming of Angelo. Once he decided to reunite Leontes with Hermione in *The Winter's Tale*, it was expedient to present Perdita's reunion with her father in narrative. In *Much Ado* it was expedient to have Borachio plot 'to undo Hero, and kill Leonato', not just 'to misuse the Prince' and 'to vex Claudio', which would have been sufficient to satisfy Don John. In *Twelfth Night* it was expedient, for the sake of surprises to come, that Viola should fail to put two and two together when Antonio takes her for Sebastian the second time (though Shakespeare might easily have avoided the absurdity by making her more obtuse on the first occasion). In *Pericles*, Cleon's imputed complicity in the attempted murder of Marina simplifies polarities of good and bad, and Lysimachus' denial of the lechery which brought him to the brothel puts him in the right camp at a relatively small cost to consistency. In *Cymbeline* it proved expedient to get rid of Cloten early on, leaving the role of defeated villain in the final scene to Iachimo, and to impose on the Queen a death-bed confession which greatly facilitates the solution.

In many of these and similar cases unconformities seem to have resulted from the author's concentrated attention on the working-out of individual scenes and his concern for their separate effect without systematic reference to their logical premises. On the other hand, we cannot picture Shakespeare sitting down to write a scene a day, or dividing his work into regular stints determined by scenic limits. The great difference in length of the scenes would in itself preclude this simple explanation. Indeed, some of the longest scenes exhibit internal incongruities (such as we have seen in the speech habits of Rosalind and Celia) which might suggest that more than a night's sleep interrupted their composition. Revision, too, would have been sporadic and liable to be performed immediately on completion of a mere passage or following a considerable interval after the whole work was finished. Where alteration produced unconformities one is tempted to suggest a sufficient passage of time to favour a slight forgetfulness, but this is no necessary assumption. Such major additions to the initially finished text as we have noticed, however (chiefly clowns' parts and masquerading divinities), would by their nature have supervened on the full completion of the plays and probably represent relatively late interpolations. External considerations such as the availability of Armin after 1599 or the tastes of more courtly audiences after the acquisition of the Blackfriars theatre would have influenced their inclusion.

Shakespeare's writing habits may be usefully illuminated by a study of the various kinds of unconformities which abound in his plays, as I hope to have shown. Above all, it is important to realise that he was not content simply to fill in the plotted outlines which he must have had in his mind. He felt his way along as he wrote and was always ready to adjust his sights to his unfolding perceptions, and if necessary to proceed by trial and error. Sometimes his absorption in what he had in hand or his prevailing moods gave a prominence to certain characters and an emphasis to certain qualities which upset the balance of his project. But even in extreme cases of unbalance such as we find in *Measure for Measure* it has often been proved that the incongruent elements of the various parts may be combined in a rare theatrical experience. In fact one reason why Shakespeare may sometimes seem careless of unconformities was surely his confidence that they could be either eliminated or overcome in performance. And his chief means of overcoming them were, first, the maturity and sophistication of his character studies, which rouse our interest and sustain it through scenes of more jejune portraiture; and, secondly, his mastery of speech in verse or prose, in forms of high poetry and lively dialogue. Both the maturity and the mastery may be easily recognised on comparison with such contemporary playwrights as Beaumont and Fletcher. It is interesting to notice that in the plays of these two collaborators there are few unconformities. The plots are too streamlined.

Theatre directors in our own day may feel that the signs of hesitation, of conflicting ideas and impulses and of incomplete revision to be found in Shakespeare's plays may justify a fair amount of plastic surgery; and in so far as they interpret the signs they may no doubt be stimulated to attempt original creative approaches within the ambit of possibilities offered by the versions of Shakespeare's texts which devotion and chance have made available to us. In one area in particular, that of passages which should evidently never have gone into print, they may amputate with considerable assurance that Shakespeare would have approved. Meanwhile readers are hardly the worse off for catching Shakespeare with his points trailing. The more Shakespeare he.

Appendix

In the course of writing four books on 'unconformities' in the plays of the Shakespeare canon, I have frequently had occasion to indicate a duplication of phrases and lines which may be associated with irregular composition and revision on the part of the author. In particular the use of identical or very similar words and lines before and after a passage which may seem superfluous or imperfectly integrated in its context reveals, on the evidence, a habit of going back to pick up a speech or part of a speech to cover an intended excision or to bridge an interpolation. Often the occurrence of such repetition in itself calls attention to irregularities of composition and, most interestingly, to the fact that a fair number of excisions intended by the author were not observed in the printing of the plays.

In the present appendix I have gathered up examples from all the plays of what may perhaps be called 'incidental duplication'. The list is more comprehensive than in all cases demonstrably significant in the sense I have explained, but it is not intended to include examples of repetition or duplication which are indisputably organic elements of the dialogue.

Quotations are from the First Folio unless otherwise indicated, the line numeration as in the Arden edition.

INCIDENTAL DUPLICATION

Titus Andronicus

I.i.91/151
    And sleepe in peace, slaine in your Countries warres:
    Romes readiest Champions, repose you heere in rest,

I.i.294/343–4
    Nor thou, nor he are any sonnes of mine,
    ... No sonne of mine, / Nor thou, nor these ...

I.i.299–300/343–4
    No *Titus*, no, ... / Nor her, nor thee, ...
    No foolish Tribune, no: ... / Nor thou, nor these...

IV.iii.96–7/105
Tell mee, can you deliuer an Oration to the Emperour with a
Grace?
Sirrah, can you with a Grace deliuer a Supplication?

V.iii.141/146
Mar. Lucius, all haile Romes Royall Emperour,
Lucius all haile to Romes gracious Gouernour.

2 Henry VI

I.i.215/237
Aniou and *Maine* are giuen to the French,
Aniou and *Maine* both giuen vnto the French?

III.i.58–64/104–6, 121–2, 133
Card. Did he not, contrary to forme of Law,
Deuise strange deaths, for small offences done?
Yorke. And did he not, in his Protectorship,
Leuie great summes of Money through the Realme,
For Souldiers pay in France, and neuer sent it?
By meanes whereof, the Townes each day reuolted.
Buck. Tut, these are petty faults to faults vnknowne,

Yorke. 'Tis thought, my Lord,
That you tooke Bribes of France,
And being Protector, stay'd the Souldiers pay,
By meanes whereof, his Highnesse hath lost France.

Yorke. In your Protectorship, you did deuise
Strange Tortures for Offendors, neuer heard of,

Suff. My Lord, these faults are easie, quickly answer'd:

IV.i.68/102/131
Conuey him hence,
away, conuey him hence.
Hale him away,

1 Henry VI

IV.v.12–14/vi.38, 52

Is my name *Talbot*? and am I your Sonne?
And shall I flye? O, if you loue my Mother,
Dishonor not her Honorable Name,

In thee thy Mother dyes, our Households Name,

And if I flye, I am not *Talbots* Sonne.

IV.v.18/vi.30
   Flye, to reuenge my death, if I be slaine.
   Flye, to reuenge my death when I am dead,

IV.vi.4/vii.2
   Where is *Iohn Talbot*?
   O, where's young *Talbot*? where is valiant *Iohn*?

IV.vi.55/vii.16
   Thous *Icarus*,
   My *Icarus*,

Richard III

IV.iv.236–8/397–9
   Madam, so thriue I in my enterprize
   And dangerous successe of bloody warres,
   As I intend more good to you and yours,

   As I entend to prosper, and repent:
   So thriue I in my dangerous Affayres
   Of hostile Armes:

V.iii.50, 53, 64 / 73, 76–7
   [*King.*] Giue me some Inke and Paper:

   Cat. It is my Liege: and all things are in readinesse.

   [*Rich.*] Fill me a Bowle of Wine:

   King . . . . Giue me a Bowle of Wine,

Is Inke and Paper ready?
Rat. It is my Lord.

V.iii.135–6/163–4
To morrow in the battell thinke on me,
And fall thy edgelesse Sword, dispaire and dye.

To morrow in the Battaile, thinke on me,
And fall thy edgelesse Sword, dispaire and dye:

The Two Gentlemen of Verona

II.i.14–15/41–2
Goe to, sir, tell me: do you know Madam *Siluia*?
Speed. Shee that your worship loues?

But tell me: do'st thou know my Lady *Siluia*?
Speed. Shee that you gaze on so, . . .

Love's Labour's Lost

IV.iii.292–300/314–19, 346–8
And where that you haue vow'd to studie (Lords) [etc.]
O we haue made a Vow to studie, Lords, [etc.]

King John

III.iii.61/68
Binde vp those tresses . . .
Binde vp your haires.

V.vi.39–42/vii.61–4
· halfe my power this night
Passing these Flats, are taken by the Tide,
These Lincolne-Washes haue deuoured them,
My selfe, well mounted, hardly haue escap'd.

For in a night the best part of my powre,
As I vpon aduantage did remoue,

Were in the *Washes* all vnwarily,
Deuoured by the vnexpected flood.

Romeo and Juliet

I.iv.11/35–6
Giue me a Torch, I am not for this ambling.

A Torch for me, let wantons light of heart
Tickle the sencelesse rushes with their heeles:

III.iii.147/166
But looke thou stay not till the watch be set,
Either be gone before the watch be set,

V.iii.108+/119–20
Heere's to thy health, where ere thou tumblest in.
O true Appothecarie!
Thy drugs are quicke. Thus with a kisse I die.

Heere's to my Loue. O true Appothecary;
Thy drugs are quicke. Thus with a kisse I die.

V.iii.173–4/194–6
Pittifull sight, here lies the Countie slaine,
And *Iuliett* bleeding, warme and newly dead

Soueraigne, here lies the Countie *Paris* slaine,
And *Romeo* dead, and *Iuliet* dead before,
Warme and new kil'd.

A Midsummer Night's Dream

I.i.114–16/123–6
But *Demetrius* come,
And come *Egeus*, you shall go with me,
I haue some priuate schooling for you both.

Demetrius and *Egeus* go along:
I must imploy you in some businesse
...   and conferre with you
Of something neerely that concernes your selues.

2 Henry IV

IV.iv.15/52
  And how accompanied?
  And how accompanyed?

IV.iv.19–20/50
             Thomas of Clarence
  How chance thou art not with the Prince, thy Brother?

  Why art thou not at Windsor with him (*Thomas*?)

Henry V

I.i.76, 79–81 / ii.132–5
  Vpon our Spirituall Conuocation,
  ...   to giue a greater Summe,
  Then euer at one time the Clergie yet
  Did to his Predecessors part withall.

             we of the Spiritualtie
  Will rayse your Highnesse such a mightie Summe,
  As neuer did the Clergie at one time
  Bring in to any of your Ancestors.

I.ii.222/234
  Now are we well resolu'd, ...
  Now are we well prepar'd ...

II.iv. 114–15/140
  To morrow shall you beare our full intent
  Back to our Brother of England.

To morrow shall you know our mind at full.

IV.i.27/293
> Desire them all to my Pauillion.

>   collect them all together
> At my tent....

The Merchant of Venice

I.i.70–1/105
> We two will leaue you, but at dinner time
> I pray you haue in mind where we must meete.

> Well, we will leaue you then till dinner time.

V.i.36–8/49
> But goe we in I pray thee *Iessica*,
> And ceremoniously let vs prepare
> Some welcome for the Mistresse of the house,

> Let's in, and there expect their coming.

Julius Cæsar

IV.iii.141/157
> *Lucius*, a bowle of wine.
> Giue me a bowl of wine,

IV.iii.148/188
> She is dead.
> For certaine she is dead,

As You Like It

I.i.3–7, 21–4 / 67–71
> charged my brother on his blessing to breed mee well...he
> keepes me rustically at home...the spirit of my Father, which I
> thinke is within mee, begins to mutinie against this seruitude. I
> will no longer endure it...

my father charg'd you in his will to giue me good education:
you haue train'd me like a pezant...the spirit of my father
growes strong in mee, and I will no longer endure it...

Twelfth Night

II.iii.14/119
> *Marian* I say, a stoope of wine. [Maria has no entry here.]
> A stope of wine *Maria*.

II.iii.18/59
> ...now let's haue a catch.
> Shall wee rowze the night-Owle in a Catch...

II.iv.3/42–3
> That old and Anticke song we heard last night;
>
> O fellow come, the song we had last night:
> Marke it Cesario, it is old and plaine;

Hamlet

III.iv.161, 172, 179, 215, 219
> Good night... Once more goodnight...so againe, good night...
> Mother goodnight... Good night, Mother.

Troilus and Cressida

III.ii.60/98
> Will you walke in my Lord?
> Will you walke in my Lord?

IV.v.94/113
> They are oppos'd already.
> They are in action.

IV.v.96+/108
> ...they call him *Troylus*;
> They call him *Troylus*;

V.iii.112+/x. 32-4
> *Pand.* Why, but heare you?
> *Troy.* Hence brother lackie; ignomie and shame
> > Pursue thy life, and liue aye with thy name.

> *Pand.* But heare you? heare you?
> *Troy.* Hence broker, lackie; ignomy, and shame
> > Pursue thy life, and liue aye with thy name.

V.x.21/30
> ... But march away,
> Strike a free march to Troy,

Othello

I.iii.189–90/198, 220
> God be with you: I haue done.
> Please it your Grace, on to the State Affaires;

> ... I haue done my Lord.
> I humbly beseech you proceed to th'Affaires of State.

V.ii.33–4/58
> *Des.* Then Heauen haue mercy on mee.
> *Oth.* Amen, with all my heart.

> *Des.* O Heauen haue mercy on me.
> *Oth.* I say, Amen.

V.ii.49–50/68
> No by my Life, and Soule: send for the man,
> And aske him.

> I neuer gaue it him: Send, for him hither:

Measure for Measure

I.ii.56–7/79
> ... there's one yonder arrested, and carried to prison,
> Yonder man is carried to prison.

I.ii.66–7/84

... it is for getting Madam *Iulietta* with childe.
... is there a maid with child by him?

II.i.65–9/76–8
which, I thinke is a very ill house too.
Esc. How know you that?
Elb. My wife Sir?

for it is a naughty house.
Esc. How do'st thou know that, Constable?
Elb. Marry sir, by my wife,

III.i.50/172–3
Prouost, a word with you.
Prouost, a word with you.

V.i.281/302
here comes the rascall I spoke of,
This is the rascall: this is he I spoke of.

King Lear

I.iv.250/256
Saddle my horses:
Prepare my Horses.

I.iv.252/303
Yet haue I left a daughter.
I haue another daughter,

I.iv.270/287 Q
... goe goe, my people?
... goe, goe, my people?

III.vii.3/22
seeke out the Traitor Glouster.
go seek the Traitor Glouster,

Antony and Cleopatra

II.v.81, 84/III.iii.1–2
*Char.*He is afeard to come.

Cleo. . . . Come hither Sir.

Alex. Halfe afeard to come.
Cleo. . . . Come hither Sir.

IV.xv.12–13/30–1
Helpe *Charmian*, helpe *Iras* helpe: helpe Friends
Below, let's draw him hither.

Helpe me my women, we must draw thee vp:
Assist good Friends.

IV. xv.18/41
I am dying Egypt, dying;
I am dying Egypt, dying.

Timon of Athens

II.ii.50/127
Pray draw neere.
Pray you walke neere.

IV.iii.291/396
Tell them there I haue Gold,
Ile say th'hast Gold:

Coriolanus

IV.v.7–9/12, 24, 32–3
What would you haue Friend? whence are you?
Here's no place for you: Pray go to the doore?

Whence are you Sir?
What haue you to do here fellow?

Heere's no place for you, pray you auoid:

Pericles (Q)

I.i.109–10/ib.144–5 Q
Heauen, that I had thy head; he ha's found the meaning:

He hath found the meaning,
For which we meane to haue his head:

V.iii.24–7/65–7
 Cer. ... found there rich Iewells, recouered her, and plac'ste her heere in *Dianaes* temple.
 Per. May we see them?
 Cer. Great Sir, they shalbe brought you to my house, whither I inuite you, ...

 Cer. ... beseech you first, goe with mee to my house, where shall be showne you all was found with her. How shee came plac'ste heere in the Temple, ...

Cymbeline

V.iii.94/193–4
 ... bring him to th' King.
 ... bring your Prisoner to the King.

The Tempest

I.ii.22–3/33
 'Tis time
 I should inform thee farther.

 For thou must now know farther.

Henry VIII

II.i.55–78/104–132
 All good people ... let it sincke me .... The law ... has done vpon the premises, but Iustice ... my guiltlesse blood must cry against 'em ... your prayers ....

 And with that bloud will make 'em one day groane for't ...
 I had my Tryall,/ And must needs say a Noble one ... to sinke ye: all good people / Pray for me

Notes

Abbreviations
Titles of Shakespeare's plays are abbreviated as in the *SQ Annotated World Bibliography*. Periodicals are referred to by standard or easily recognisable abbreviations, but the following may be noted:
  SS : *Shakespeare Survey*
  SSt: *Shakespeare Studies*.
Sources stands for Geoffrey Bullough, *Narrative and Dramatic Sources of Shakespeare*.
Modern editions of Shakespeare's plays are referred to as follows:
  Arden: The Arden Shakespeare, new series inaugurated in 1951.
  Cam.: The New Shakespeare edited by Sir Arthur Quiller-Couch ('Q') and John Dover Wilson.
  New Cam.: The New Cambridge Shakespeare inaugurated in 1984.
  Oxf.: The Oxford Shakespeare inaugurated in 1982.

1 INTRODUCTION

1. In *The Decameron*, which is Shakespeare's source for this episode, Ambrogiuolo describes 'no especiall note or marke... whereof he might make credible report' on the body of Bernardo's wife, 'but onely a small wart upon her left pappe, with some few haires growing thereon, appearing to be as yellow as gold'. He accordingly reports this in detail to Bernardo on his return to Paris (*Sources*, VIII, pp. 55–6). Shakespeare's Iachimo describes the mole more poetically to himself. It is 'cinque-spotted: like the crimson drops/I th' bottom of a cowslip' (II.ii.38–9). It is all the more remarkable that he does not give Posthumus this detailed description, but Shakespeare may have decided to work on the idea of the mole as a 'stain', see II.iv.138–40.
2. See e.g. Jones, *Scenic Form in Shakespeare* (1971, 1985) and Rose, *Shakespearean Design* (1972).
3. Price, 'Measure for Measure and the Critics', *SQ* XX.2 (1969), p. 203.
4. Gesner, *Shakespeare and the Greek Romance/A Study of Origins* (1970); Bulman, *The Heroic Idiom of Shakespearean Tragedy* (1985).
5. Traditional assumptions about the credentials of the play-texts have been energetically questioned by such modern scholars as Honigmann and Taylor (see Bibliography). The need for a thoroughly sceptical revision of commonly-held theories concerning 'foul papers' and 'bad quartos' is argued by Werstine in 'Narratives About Printed Shakespearean Texts', *SQ* 41.1 (1990), 65–86. In the same issue of *SQ*, Trousdale advances a completely relativistic view of texts and productions of plays as occasions in a diachronic process of becoming:

'A Second Look at Critical Bibliography and the Acting of Plays' (87–96).

6. Relevant quotations from Jonson, Manningham, etc. are conveniently collected in Chambers, *William Shakespeare: A Study of Facts and Problems* (1930), Vol. II, pp. 207–10, 328–44. There are photo-reproductions of the Swan sketch and the *Titus* scene in Thomson, *Shakespeare's Theatre* (1983), plates 4 and 11.

7. 'Unconformity' is a term borrowed from geology and was first used in a Shakespearean connection by Rossiter – see Smidt, *Unconformities in Shakespeare's History Plays* (1982), p. 1.

8. Foakes, *Shakespeare: The dark comedies to the last plays* (1971), p. 3.

9. Ibid., p. 97.

10. Frye, *A Natural Perspective* (1965), p. 13.

11. Ibid., p. 123.

12. See Bibliography. Among the characteristics which distinguished Shakespeare's plays, Coleridge listed first 'Expectation in preference to surprize': 'God said, let there be LIGHT: and there was LIGHT. not there *was* Light. As the feeling with which we startle at a shooting star, compared with that of watching the Sunrise at the pre-established moment, such and so low is Surprize Comp. with Expect.' (Coburn, ed., *The Collected Works of Samuel Taylor Coleridge*, 5, 1987, p. 129.)

13. See Baldwin, *Shakspere's Five-Act Structure* (1947, 1963), pp. 576, 668.

14. See Herrick, *Comic Theory in the Sixteenth Century* (1950, 1964), pp. 109, 119.

15. See Salingar, *Shakespeare and the Traditions of Comedy* (1974), pp. 187, 223.

16. Ibid., pp. 31–3, 47, 67.

17. See Bradbrook, *The Growth and Structure of Elizabethan Comedy*, New edn (1973, 1979), pp. 4–5, 119.

18. Frye, *The Myth of Deliverance* (1983), pp. 14–15. See also Smidt, *Unconformities in Shakespeare's Early Comedies* (1986), p. 14.

19. Frye, op. cit., pp. 5–6.

20. I find somewhat strained the effort of Clifford Leech to demonstrate that *Per.*, *Cym.* and *Tmp.* have a cyclical pattern in that the ending in each case 'is not truly a point of finality' (whereas *WT* has a crisis structure in that 'it achieves a sense of finality') ('The Structure of the Last Plays', *SS* 11, 1958, pp. 19–30).

21. Gesner, op. cit., pp. 120–1. See also Smidt, op. cit., p. 14.

22. Barber, *Shakespeare's Festive Comedy* (1959).

23. Pettet, *Shakespeare and the Romance Tradition* (1949, 1970), pp. 122–8.

24. Boas, *Shakspere and his Predecessors* (1896).

25. Lawrence, *Shakespeare's Problem Comedies* (1931, 1969); Tillyard, *Shakespeare's Problem Plays* (1950, 1970).

26. Lawrence, op. cit., pp. 21–4, 78.

27. Tillyard, op. cit., p. 10.

28. Pettet, op. cit., p. 157.

29. Salingar points to the derivation of many of Shakespeare's plots from Italian *novelle* and to the features of 'broken nuptials and a legal crisis' which the problem comedies in his classification (he includes *MV* and *Ado*) have in common – op. cit., pp. 301–5.

30. Frye, op. cit., pp. 15, 32–3.
31. Lawrence, op. cit., p. 30.
32. Ibid., p. 202.
33. Foakes, op. cit., pp. 3–4.
34. Lawrence, op. cit., p. 202. See also Pettet, op. cit., pp. 198–9.
35. See Lawrence, op. cit., pp. 172–3. I prefer to leave open the question of Shakespeare's debt to Beaumont and Fletcher in *Cymbeline*.
36. Pettet, op. cit., pp. 162–4.
37. Ibid., pp. 176–7, 179, 182, 185–6.
38. Arden *Per*. (1963, 1969), pp. lxxii–lxxv.
39. Tillyard, *Shakespeare's Last Plays* (1938). See also Mowat, *The Dramaturgy of Shakespeare's Romances* (1976), p. 6.
40. Pettet, op. cit., pp. 174, 190–5.
41. Frye, op. cit., pp. 8, 32; and *A Natural Perspective*, p. 8.
42. Arden *Per.*, p. lxxv. Nosworthy sees *Pericles, Cymbeline*, and, 'to a certain but insignificant extent, *The Winter's Tale*', as 'the pioneer colonizing efforts of a Shakespeare more completely without a reputable model than he had ever been', Arden *Cym.*, p. xxxi.
43. Mowat, op. cit., pp. 26–7.
44. Ibid., pp. 69, 83–4, 59, 64; 25, 43; 69, 75, 100.
45. Ibid., pp. 65, 69.
46. The most evident exceptions are *Ado* and *Per*. *Ado* was 'set to all appearances from Shakespeare's "foul papers"' (Arden, p. 77). *Per*. is held by some, notably Philip Edwards, to be a reported text, see Arden *Per.*, pp. xxxiii–xxxvii. *MM* was probably printed from a transcript by Ralph Crane but still bears many marks of an origin in foul papers. As regards the 'foul papers' category, see Werstine's article (n. 5 above).
47. See Bethell, Raleigh and Strachey quoted by Edwards in 'Shakespeare's Romances: 1900–1957', *SS* 11 (1958), pp. 2–3.

2   AGAINST THE BRIDAL DAY

1. '[T]he relation between report and event that is central to the play's concern' – Mares in the New Cam. *Ado* (1988), p. 149.
2. Humphreys has given a good account of these irregular details in the Arden *Ado* (1981), pp. 65, 77–80. See also Mares, op. cit., pp. 146–53.
3. 'It is a nice point to consider why he [Antonio] is not included in the Q stage directions for the wedding, and whether the Antonio who challenges Claudio in 5.1 believes Hero dead or knows that she is alive.' Mares, op. cit., p. 149. Smallwood points out that directors often bring him on to help produce a respectable congregation for the wedding. He also informs me that in the 1990 RSC production of *Ado*, Leonato's statement in V.i to Claudio that Hero is dead was clearly news to Antonio, and this very neatly explained the suddenness of his entry into the quarrel.
4. '*And Balthasar, or dumb Iohn*' (Q and substantially F) could be a

misinterpretation by the scribe of *'and Bor* for *Borachio, Don Iohn'*. See Dover Wilson, Cam. *Ado* (1923, 1980), pp. 94–5.

5. *Sources*, II, p. 114.

6. Thus there is a George Seacoal in III.iii and a Francis Seacoal in III.v., both perhaps identical with the 'Sexton' of IV.ii. There is also a Friar Francis in IV.i.

7. This form of address seems not to be used after II.i, but Dogberry in one scene presents himself and Verges as 'the poor Duke's officers' (III.v.18–19), rather suggesting that they are not the Governor's (i.e. Signior Leonato's) men but the Prince's. See also III.iii.72–3 and 159. However, Dogberry reports to Leonato in III.v; and Leonato takes charge in V.i.

8. In stage directions he is twice in the initial scene introduced as *'Don Pedro'* (87, 188), then at II.i.78 as *'Prince, Pedro'* in both Q and F, the comma perhaps suggesting that the Prince title was unexpectedly introduced at this point and that the compositor thought the Prince and Pedro were separate persons.

9. See my *Unconformities in Shakespeare's Early Comedies* (1986), pp. 49, 81, 162.

10. Not till IV.i.188 and V.i.187 is Don John spoken of in the dialogue as the Bastard (by Benedick).

11. Rees, *Shakespeare and the Story* (1978), p. 28.

12. Cam. *Ado*, pp. 102–4.

13. Wilson, *Shakespeare's Happy Comedies* (1962, 1963), p. 138.

14. Chambers, *Shakespeare: A Survey* (1925, 1948), pp. 134–5.

15. Wilson, op. cit., pp. 123–6.

16. Leggatt, *Shakespeare's Comedy of Love* (1974), pp. 164–6.

17. Arden *Ado*, pp. 62–5, 69–70. See also Muir, *Shakespeare's Comic Sequence* (1979), pp. 72–3; Rossiter, *Angel with Horns* (1961), p. 77; Van Doren, *Shakespeare* (1939, 1953), pp. 119–20.

18. Cam. *Ado*, p. xviii. Bradbrook, however, finds no difficulty in understanding Don John: he 'hates Claudio because he won glory in the wars by Don John's overthrow.... His bastardy... explains his malignity' (*Shakespeare and Elizabethan Poetry*, 1951, p. 266, n.19). Similarly Wilson, op. cit., p. 126.

19. Huston, *Shakespeare's Comedies of Play* (1981), p. 146. So also Foakes: 'Don John... has no personal interest in Claudio or Hero; he is a professed enemy of good, a "plain-dealing villain", who has an abstract love of mischief. He needs no motive, even though he finds one in that Claudio overcame him in battle' (Penguin *Ado*, p. 17). Leggatt agrees on more practical, dramaturgical grounds, see op. cit., pp. 156–7. And Berger sees Don John simply as 'a comic villain... The ease with which his practice... succeeds, therefore, tells us more about the susceptibility of Messina than about the Bastard's motiveless malignity' ('Against the Sink-a-Pace...', *SQ* 33.3, 1982, p. 311).

20. Allen, 'Dogberry', *SQ* XXIV.1 (1973), pp. 39–40.

21. See pp. 23–4 above and n. 4. Mares, however, argues 'for the propriety of Balthasar's participation' in the dance and refers further to A. T. Brissenden; see his 'Textual Analysis' in the New Cam. *Ado*, p. 150.

Another masked dance possibly caused a confusion of speech attributions in *LLL*, II.i, but see my *Unconformities in Shakespeare's Early Comedies*, pp. 90–4.

22. Nevertheless, there are indications that Margaret was meant to appear with Hero in the gulling scene. Claudio remarks at III.ii.68–9: 'Hero and Margaret have by this played their parts with Beatrice', and Beatrice refers to 'my cousin, Margaret, and Ursula' for confirmation of Benedick's love (V.iv.78).

23. Kirschbaum thinks there are two Margarets, who are psychologically completely incompatible (reported by Muir, op.cit., p. 73). McCollom thinks this is a matter of genre decorum: 'the Elizabethans were frequently ready to drop consistency of characterization for tonal or other reasons', and Margaret 'is a witty lady-in-waiting, on excellent terms with both Hero and Beatrice, but the plot demands that she play her foolish part in the famous window scene that almost destroys Hero' ('The Role of Wit in *Much Ado About Nothing*', *SQ* XIX.2, 1968, p. 167). Huston senses ambiguity: 'the fact that our knowledge of Margaret's innocence depends exclusively on the testimony of a single person, and he a villain, may not be altogether irrelevant in a play whose principal action has to do with false testimony.' He also thinks that Margaret's confusing behaviour makes for greater realism: the confusion in the play in general 'suggests the complexity of motive and action we associate with real human beings, and makes the world of this play the most realistic so far encountered in the comedies' (op.cit., pp. 123–5). Wilson suggests a lost, older play giving a fuller explanation (Cam. *Ado*, pp. 194–7). Richard Levin provides Margaret with a motive for wickedness, 'resentment against her social betters' (*Love and Society in Shakespearean Comedy*, 1985, p. 114). (Levin, incidentally, takes a dark view of everyone in the play.)

24. 'Q' in Cam. *Ado*, p. xii. 'Q' thinks this 'weakens our sympathy with Claudio in the chapel-scene' (p. xiii).

25. *Sources*, II, p. 76.

26. Parrott, *Shakespearean Comedy* (1949, 1962), p. 157. Beaumont and Fletcher's farcical comedy *The Woman Hater* (1607) has a slandered mistress (Oriana, courted by the Duke of Millaine and defamed by Gondarino, the Woman Hater). There is a scene in which she is seen to sit in the window of a brothel, to which she has been abducted by Gondarino's servants.

27. *Sources*, II, p. 76.

28. Carroll, Letter to Ellen Terry, 20 March 1883, quoted by Mares in New Cam *Ado.*, pp. 157–8 and (with slight differences) by Humphreys in the Arden *Ado*. pp. 65–6.

29. It is perhaps interesting to note that this would be the second time someone impersonated Claudio, supposing the Prince did so in II.i. If Claudio has a somewhat foppish appearance (see p. 34) the disguise would be simple. His role being so easily taken over by others also detracts somewhat from our sense of his independent personality.

30. Humphreys has the following note on the passage in question:
     Theobald and some others read 'Borachio' for 'Claudio', arguing that

to hear (supposed) Hero call a wooer 'Claudio' would suggest not that she was false but that she was herself deluded by an impersonator. But Borachio means to persuade Margaret to disguise as her mistress, and to act with him a love-scene in which the servants masquerade as their 'betters'. (Arden *Ado*, p. 131)

This, it seems to me, makes the charade only more unbelievable. There is more logic in the corresponding Penguin explanation (Foakes), but it is rather too subtle for the psychological level of the play:

> Margaret is to be persuaded to impersonate Hero, while Borachio pretends to be Claudio. Thus she will not suspect villainy, and the Prince and Claudio will think that Hero is mocking Claudio as well as deceiving him, by play-acting with another lover under his name. (Penguin *Ado*, p. 139)

31. Graves, 'Making sound sense of Shakespeare', *Sunday Times*, 14 February 1965.
32. Modern critics who have taken a censorious view of Claudio's character and behaviour include John L. Palmer (*Comic Characters of Shakespeare*, 1946), Parrott (*Shakespearean Comedy*, 1949), Frye (*A Natural Perspective*, 1965) and Richard Levin (*Love and Society in Shakespearean Comedy*, 1985). Parrott considers Claudio 'anything but a true lover in the Elizabethan mode' and goes on: 'It is, perhaps, too hard to call Claudio, as Swinburne does, "a pitiful fellow", but only in romantic comedy could such a character be at last rewarded with the hand of the lady he had so publicly slandered' (p. 157). Levin observes that Claudio 'accepts evidence that would hardly deceive a four-year-old child, and repudiates Hero in the most public and humiliating way possible'. Moreover, he is 'unaffected emotionally' by her apparent death 'and ridicules Hero's father for taking his daughter's death seriously' (p. 46).

A vigorous defence of Claudio appeared in 1952, Neill's 'More Ado About Claudio: An Acquittal for the Slandered Groom' (*SQ* III.2, pp. 91–107). In Shakespeare's handling of the Claudio/Hero material the 'proof' of Hero's unchastity is made to seem much stronger than in his sources, and Claudio, whose 'love is neither carnal nor mercenary' and 'whose affections are deeply moved towards a woman who seemed to fulfill his high ideal', cannot, according to Neill, be blamed for believing it. We have trouble in fully accepting his behaviour only because his character, for reasons involving the economy of the whole play, is weakly developed. In fact, says Neill, 'The only scene where Claudio's part is allowed any emotional range is in the repudiation of Hero, where he washes his accusations with tears.' There is positive enthusiasm for Claudio's merits in a 1959 article by Schoff, 'Claudio, Bertram, and a Note on Interpretation' (*SQ* X.1, pp. 11–23). Schoff wishes to demonstrate that Claudio appears 'conclusively and steadily an admirable hero on the evidence of the play itself'. He 'proves under stress to be a good Christian and a good subject' and is 'one of

Shakespeare's fresh and innocent young lovers, fit company in his shy way for Orlando, Bassanio, Romeo, and their friends'. A note of even greater idolatry is sounded by Paul and Miriam Mueschke in their 1967 article 'Illusion and Metamorphosis in *Much Ado About Nothing*' (*SQ* XVIII.1, pp. 53–65). Centring the play on the question of honour, they find that the virtuous regard for honour in Claudio subjectively justifies his repudiation of Hero: 'Throughout his incisively truncated recantation, Claudio does mourn; throughout his rapt vigil he mourns the martyr slain by slanderous tongues.' Thus 'the recantation scene not only ennobles Claudio, who lost stature in the repudiation scene, but also sanctifies his delayed union with Hero'. A more balanced defence of Claudio is provided in the new Arden and Penguin editions of *Ado*. Humphreys justifies Claudio's credulity by reference to dramatic convention (the traducer conventionally believed), and the publicity and fierceness of the denunciation in the chapel by theatrical expediency (pp. 56–7). Foakes, like Neill, finds that the weight of the evidence of Hero's guilt in Shakespeare's elaboration of the hoax has the effect of removing 'all censure for his rejection of Hero from Claudio', but thinks that Shakespeare precisely intended to portray Claudio 'as a most conventional young man, who loves by the rules, woos through intermediaries, and seems as much concerned about Leonato's wealth as he is about Leonato's daughter' (pp. 15–16).

33. Of course, Shakespeare also needed the Prince to share with Claudio both responsibility for the contract and outrage at the supposed disgrace.

34. There are few exceptions to this rule, which is borne out by the use of 'thou' in speaking to obvious social inferiors, like servants and constables. Leonato and Antonio say 'you' to one another, as do Hero and Beatrice. Here is a typical exchange between Claudio and Benedick (with my italics):

> *Claud. Thou* thinkest I am in sport: I pray *thee* tell me truly how *thou* lik'st her.
> *Bene.* Would *you* buy her, that *you* inquire after her?

> (I.i.165–7)

It is remarkable that Benedick suddenly 'thous' both Don Pedro and Claudio right at the end of the play. Shakespeare obviously wishes to emphasise Benedick's feeling of being on top of the world:

> I'll tell thee what, Prince; a college of wit-crackers cannot flout me out of my humour. Dost thou think I care for a satire or an epigram?... For thy part, Claudio, I did think to have beaten thee, but in that thou art like to be my kinsman, live unbruised and love my cousin. (V.iv.99–110)

Commenting on the ending, Levin points out that 'Benedick, pleased that he is marrying (as he thinks) despite social pressures, usurps Leonato's role as master of ceremonies', but he goes on to declare that

Benedick's last words to the Prince ('get thee a wife./There is no staff more reverent than one tipp'd with horn') are 'the taunt of an insecure man' (op. cit., p. 116). I fail to see this insecurity in Benedick's final euphoria.

For the use of 'thou' and 'you' by Celia and Rosalind in *AYLI*, see p. 53 and nn 10, 11.

35. I cannot accept Humphreys' statement that 'Among other main differences from Bandello are [sic] the equalizing of rank between Claudio and Hero' (Arden *Ado*, p. 11). Shakespeare reduces the social difference but retains a general sense of it. Probably Don John insinuates Hero's inferiority in relation to Claudio as well as to the Prince when he maliciously confides to the former (who is in disguise) that the Prince 'is enamour'd on Hero', but 'she is no equal for his birth' (II.i.152–3).

36. See also Palmer, op. cit., p. 113.

37. Benedick soliloquising on Claudio turned lover: 'I have known when he would have walked ten mile afoot to see a good armour, and now will he lie ten nights awake carving the fashion of a new doublet' (II.iii.15–18; see also II.i.176–8). 'The influence of fashion in social intercourse, as opposed to that of genuine character, is a major target of the satiric arsenal in *Much Ado*', Allen, op. cit., p. 40.

38. Berger, 'Against the Sink-a-Pace . . .', *SQ* 33.3 (1982), p. 303.

39. Leggatt, *Shakespeare's Comedy of Love* (1974), p. 159.

40. Berger, op. cit., pp. 305–6.

41. III.iv.6–23, 57–8, 92. See also III.i.102–3.

42. III.iii.114–34. Conrade does not quite see what Borachio is driving at, and we, too, may be puzzled by his digression from his tale (137–8), though we grasp the thematic connection when we hear Hero talk of fashions in the next scene. Shakespeare may not have worked out Borachio's bit of moralising finally.

43. Ormerod, 'Faith and Fashion in "Much Ado About Nothing"', *SS* 25 (1972), pp. 94, 96. On the theme of fashion see also McCollom, op. cit., pp. 173–4; Allen, op. cit., pp. 40–51; Berger, op. cit., pp. 308–10.

44. A less worldly Hero may be seen reflected in the Mariana of *Measure for Measure*, another woman deserted, at least ostensibly, because of false reports of unchastity and presented incognita to her husband. In Beatrice's opinion Benedick is included in the judgement of worldliness (see I.i.68–70), though he ridicules Claudio for his vanity (II.iii.15–18). See also Pedro's and Claudio's baiting of the love-smitten Benedick at III.ii.29–47.

45. See I.ii.88–90, 189–90.

46. See the Appendix on 'The Proxy Wooing' in the Arden *Ado*, pp. 230–1.

47. Arden *Ado*, p. 230.

48. Evans, *Shakespeare's Comedies* (1960), pp. 71–2.

49. There may also be an intimation of this kind of betrayal in *The Shrew*, see my *Unconformities in Shakespeare's Early Comedies*, pp. 75–6.

50. Evans, op. cit., p. 72.

51. 'At 2.1.48 it appears that she [Hero] is, without protest, expecting a proposal of marriage from the prince. At 226–8 she is handed over to Claudio, equally without comment or protest', Mares, New Cam. *Ado*, p. 149.

52. Leggatt, op. cit., p. 154.
53. Palmer, op. cit., p. 126. See also Rees, op. cit., p. 30.
54. The time-scheme is excellently set out by Mares in Appendix I, New Cam. *Ado*, pp. 154–6.
55. Benedick resents being called a fool and makes an egregious fool of himself. Dogberry resents being called an ass and is unaware of his asininity.

3   ALL EVEN IN ARDEN?

1. See Barnet's closely-argued essay '"Strange Events" : Improbability in *As You Like It*', *SSt* IV (1968), pp. 119–31.
2. *Sources*, II, p. 183.
3. Ibid., pp. 199, 220.
4. Jenkins, '*As You Like It*', *SS* 8 (1955), p. 41.
5. He would also have omitted Orlando's specific mention of 'poor a thousand crowns' as his inheritance from his father, leaving Oliver's later denial of a 'thousand crowns' without a reference, but this would cause no problem.
    Several critics have identified the Jaques who appears in the Duke's company in Arden with Orlando's brother in Shakespeare's first conception of this character. Thus Jenkins: 'It seems clear enough that these two men with the same name were originally meant to be one. As things turned out Jaques could claim to have acquired his famous melancholy from travel and experience, but I suspect that it really began in the schoolbooks which were studied with such profit by Jaques de Boys' (op. cit., p. 42).
6. Thus, following Theobald, e.g. the Arden, Penguin, Signet and Riverside editions.
7. Adam, too, characterises Duke Frederick as 'humorous' at II.iii.8. It should be added that Le Beau suggests a cause for the Duke's hatred of Rosalind (though not for its sudden eruption) – her popularity with the people, who, 'pity her for her good father's sake' (I.ii.270–1); and that Frederick himself enlarges on this in I.iii.73–8.
8. Cam. *AYLI* (1926, 1948), pp. 94–8.
9. Ibid., pp. 98–103. Wilson thinks that 'the time which elapsed between the first and the second draft must have been long enough for changes in the cast to have intervened and for Shakespeare to have forgotten some material points in the plot' (p. 96).
10. McIntosh, '"As You Like It": a grammatical clue to character', *REL* 4.2 (1963), pp. 68–81. In the first half of the play Celia says 'thou' to Rosalind 34 times and 'you' 12, while Rosalind says 'you' to Celia 10 times and 'thou' once; in the second half Celia says 'you' to Rosalind 17 times and 'thou' 3, while Rosalind says 'thou' to Celia 16 times and 'you' 7. (Oblique forms of the pronouns are included in these counts.)
11. See p. 33 above. In *TN* Sir Toby advises Sir Andrew to write a taunting challenge to 'Cesario': 'If thou thou'st him some thrice, it shall not be amiss' (III.ii.43–4). Though Shakespeare's use of second-person

pronouns may sometimes seem haphazard, he was quite conscious of their potentials as social and emotional markers. An amusing comment on the implications of using the 'thou'-pronoun in the mid-sixteenth century is provided by Thomas Gilbert:

> But he, despising reverence
> To prince or any state,
> Not them regards, but used terms
> As each had been his mate.
> For he did thou each wight the which
> With him had any talk.
> Thus did his tongue most devilishly
> With defamy still walk.
> ('A declaration of the death of John Lewes ... ', 1583.

Table 3.1
Occurrences of 'thous' and 'yous' and their oblique forms in the conversations of Rosalind and Celia

	thou		*you*	
	Ros.	*Cel.*	*Ros.*	*Cel.*
I.ii	1	15	6	2
I.iii	0	16	3	10
III.ii.160–75	0	3	1	0
176–423	14	2	1	8
III.iv	0	1	2	1
IV.i	2	0	2	5
IV.iii	0	0	2	3

12. In spite of his objection to blank verse, Jaques himself speaks it in II.vii and reverts to it at the very end of the play. I also take the first part of the conversation between Jaques and Orlando at III.ii.249–54 to be blank verse. It almost looks as if Orlando tends to be ushered in in blank verse.
13. McIntosh, op. cit. Hapgood, 'Shakespeare's AS YOU LIKE IT, III.ii', *Explicator* XXIV.7 (March 1966), Note 60.
14. *Sources*, II, p. 198.
15. 'This sharp and surprisingly serious rebuke contrasts with the Duke's usual indulgence of Jaques', Leggatt, *Shakespeare's Comedy of Love* (1974), p. 201.
16. There is one main exception in the case of Touchstone: his dialogue with Audrey before the arrival of Sir Oliver Martext. But this is for the comedy of the illiterate Audrey echoing Touchstone's classical invocations (III.iii.1–41).
17. Jaques's advice to Touchstone, 'Get you to church, and have a good priest that can tell you what marriage is' (III.iii.75–7), inevitably brings to mind the Roman Catholic view of marriage as a sacrament. See the

Arden note to line 37. The setting of *AYLI* is ostensibly France, but Martext can only be an English puritan, and the name hints at the Marprelate controversy.

18. 'It is left to the producer to decide whether the masque shall be plainly a charade got up by Rosalind, or whether it is pure magic, like the masque in *The Tempest*, in which the actors were "all spirits"' Arden note to V.iv.106 stage direction. 'The fact that Amiens is given an entry at the head of the scene in F. but has nothing to say or sing in the received text suggests that his original part was cut by the reviser in order that the actor who played him might come on as Hymen', Dover Wilson in Cam. *AYLI*, p. 163. Smallwood has seen the role of Hymen played by Corin (even taking a prompt from Rosalind, who had obviously written his speech), and also by Adam, who otherwise simply disappears on joining the Duke's entourage.

19. Were the religious uncle and the magician supposed to be the same person (whom we might then naturally identify, too, with the 'old religious man' who converts Duke Frederick)? Perhaps this assimilation was made only belatedly, see Orlando's speech at V.iv.30–4.

>   this boy is forest-born,
> And hath been tutored in the rudiments
> Of many desperate studies, by his uncle,
> Whom he reports to be a great magician,
> Obscured in the circle of this forest.

In Lodge's story there is no religious uncle, but Ganimede says 'he' has 'a friend that is deeply experienst in Negromancie and Magicke' (*Sources*, II, p. 246).

20. 'Yet even after a lion and a snake, these classical nuptials seem wildly incongruous with the English Arden Shakespeare has evolved for us out of his young memories. It may very well be that, as our texts reach us, they were adapted out of Christian to Pagan ceremonial in obedience to royal wish or statute', 'Q' in the Introduction to the Cam. *AYLI*, pp. xvii–xviii. 'The appearance of Hymen is completely unexpected, seeing that what we have been led to anticipate is a magician.... Hymen's words, whether spoken or sung, do not seem to us in the least Shakespearian; and they might all be omitted without loss to the context', Wilson in the Cam. *AYLI*, p. 163. See also p. 108.

21. Adam has been missed by some readers in the final scene. Anne Barton thinks 'Adam is simply too old to help initiate the new social order' (Riverside, p. 367), though his counterpart in Lodge becomes 'Captaine of the Kings Gard' (*Sources*, II, p. 256). It may merely have been necessary to save some actors' parts. With enough actors, of course, Adam could come on even if he does not speak. As for Duke Frederick, he may be said to be present by report.

22. In other passages of Act V, too, the style may seem unworthy of Shakespeare. Dover Wilson points to Rosalind's speech in which she asks for credence of her knowledge of magic arts (V.ii.51–68),

and Wilson thinks it 'ludicrous, for instance,... that Rosalind should suddenly assure Orlando that he is "a gentleman of good conceit"' (Cam. *AYLI*, p. 157).

23. 'We may indeed ask why the third De Boys should be dragged in here at all when a messenger would have done equally well; perhaps he played a more considerable part in the original draft', Wilson, Cam. *AYLI*, p. 164. The little notice that is taken of the messenger would have been more natural if the message was brought by Le Beau – a transfer of the part which could easily be made in the theatre and probably has been on occasion.

24. Actually, of course, Oliver's house and lands were seized by Duke Frederick (III.i.9–18) and we do not yet know of Frederick's conversion. When the second brother has delivered his message Duke Senior shows that he is aware of the sequestration of Oliver's lands and now assumes that Oliver will take possession of them again. Oliver's bequest to Orlando is obviously premature.

25. In Lodge's *Rosalynde* the unregenerate Saladyne salves his conscience with the following thought for his middle brother: 'As for *Fernandyne* thy middle brother he is a scholer, and hath no minde but on *Aristotle*; let him reade on *Galen* while thou riflest with gold, and pore on his booke til thou doost purchase lands: wit is great wealth, if hee have learning it is enough; and so let all rest.' And Fernandyne is not forgotten in the happy ending, for the King 'created *Rosader* heir apparent to the kingdom: he restored *Saladyne* to all his fathers lande, and gave him the Dukedom of *Nameurs*, he made *Fernandyne* principall Secretarie to himselfe'! (*Sources*, II, pp. 166, 256).

4 OR, WHAT YOU WILL

1. Parrott, *Shakespearean Comedy* (1949, 1977), p. 178.
2. Mahood surveys a number of different stage interpretations and readings of *TN* in the New Penguin Introduction (1968), pp. 31–9.
3. Both James I and Charles I may have known the play as 'Malvolio'. It was performed at court under that title in February 1623, and in Charles I's copy of the 1632 Folio 'the name Malvolio is written opposite the title in the list of contents' – see Chambers, *William Shakespeare: A Study of Facts and Problems*, II (1930), p. 346, and Arden *TN* (1975), pp. 1xxix–1xxx.
4. E.g. I.ii.28, I.iii.107, II.iv.27–9, V.i.242. See also Turner, 'The Text of *Twelfth Night*', *SQ* XXVI.2 (1975), p. 134.
5. Olivia's self-confident awareness of her rank is hinted at in her remark to Sebastian, 'What time we will our celebration keep/According to my birth' (IV.iii.30–1).
6. Craik seems to half-accept R. K. Turner's statement that the titles of duke and count 'are not employed synonymously by Shakespeare', but he rather unconvincingly suggests by way of compromise that 'in this play [*TN*] alone, Shakespeare did allow the same person to be both duke

and count according as he exhibited the different aspects of his personality and office' (Arden *TN*, p. xxii). It may be of interest to note that the Florentine Mariana in *AWW* calls Count Bertram an earl (III.v.12, 17), but count and earl were more equivalent than count and duke.

7. There seems to be some confusion in *Ado* concerning the title of Don John, however, see p. 25 above.

8. Turner, op. cit., pp. 134–5, 131. (Turner uses Hinman's line numbering in the Norton Facsimile).

9. See my *Unconformities in Shakespeare's Early Comedies* (1986), pp. 47–9, 80–2, 161–2.

10. The word 'jester' is relatively rare in Shakespeare, and the occurrence in *TN* may be the only time a living character is called a jester without irony.

11. Repetitions signalling omitted or inserted matter have been frequently pointed out in my earlier books in this 'Unconformities' series. See also my 'Repetition, Revision, and Editorial Greed in Shakespeare's Play Texts', *Cahiers élisabéthains* 34 (1988), 25–37.

12. See also Wilson, Cam. *TN* (1930, 1974), pp. 91–4; and Parrott, op. cit., p. 179.

13. See Bethell, *Shakespeare and the Popular Dramatic Tradition* (1944, 1948), pp. 140–3. Bethell is supported by Craik, Arden *TN*, pp. xxii–xxiv. See also Mahood, New Penguin *TN*, p. 20.

14. Arden *TN*, p. 2.

15. See Wilson, Cam. *TN*, p. 94. Wilson is supported by Mahood (New Penguin *TN*, p. 20). Bill Alexander opines that Shakespeare had to 'introduce another character, because he wanted to hold Feste back for the climactic dark-house scene' (Billington, ed., *Directors' Shakespeare: Approaches to Twelfth Night*, 1990, p. 101). Peter Thomson sensibly comments:

> It has sometimes been suggested that the substitution of Fabian for Feste in the letter scene (II.v.) reflects Shakespeare's nervousness that the audience might be *too* interested by Feste, and that the scene's focus might therefore be blurred. I find that unconvincing. Shakespeare never lacked confidence in his actors; and Armin was certainly no Will Kempe, mercilessly improvising for the sake of a laugh.... We have to accept the sudden introduction of Fabian as a playhouse mystery, a rehearsal decision preserved in the text.
>
> (*Shakespeare's Theatre*, 1983, p. 91)

– that is, if we accept Fabian as the interloper, which for reasons given below I cannot do.

16. Compare Brutus' repeated call for a bowl of wine framing an inserted passage in *JC*, IV.iii.141, 157.

17. Craik offers an explanation of this oddity, Arden *TN*, xx–xxi, n. 5.

18. 'Feste knows as well as Viola the importance of waiting for the right moment' – Levin, *Love and Society in Shakespearean Comedy* (1985), p. 147. There is nothing in the text to support this explanation.

19. Walker asks, 'Was not Maria, rather than Fabian, meant to say "myself and Toby/Set this device against Malvolio here"?' ('The Whirligig of Time: A Review of Recent Productions', *SS* 12, 1959, p. 130, n. 15.)
20. The belief that Feste was in the carousal scene when it was first composed will not explain either the apparent textual interpolation in that scene or Feste's mysterious disappearance before it ends. Since most critics at least agree that Feste supplanted Viola in II.iv, they should have no difficulty in supposing that he also supplanted Fabian in some scenes.
21. One may suspect a remnant of such a scene in the conversation of Fabian and the two knights at II.v.4–12.
22. New Penguin *TN*, p. 20.
23. Maria says he will be hanged but Olivia makes no reference to his delinquency. Compare the late appearance of the Fool in *Lear*.
24. Cam. *TN*, p. 94. Is this 'official diploma', as Wilson calls it, Shakespeare's way of introducing Armin to the public, or is the passage non-Shakespearian?
25. See, however, Bradley, 'Feste the Jester' in Palmer, ed., *Twelfth Night: A Casebook* (1972), pp. 67–8. Olivia accuses Feste of growing dishonest (I.v.39) and we may suspect him of both drunkenness (I.v.40) and unchastity ('I did impeticos [impetticoat?] thy gratillity', I.iii.27); perhaps the causes of his truancy. But he never actually demonstrates these failings, though Toby repeatedly calls him a 'sot'. His scrounging for tips may have been adopted as a kind of hallmark for him. There is more to be said for the sense of loneliness that pervades him (see Bradley), and there is a sadness about him which is emphasised by his songs, particularly the concluding song which is ostensibly about himself.
26. This is Wilson's suggestion (Cam. *TN*, p. 97). But Wilson finds a 'frequent use of "Jove" in the play' and does not see that it is practically limited to Malvolio. Craik, on the other hand, seems to think the use of 'God' less frequent than it actually is (Arden *TN*, n. to III.iv.75). 'God' occurs 12 times, most frequently in the long fourth scene of Act III, where also Malvolio's most fervent invocations of Jove occur. We also find 'Lord' and 'Heaven(s)' in a number of ejaculations, as well as 'Dieu' and "Slight' ('God's light') once each. There is a very obvious substitution of Jove for God in *AWW* IV.ii.25, where there can be no suspicion of intentional absurdity. Diana says to Bertram, 'If I should swear by Jove's great attributes/I lov'd you dearly...'
27. Antonio and Sebastian confuse the time-scheme a little. They appear in the city in II.i, which in the context of the main wooing plot is the first day of the action. Sebastian is then 'bound to Count Orsino's court' (41–2). When we meet him again in III.iii he has not yet been to his lodging (20, 39–40) and now merely plans to go sightseeing (18–24, 41–2), yet this must be day two of the main action. Next, in V.i, Antonio states that the person he takes to be Sebastian came to town 'today' (92). So Sebastian's and Antonio's one day corresponds to the two days of Viola and the rest. See also Billington, ed., op. cit., pp. 4–5.
28. 'That it should all depend on there being an indistinguishable twin

brother always troubles me when I think about it, though never when I watch the play', Barber, *Shakespeare's Festive Comedy* (1959), p. 244. See also p. 246.

29. See also my Preface to the present book, p. x. Barton emphasises Viola's passivity, which turns out to be expedient, since 'Time does untangle the knot without her help', as Viola had hoped (*Riverside Shakespeare*, 1974, p. 406). Levin thinks her calculating (op. cit., pp. 146–7). Taylor admires the way in which Shakespeare manages to seem 'despite these inconsistencies not only plausible but uniquely and intensely real'. 'The inconsistencies', he says, 'have been called carelessness; they seem to me the products of great care, for each solves a serious dramatic problem, and each has been painstakingly concealed.' (*Moment by Moment by Shakespeare*, 1985, p. 84). Taylor's argument, however, is far from compelling.

30. See Cam. *TN*, p. 165. If Wilson is right, the puzzle of the two encounters with Sebastian passed unobserved till Wilson remarked on it in 1929; but it does not follow that 'dramatically it has no importance', as he concludes. Craik's comment in the Arden *TN* is typical: 'As so often, [Shakespeare] sacrifices rational consistency for dramatic effect, knowing that the inconsistency will go unnoticed in the theatre' (p. lxxvii, n. 2).

31. On the whole, Maria behaves more like a chambermaid than a gentlewoman. Levin makes a point of the difference, op. cit., p. 132. The last time she is seen and heard is at IV.ii.66–7. She could be one of the 'attendants' to enter with Olivia at V.i.94, but would hardly have remained silent; and Fabian speaks as if she is absent – having married Toby (361–3).

32. There are hints in the early part of the play that the union may be expected (I.v.26–7, II.v.182, 190–1). See also Levin, op. cit., p. 132.

33. Directors, of course, are free to put any interpretation they please on the casual treatment of Antonio, and the tendency nowadays is to be more cynical about it than Shakespeare probably intended. See n. 36 below.

34. New Penguin *TN*, p. 17. Thomson (op. cit., p. 91) speaks of 'the Captain of I.ii., in whom Viola invites us to take a disproportionate interest. Shakespeare had clearly thought of pairing the Captain with Antonio, but "lost" him somewhere .... An episode in the sub-plot is missing.'

35. 'There is a disturbingly large number of important absentees in the ending of *Twelfth Night*, more than in any other Shakespearean comedy', Barton in the *Riverside Shakespeare*, p. 407.

36. Levin, op. cit., pp. 152, 164. In the moving close of Kenneth Branagh's film version of *TN* as shown on TV (Oslo, 26 December 1990), three persons were left to exit through an iron gate after the bridal couples had entered Olivia's house: Sir Andrew, showing a bloody face, Antonio, forgotten and still in handcuffs until released by an officer, and finally Feste, who, after singing his sad song, shut the gate and peered back through the bars as the screen darkened.

5 DARK DOINGS IN TUSCANY

1. Evans, *Shakespeare's Comedies* (1960), p.166.
2. Ibid., p.152.
3. Conceivably pilgrims from central and southern Italy might be thought of as going to Saint Jaques by way of Florence, but this would not be what Shakespeare had in mind.
4. *Sources*, II, pp. 392–3.
5. Rees, *Shakespeare and the Story* (1978), p. 41.
6. See Rees, op. cit., p. 43.
7. Bradbrook, 'Virtue is the True Nobility', in Muir, ed., *Shakespeare: The Comedies* (1965, 1976), pp. 132, 120.
8. Toole, *Shakespeare's Problem Plays* (1966), pp. 130–50. Toole takes his comparison quite far: 'by substituting herself for Diana, Helena has saved Bertram from the commission of a sin. The substitution motif here, as in *Measure for Measure*, provides an analogue to the ransom paid by Christ for man'! (p.150). For a more sober view of the morality element in *AWW*, see Tillyard, *Shakespeare's Problem Plays* (1950, 1970), pp. 108–9).
9. See op. cit., pp. 94 – 5.
10. Ure, *Shakespeare: The Problem Plays* (1961), pp. 16 –18.
11. See e.g. 'Q', Cam. *AWW* (1929, 1968), pp. xxvi – xxviii; Carter, 'In Defense of Bertram', *SQ* VII.1 (1956), pp. 21–31; Halio, *'All's Well That Ends Well'*, *SQ* XV.l (1964), pp 33–43; Smallwood, 'The Design of *All's Well That Ends Well'*, *SS* 25 (1972), pp. 56–61.
12. E.g. Rees, see op. cit., p. 45.
13. Ure, op. cit., p. 15.
14. Evans, op. cit., pp. 158–9. Joan Rees finds 'a failure of story-telling technique' in the latter half of the play and blames it on Shakespeare's 'use of a programme' contained in the conditions set down by Bertram for an acceptance of Helena and her determination to fulfil them. This 'programming device' does not leave Shakespeare free to develop his characters, but on the contrary fetters him (Rees, op. cit., pp. 46–7).
15. Smallwood, op. cit., pp. 56–61. Smallwood instances Trevor Nunn's 'splendid production' a few years ago – see his review reprinted in Cox and Palmer (eds), *Shakespeare's Wide and Universal Stage* (1984), pp. 98–103.
16. See Arden *AWW*, pp. xv–xvi.
17. For Hunter's explanation of the confusion of speech prefixes see Arden *AWW*, pp. xv–xvii. It is remarkable that only after the capture of Parolles, when the brothers are given an interval of conversation while they are waiting for Bertram, are we told that Cap. E. has delivered the letter to Bertram that the Countess charged him with at Rossillion (III.ii.94–5, IV.iii. 1–2). Cap. E. thinks 'there is something in't that stings his [Bertram's] nature, for on the reading he chang'd almost into another man' (IV.iii.2–4), but this is more likely to refer to the letter containing news of Helena's self-banishment which the Countess asks Reynaldo to write and to dispatch by 'the most convenient messenger' (III.iv. 29–34). Cap. E. says he delivered the letter to Bertram 'an hour

since', but we see no effects of the reading of the letter in the behaviour of Bertram when he re-enters the stage.

18. On the basis of these two months Evans constructs a rather far-fetched explanation, op. cit., pp. 154, 163–4.
19. Cam. *AWW*, p. xxv.
20. See also Arden *AWW*, p. xxxv.
21. F's entry for 'Count' and one speech prefix for 'Ros.' (Rossillion) in this scene are apparently a mistake, though the Arden editor thinks differently (n. to II.iii.S.D.).
22. Parrott, *Shakespearean Comedy* (1949, 1977), p. 348.
23. 'Helena has possessed this token of supreme authority ever since she cured the King's fistula and has kept the fact from us', Evans, op. cit., p. 165.
24. V.iii.198–201. The King refers to a prior mention of Parolles by Diana which we have not heard. Possibly a few lines could have been lost or cancelled, but see Arden n. to lines. 198–9.
25. Giletta in Painter's version of the story is 'brought abedde of twoo sonnes, whiche were very like unto their father' (*Sources*, II, pp. 395–6). Shakespeare changed the wording of Bertram's letter as first read out in III.ii, or made Helena misquote it. It now reads: '*When from my finger you can get this ring / And is by me with child, &c.*' (V.iii.306–7). Even if Helena is only pregnant and has not yet given birth, she already 'feels her young one kick' (296) and must be visibly expecting. But Shakespeare has not really allowed time for this since the ladies break up from Florence immediately after the bed-trick (IV.iv.14, 33–5) and travel by 'exceeding posting day and night' (V.i.1) by way of 'Marcellus' (Marseilles) to Rossillion (IV.v.77, V.i.22–38).
26. Arden *AWW*, p. liv.
27. Bradbrook, op. cit., pp. 120, 131–2.
28. Cam. *AWW*, p. xxxi.
29. Ibid., p. xxxiii.
30. Arden *AWW*, pp. liv–lv.
31. Bradbrook, op. cit., p. 132.
32. Everett, Penguin *AWW* (1970), pp. 35–9.
33. Edwards thinks *AWW* and *MM* are failures 'in their insistence on a happy ending in spite of the evidence'. Shakespeare realised as he approached the ending that his human material was intractable:

> Helena never saves Bertram. He is unredeemable. Shakespeare could not save him. It is not a matter of failing to write the lines that would have changed the soul of the play: it is a matter of not being able to force one's conscience to alter a character whose alteration would be, simply, incredible.

Hence the hurried dismissal of Bertram after his brief and unsatisfactory remarks at the end. (*Shakespeare and the Confines of Art*, 1968, pp. 109–15). This interpretation is undeniably attractive but takes the ending far too seriously after the play has demonstrably lost much of its seriousness.

34. Cam. *AWW*, p. vii–xii, 105. '*All's Well* is largely a palimpsest and over-written upon juvenile work after a considerable interval of time' (p. vii).
35. Parrott, op. cit., pp. 347–8.
36. E.g. I.i.212–25, iii. 123–30, II.iii. 118–41.
37. Tillyard, op. cit., p. 100.
38. See my *Unconformities in Shakespeare's History Plays* (1982), pp. 50–1.
39. Passages in rhyming couplets or, more rarely, in laced rhyme occur par-ticularly in I.i.iii, II.i.iii and at the conclusion of the play. The distribu-tion of verse and prose does not throw much light on a possible stratification (though Wilson finds 'some very obvious joins', see Cam. *AWW*, pp. 104–5). By a very rough estimate there is about an equal amount of verse and prose in *All's Well* and both are used much as one might expect according to the degree of seriousness and dignity of scenes and characters. There is a tendency exemplified in the opening episode to begin the scenes in prose before modulating into verse, but this probably means no more than a general attempt to create heighten-ing effects in the substructure of the comedy as a part of the ultimate design.
40. '[I]f Shakespeare chose to use chunks of earlier work these must be considered no less organic to his scheme than the actual insects or postage stamps or leaves gummed on to the canvas of a surrealist picture', Tillyard, op. cit., p. 100.
41. So also the King's speech on virtue and honour at II.iii. 118–41, but there is here no clash with the context.

6 THE DIVIDED WORLD OF VIENNA

1. For Rosaline, see my *Unconformities in Shakespeare's Early Comedies* (1986), pp. 103–6.
2. It is generally agreed that the copy for the F text was Shakespeare's 'foul papers' or 'rough draft' as transcribed by Ralph Crane, though Jowett argues strongly for prompt-book copy (Wells and Taylor, *William Shakespeare: A Textual Companion*, 1987, p. 468). Crane may have regularised speech prefixes and some other features. See the Arden *MM* (1965, 1976) pp. xi–xii, xxiv. Lever has listed and commented on most of the anomalies of *MM* in his Arden edition, pp. xiii–xxxi, lxvi, lxxix, lxxxii, lxxxvii, xc, xciv–xcvi.
3. Judging by Isabella's statement to Claudio when she sees him in prison, Angelo has also demanded gratification of Isabella that very night:
    This night's the time
    That I should do what I abhor to name;
    Or else thou diest tomorrow.
    (III.i.100–2)
    See also III.i.263–4.
4. This difference between the time-schemes of main and subsidiary plots must not be confused with what has become known as 'double time',

which chiefly relates to different parts or developments of the main action, as in *Othello*.

5. Harbage amusingly comments on bardolatrous explanations of the discrepancy between Claudio's 'nineteen zodiacs' (I.ii.157) and the Duke's 'fourteen years' (I.iii.21), concerning the time when the laws of Venice have slept. See his 'Shakespeare and the Myth of Perfection', *SQ* XV.2 (1964), p. 3.

6. The name of Friar Thomas occurs only in the SD for I.iii and in F's appended list 'of all the Actors', where Thomas and Peter are bracketed as '2. Friers'. It seems reasonable to suppose that the Friar Peter of Acts IV–V is meant to be the same as the Friar in whom the Duke confides in I.iii. Whether Isabella is acquainted with Friar Peter, as may be suggested by her being asked to take a letter to him (IV.iii.137) is another minor problem.

7. The introduction of Barnardine, who refuses to be beheaded and is replaced by Ragozine (who has died of a 'cruel fever', IV.ii–iii) may seem entirely gratuitous. It could be meant as a sign of justice and clemency in the Duke when a dead body is decapitated instead of a living man, and no doubt the spirit of comedy gains by this exchange. But this strange business may have begun as a case of second thoughts. In Shakespeare's main source, *Promos and Cassandra*, the prisoner whose head is to replace Claudio's has already been executed (*Sources*, II, p. 171). Lever comments humanely on the Barnardine business in his Arden Introduction, pp. lxxxix–xc.

8. Lever thinks that 'One can only conclude that the book-keeper or some other member of the company noticed that a necessary soliloquy was missing and patched up the empty place as best he could.' Lever curiously suggests that either 'Shakespeare here showed an unusual degree of neglect' or 'he wrote a speech for the Duke which his colleagues or the censor found unacceptable', Arden *MM*, p. xxii. Dover Wilson proposes a theory of abridgment and thinks the lines of the Duke's soliloquy 'have been carried over from one scene to another in order to cover, however inadequately, a join in the text', Cam. *MM* (1922), p. 98. Jowett and Taylor, on the contrary, argue that the song beginning Act IV and the Duke's dialogue with Mariana were interpolated by an adapter, who also introduced the act-break before this scene. The adapter transposed a fragment of soliloquy from the preceding scene 'with the longer and more appropriate soliloquy' which he found in the original Mariana scene and which he now moved to create 'a theatrically convincing lead into the new act-break', Wells and Taylor, op. cit., p. 468.

9. Musgrove, 'Some Composite Scenes in *Measure for Measure*', *SQ* XV.1 (1964), pp. 67–74.

10. This may be generic, as Lever points out (Arden, n. to I.ii.104), but Pompey has no other name in this scene. He is merely 'Clown' in SDs and speech-prefixes throughout the F text.

11. The stage is theoretically left empty for a moment and F here begins a new scene, 'Scena Tertia', while modern editors continue scene ii. The Clown points out 'Madam Juliet' (107) and she is included in the entry direction but there is no other indication of her presence, and Claudio

speaks of her to Lucio ('You know the lady', 136) as if she is absent. She first definitely appears, accompanied by the Provost, in II.iii. See also Arden *MM*, p. xvii.

12. Jowett in Wells and Taylor, op. cit., p. 468. Lever suggests omitting only lines 79–85, containing the Clown's news of the arrest and the reason for it, leaving his information concerning the import of the proclamation and allowing him to be introduced to us in this early scene (Arden *MM*, p. xx). Musgrove thinks the whole scene 'is an unskilful piece of patching' and proposes a rearrangement of its parts (op.cit.). But where so much is theoretically possible, speculation as to original intentions is not very tempting.

13. At III.i.152, i.e. near midway. There are 1375 lines before this point and 1563 after (Hinman's numbering). Compare the somewhat similar switch in *AYLI*, see p. 54 above.

14. Rossiter, *Angel with Horns* (1961), p. 164.

15. Barnardine refusing to be executed and being let off is surprising enough but of little importance to the intrigue even if it has other effects (see n. 7 above).

16. See also Leech, 'The "Meaning" of *Measure for Measure*', *SS* 3 (1950), p. 68. Pettet finds 'something peculiarly unsatisfying in the play's treatment of evil' and instances the deflation of 'Angelo's unbridled lust' in the latter half of the play (*Shakespeare and the Romance Tradition*, 1949, 1970, pp. 157–8).

17. See also Rees, *Shakespeare and the Story* (1978), p. 58.

18. Soon after this speech Isabella alludes to Jove as the ruler of Heaven (11–14) but this seems to be because her image of Jove's thunder requires it, not because 'Jove' is substituted for 'God'. There is obviously a tremendous irony in Angelo's appeal to Isabella's Christian charity in their dispute at II.iv. 63–8.

19. Arden *MM*, p. lxxix.

20. Stevenson cites R. W. Chambers (1937), R. W. Battenhouse (1946), E. M. Pope (1949), Madeleine Doran (1954) and above all 'the most ardent of the Christian apologists', Virgil Whitaker (1953). Stevenson himself sees *MM* as 'intellectual comedy', where Isabella's Christian virtue is used dramatically as a foil to Angelo's vice and where 'neither Isabella nor the audience can be allowed to succumb to the emotional violence which her surrender to Angelo would evoke', *The Achievement of Shakespeare's 'Measure for Measure'* (1966), pp. 98–9, 23.

21. Thus Rossiter (*Angel with Horns*, 1961, p. 160), Kirsch ('The Integrity of "Measure for Measure"', *SS* 28, 1975, p. 97), Rees (op. cit., 1978, p. 57). Sexual inhibitions and neurosis are emphasised by Wilson Knight (*The Wheel of Fire*, 1930, 1960, p. 93) and Hawkins ('"The Devil's Party": Virtues and Vices in "Measure for Measure"', *SS* 31, 1978, p. 112).

22. 'In terms of plot-mechanics, it may be noted, Isabella's participation was by no means necessary: a message to Angelo, and the Duke's own visit to Mariana, would have been enough to operate the substitution device', Lever, Arden *MM*, p. lxxxii. Lever thinks 'Isabella is being re-educated in the function of virtue as an active force in the world' (loc. cit.).

23. Nuttall is enlightening on Elizabethan marriage contracts: see his '"Measure for Measure": The Bed-Trick', *SS* 28 (1975), 51–6.
24. Isabella could supposedly be dressed as a novice in the first half of the play and in secular clothes in the second half. It obviously makes a great difference to the play in performance which way this decision goes.
25. Rossiter, op. cit. p. 162. Edwards, who sees *MM* as 'a drama of choice and decision', acutely observes that choice and decision at the crucial moment are taken out of the hands of the two principals, Angelo and Isabella, by 'the devices and intrigues of a controlling superhuman figure': 'we are thoroughly cheated. We are never shown the consequences of the two great decisions', *Shakespeare and the Confines of Art* (1968), pp. 117–18.
26. See Evans, *Shakespeare's Comedies* (1960), pp. 217–18. Tillyard rejects this idea of a moral education as represented by R. W. Chambers, even though, as he ironically remarks, 'Nothing could be more ingenious and plausible than Chambers's notion of Shakespeare's keeping Isabella ignorant of her brother's survival and filled with justified fury at Angelo's having done him to death, in order that her powers of forgiveness might be tested to the uttermost when she brings herself to join Mariana in pleading for Angelo's life' (*Shakespeare's Problem Plays*, 1950, 1970, p. 121).
27. See n. 11 above.
28. For the Christ-analogy and the Providential view of the Duke see e.g. Wilson Knight (op. cit., 1930, pp. 74, 79–82), Battenhouse ('*Measure for Measure* and Christian Doctrine of the Atonement', *PMLA* LXI, 1946, pp. 1029–59), Toole (*Shakespeare's Problem Plays*, 1966, p. 192), Kirsch (op. cit., p. 104). On the other side, e.g. Leech (op. cit., pp. 112–16) and Weil ('Form and Contexts in *Measure for Measure*', *CQ* 12.1, 1970, pp. 61–7). A balanced view is that of Rossiter, who sees the Duke as the representative of 'degree' and order (op. cit., 1961, p. 156). This is not far from the view of the Arden editor (the Duke as 'the representative of true secular and spiritual authority'), but Rossiter rejects (p. 156) Lever's opinion that 'the Duke belongs to quite another level of dramatic presentation than that on which the other characters act and suffer' (Arden *MM*, p. xciv).
29. See also Lawrence, *Shakespeare's Problem Comedies* (1931, 1969), pp. 105–7.
30. E.g. by Coghill, 'Comic Form in *Measure for Measure*', *SS* 8 (1955), pp. 23–4. See *MM* I.iv.50–5, III.ii.85–90, 145–8, IV.iii.154–5. It should be observed that if Lucio did see through the Duke it would spoil the dénouement, in which Lucio is obviously unprepared for the Duke's reappearance.
31. Arden *MM*, p. lxxxvii.
32. The fear that Claudio feels in III.i.117–31 is chiefly aroused by visions of hell. These the Duke evidently wishes to dispel.
33. V.i.489–90 and 531–4. The second proposal, coming right at the end of the play, is worded as if it is the first:

> Dear Isabel,
> I have a motion much imports your good;
> Whereto if you'll a willing ear incline,
> What's mine is yours, and what is yours is mine.

34. Stevenson, op. cit., p. 130. See also Arden *MM*, p. xcvi.
35. At V.i.137–8 he also says that he saw Isabella and the friar at the prison 'but yesternight'. Lever remarks that 'the change of time from morning to evening' at the end of IV.iii implies that this section 'was written on another occasion than the rest of the scene', Arden *MM*, p. xxiii.
36. But Wiles thinks Armin played Pompey, not Lucio, see *Shakespeare's Clown* (1987), pp. 150, 162.
37. E.g. Leavis in 'The Greatness of *Measure for Measure*', *Scrutiny*, 10 (1941–2), pp. 234–47; Knight, op. cit., p. 96, Stevenson, op. cit., pp. 5, 11, 128.
38. See also Tillyard, op. cit., pp. 129–31.
39. In the prison-scenes of Act IV (ii–iii) we have a succession of prose (1–57), verse (58–98), prose (99–105), verse (rhymed, 106–11), prose (112–209 and next scene 1–55), verse (56–7), prose (58–62), verse (63–148), prose (149–77). If we examine the whole play we find that the Duke usually speaks verse and even has isolated verse speeches in a prose context in III.ii. Extraordinarily he speaks prose with Isabella, Claudio and the Provost in the last part of III.i (from line 153), and this is the only place in the play where Isabella and Claudio speak in prose. The Duke also speaks prose with Lucio in III.ii, IV.iii and V.i, with the Provost in part of IV.ii, with Barnardine in IV.iii, and with Mariana in IV.i. Lucio usually speaks prose and has isolated prose speeches in verse contexts in the last part of I.ii (talking to Claudio) and at the end of V.i (talking to the Duke). However, he speaks verse with Isabella in I.iv and II.ii, and with the Duke at V.i.77–85. Escalus speaks both verse and prose. In the examination-scene (II.i), which is in prose, he has a tendency to introduce sporadic one-line speeches in blank verse. Rhyme occurs in *MM* particularly in soliloquies and asides, in gnomic utterances, and at scene endings.
40. See especially the Duke's conversation in verse with Pompey at III.ii.18–39 immediately after conversing with Isabella in prose.
41. In Rossiter's words:

> I believe that *Measure for Measure* was intended to finish as a play of higher ethic, and that ethic 'Christian'. But this remains largely an aim: achievable by manipulation of the plot (which is why you can take out 'the moral fable' and talk about that), but carried out neither by character-development, nor (more important) by the texture of the writing. (Op. cit., pp. 168–9)

7 FORTUNE AGAINST LIFE-FORCE: THE PAGAN WORLD OF *PERICLES*

1. Hoeniger exemplifies both 'the extreme unevenness in the literary

quality' of *Pericles* and 'the highly irregular manner in which it is set up', Arden Introduction, pp. xxviii–xxxiii.

2. See Frye, *A Natural Perspective* (1965), p. 28.

3. The Fishermen's comic dialogue in II.i has been particularly singled out as 'not unworthy of Shakespeare', see Arden *Per.*, p. liv. I would personally suggest the possibility that Shakespeare wrote or rewrote the beginning of I.iii. There is a clue in the fact that throughout the first two acts, with the exception of this one scene, Pericles is consistently addressed as 'Prince', whereas in the rest of the play, considered to be Shakespeare's original work, and in I.iii, he is addressed and spoken of as 'King'. Shakespeare sometimes altered ranks and honorifics in the course of a play, usually to upgrade them, but in this case there is an interesting correspondence with *Confessio Amantis*, which changes from 'prince' to 'kynge' quite systematically, if we compare the episodes leading up to Apollinus's arrival in Pentapolis with those following upon Thaise's abduction to Mytilene. Twine's *Patterne of Painefull Adventures* changes from 'prince' to 'king' only in the last two chapters. Wilkins, on the other hand, retains 'Prince' throughout. See *Sources*, VI, pp. 375–546. The prince/king variance does not necessarily indicate a difference in rank, but it is arguable that Shakespeare preferred the more royal title. Wilson Knight's reflections on the idea of royalty in Shakespeare may be relevant in this connection; see his chapter on *Pericles* in *The Crown of Life* (1947, 1965), p. 72. See also Maxwell on Pericles' 'kingly character', Cam. *Per.* (1956, 1969), pp. xxvii–xxviii.

4. Wells and Taylor, *William Shakespeare: A Textual Companion* (1987), p. 557. Hoeniger accepts the majority view that 'Shakespeare wrote most or all of Acts III–V' and that 'It is very doubtful whether [he] contributed anything to Acts I and II', but he proposes a new candidate for co-authorship along with Wilkins: John Day (Arden *Per.*, pp. 1ii–1xiii).

5. Edwards does not entirely reject the divided authorship theory but, following Wilson Knight (op. cit, p. 75), he argues that 'there is a wholeness in the design of the play, a consistency in its method and a unity in its meaning, which powerfully suggests that the play was conceived as a whole by a single mind' and that mind Shakespeare's. He attributes the unevenness in quality largely to the different talents and methods of two separate reporters, Peng. *Per.*, (1976), pp. 31–41.

6. Wells and Taylor, op. cit., pp. 557–8. Taylor and Jackson suppose on the basis of Wilkins's narrative that the lost play originally 'included a musical episode' in which 'Pericles displays his skill in playing the harp and singing at the banquet' (ibid., p. 558). In the extant play-text King Simonides only retrospectively alludes to Pericles' performance: 'sir, I am beholding to you/ For your sweet music this last night' (II.v.25–6). It seems likely that the allusion refers to an event once actually presented and for some reason lost or omitted from the surviving version of the play.

7. Hoeniger discusses Muir's theory of an 'Ur-Pericles' (Muir, 'The Problem of *Pericles*', *ES* XXX, 1949, pp. 65–83, and elsewhere), see Arden *Per.*, pp. x1vii–x1ix.

8. I agree with Edwards that there 'is a wholeness in the design of the play', etc., which indicates one master-mind behind the completed

version but I doubt whether incompetent reporting alone could have produced the inferior writing of the first two acts.

9. Davies, *'Pericles* and the Sherley brothers', in Honigmann (ed.), *Shakespeare and His Contemporaries* (1986), pp. 94–113, see esp. pp. 105–12.
10. White, *Shakespeare and the Romance Ending* (1981), p. 77.
11. See e.g. Edwards, Peng. *Per.*, p. 15.
12. Knight, op. cit., p. 37.
13. Peng. *Per.*, pp. 16–18.
14. Knight, op. cit., pp. 52, 57, 70.
15. Arden *Per.*, pp. lxxx, lxxxvii–lxxxviii.
16. Peng. *Per.*, pp. 30–1.
17. Muir, *Shakespeare's Comic Sequence* (1979), p. 155.
18. See *Sources*, VI, pp. 374–423, esp. p. 417. *Confessio Amantis* has no dream-vision of Diana. Her name occurs only twice in the actual poem in connection with her temple at Ephesus and twice in the Latin synopses of Pericles' voyage to that city. Neptune is mentioned only three times, and we once hear of 'the goddes all above' (in the plural, p. 397). No other pagan gods are named.
19. Ibid., pp. 423–82.
20. Ibid. p. 482.
21. There is an odd section of the play from I.i.109 to II.iii.21 where, for some reason, possibly having to do with divided authorship, there is either no mention at all of superhuman agencies or where, with one trifling exception ('gods' at II.i.78), they are referred to as 'heaven' (clustered in I.iv), 'the Destinies' (I.ii.108), the 'stars' (I.iv. 108, II.i.1–11) or 'fortune' (II.Chor. 37–8, i.120–1, iii.12). In the same section, at II.i.34, the First Fisherman incongruously speaks of 'parish, church, steeple, bells, and all', but this must belong to his image as a man of the people.
22. See II.v.86, III.i.38, V.i.57. In *The Painfull Adventures* there are similar invocations of 'the gods', fewer than in the play, but more frequent towards the end of the story. Wilkins twice speaks of 'the whole Sinode of the gods' (or 'the gods in their holy Synode'), but he does not mention other than Neptune, Apollo and Diana by name (except that he once lets the Bawd use a simile of Jove and Danae: *Sources*, p. 534). His first mention of Fortune coincides with that of the play and occurs in both cases in the episode of Pericles' shipwreck on the coast of Pentapolis. Wilkins only once uses 'God' in the singular, in a conventional greeting (Marina's 'God save you sir' to Pericles: *Sources*, p. 542).
23. See III.i.37 and IV.vi.107. There are also the 'holy gods' at III.iv.6 and V.i.198. One may wonder, of course, what 'divinity' Marina preaches (IV.v.4).
24. Knight, op. cit., p. 71.
25. Muir has a different opinion (*N&Q* 193, 1948, p. 362): see the Arden n. to II.v.11–12.
26. See e.g. Arden *Per.*, p. lxxxi.
27. Marina's firmness and self-reliance may even seem undramatic. Traversi complains of the weakness of the brothel scenes due to 'the

excessive clarity of the contrast' between the vividly pictured background of social and moral corruption and Marina's 'flawless
integrity':

> Marina, unlike Isabella, does not answer to the realistic conception
> of drama which still prevails in the presentation of her background.
> Her motives are not analysed, and still less subjected to the possi-
> bility of conflict; they are inflexibly simple, self-consistent, and
> therefore, in terms of the dramatic objectivity with which Boult,
> Pander, and their like are presented, artistically incompatible.
> (*An Approach to Shakespeare*, 3rd edn, Vol. 2, 1969, p. 258)

28. Arden *Per.*, pp. lxxxvi–lxxxviii.
29. Evans considers the philosophy of *Pericles* inconsistent, chiefly owing
to the failure on Shakespeare's part to impose a belief in divine purpose
on the already fatalistically impregnated action of his material. We have
had, he says,

> during Acts I and II, inconclusive evidence that in this world events
> either follow one another meaninglessly, or fit the design of a
> malevolent intelligence bent on torment and destruction. And
> during Acts III and IV, while the same ambiguity continued, we
> have been provided with growing, but still sporadic, signs of
> benign purpose. When this evidence at last prevails at the opening
> of Act V, it can hardly compensate for the preceding four acts of
> uncertainty. (*Shakespeare's Comedies*, 1960, p. 242)

30. See Smidt, *Unconformities in Shakespeare's Tragedies* (1989), p. 36.
31. Evans, op. cit., p. 224.
32. See Smidt, op. cit., p. 23.
33. *Sources*, VI, p. 421.
34. Ibid., pp. 454–5, 457. In Twine, Tharsia tells Athanagoras
(Shakespeare's Lysimachus) that Dionisiades sought her death. This is
omitted in the play.
35. In Twine the people of Tharsus stone their rulers to death; in
Shakespeare they burn them in the palace. In *Confessio Amantis* the
same rulers are 'Atteynt...by the lawe,/And demed to be honged and
drawe,/And brent'. *Sources*, VI, pp. 476, 421.
36. Q prints the whole scene as prose but in lines 91–120 and 160–8 the
blank verse shows through quite clearly, possibly as a relic of an earlier
play. For a discussion of the possible derivation of Wilkins's novel *The
Painfull Adventures* from an 'Ur-Pericles' and the bearing of this on the
use of verse and prose, see *Sources*, VI, pp. 549–64 and Arden *Per.*,
pp. xl–xlix.
37. *Sources*, VI, p. 457.
38. Muir, op. cit., pp. 153–4.
39. *Sources*, VI, pp. 534–6.
40. Wells and Taylor, op. cit., pp. 558–9.
41. Peng. *Per.*, pp. 25–6.

42. In Gower, Athanagoras (Lysimachus) speaks both to 'this maide' and 'to hir fader' for marriage and in Twine's version we learn that Tharsia is asked by her father if she is 'contented to bee wife unto Athanagoras' and that she joyfully consents. Gower practically dismisses Thaise from his story after the wedding, but in Twine Lucina at least asks for her child and there is a loving reunion. *Sources*, VI, pp. 416, 455–61, 468, 474.
43. Pettet finds a progressive 'decline of courtship in the action' of Shakespeare's comedies and maintains that 'while the romances are still very much stories of love.., their love-interest is markedly different from that of the comedies. Young lovers are far less prominent, and there is comparatively little love-making' (*Shakespeare and the Romance Tradition* [1949, 1970], pp. 124–5, 183–7). I cannot agree with Pettet that there is no humour in *Pericles* (ibid., p. 186) and would cite the Pentapolis scene in rebuttal.
44. Some of the minor irregularities may be briefly mentioned. There is a repetition in I.i–ib which is obviously redundant. At I.i.110, Antiochus exclaims, 'Heaven, that I had thy head! he has found the meaning', which anticipates his exclamation at ib.1–2, 'He hath found the meaning,/For which we mean to have his head'. Apparently the first exclamation should have been cancelled. The second may well represent Shakespeare's revision.

There is another unnecessary repetition in V.iii. At lines 23–7 Cerimon explains how he opened the coffin containing Thaisa's body, 'Found there rich jewels; recover'd her, and plac'd her/Here in Diana's temple.' Pericles asks, 'May we see them?' and Cerimon replies: 'Great sir, they shall be brought you to my house,/Whither I invite you.' Shortly afterwards, at lines 63–8, Pericles asks, 'Will you deliver/How this dead queen re-lives?' and Cerimon replies,

I will, my lord.
Beseech you, first go with me to my house,
Where shall be shown you all was found with her;
How she came plac'd here in the temple;
No needful thing omitted.

One of these two passages is definitely not 'needful' and may certainly be omitted.

There are two scenes which seem to exhibit an internal disarray as they have come down to us: I.ii and II.ii. For conjectural reconstructions see Arden *Per.*, Appendix C, pp. 180–3.

Hoeniger suspects that 'in the original text Marina made a much longer and more eloquent plea' to Lysimachus in IV.vi than what Q has retained. See Arden n. to IV.vi.91–3.

8   ROMANCE AND REALISM IN *CYMBELINE*

1. Nosworthy offers the speculation 'that the remarkable chain of dénoue-

ments which constitutes the final scene was the goal that [Shakespeare] had before him at the outset, and that he was content to tolerate incidental crudities for the sake of ultimate virtuosity', Arden *Cym.* (1955, 1976), p. xxx. Wilson Knight calls the final scene ' a *tour de force* of technical compression, [which] knits our various themes together', *The Crown of Life* (1947, 1965), p. 165.

2. See Arden *Cym.*, pp. xxv–xxvii.
3. Gesner, *Shakespeare and the Greek Romance* (1970), pp. 98–115.
4. See also Nosworthy, Arden *Cym.*, pp. xxvi–xxvii. Maxwell, however, treats 'the wager story as the main plot'. It is certainly, he says, 'the part of the play for which Shakespeare has most purposefully combined his source-material', Cam. *Cym.*, pp. xxxviii–xxxix.
5. See *Sources*, VIII, pp. 13–19; Arden *Cym.*, pp. xx–xxiv; Cam. *Cym.*, pp. xvi–xix.
6. See *Sources*, VIII, pp. 23–4.
7. Much of his explanation is repeated in his confession to the King in the final scene.
8. See II.i.57, V.v.65–7, 463–6.
9. II.iv.10–26, III.i, v.1–29, viii.
10. We would have to disregard certain anachronisms, of course, like Cloten playing at bowls in II.i. (though doubts have been raised as to whether Shakespeare wrote that scene, see Arden *Cym.*, p. 45 n.)
11. Arden *Cym.*, p. xxxii. Nosworthy also mentions the spatial distance between 'Augustus' Rome and Cymbeline's Britain'.
12. Arden *Cym.*, pp xlix–1.
13. Rees, *Shakespeare and the Story* (1978), p. 142.
14. See also Lawrence, *Shakespeare's Problem Comedies* (1960, 1969), pp. 172–3.
15. See also White, *Shakespeare and the Romance Ending* (1981), pp. 91–2. But compare Arden *Cym.*, pp. lix–lxi, especially Nosworthy's analysis of Imogen. There are brief comments on the lack of continuity in the portrayal of Posthumus and Iachimo in Granville-Barker, *Prefaces to Shakespeare* 10 (Vol.II) (1930, 1963), p. 89; Parrott, *Shakespearean Comedy* (1949, 1977), p. 379; Pettet, *Shakespeare and the Romance Tradition* (1949, 1970), p. 178; and Rees, op. cit., p. 143.
16. See also Arden *Cym.*, p. lii; Rees, op. cit., pp. 142–3; Foakes, *Shakespeare: The dark comedies to the last plays* (1971), p. 107.
17. Granville-Barker, op. cit., p. 145; see also pp. 128–31.
18. Foakes, op. cit., pp. 104–7. See also Parrott, op. cit., p. 379, and Rees, op. cit., pp. 142–3.
19. Foakes, op. cit., p. 103.
20. Arden *Cym.*, p. 1.
21. Parrott, op. cit., p. 378.
22. Evans, *Shakespeare's Comedies* (1960), pp. 284, 286. Gesner explains the Jupiter episode, as well as other puzzling incidents in *Cym.*, as reminiscences of Greek romances which Shakespeare may have read in English translations, especially Heliodorus' *Aethiopica*. She takes this as 'evidence against the contention that the scene [containing the comic banter of Posthumus with his jailers and his subsequent oracular

dream] is not from Shakespeare's pen', although, she admits, 'it is not thus artistically commended'. See op. cit., esp. pp. 113–15.

23. Thus Foakes, op. cit., p. 118, and White, op. cit., pp. 100–1.

24. III.iii.2–9, 72, 99, V.v.351. Belarius also sees Nature as a goddess, IV.ii.169–70; see also III.iii.79, 84, IV.ii.27.

25. III.v.85, II.iii.136, IV.i.23.

26. In his address to the gods at V.i.7–17, Posthumus sees their treatment of the virtuous and the wicked as completely arbitrary. Jupiter himself explains his conduct by the specious argument, which for being an ancient one is not more acceptable to either good sense or religious feeling, that 'Whom best I love I cross; to make my gift,/The more delay'd, delighted' (V.iv.101–2).

27. Cupid, Venus (or Cytherea), Saturn, Minerva, Phoebus, Mars, Lucina, Neptune, Titan and Hercules are all mentioned at least once in various connections. We are told by Jupiter at V.iv.105–6 that Posthumus and Imogen were married in his temple. There would have been excellent opportunities to mention this fact in one of the first two scenes if the care of Jupiter for his worshippers was intended to be important.

28. 'Since Posthumus, who is quite one of the dullest of Shakespeare's heroes, never really comes to life, it should not be difficult for him to sustain this role of perfect knighthood, and we should never call his honour and virtue into question. But we do.' (Nosworthy in Arden *Cym.*, p. lix)

29. Compare the endings of *RJ* and *Per.*, see p. 116 above. There is a certain negative preparation for this pious ending in Posthumus' soliloquies in the first and fourth scenes of Act V, in which he addresses the gods somewhat ambivalently, reproaching them and praying for death.

30. I cannot make sense of the garment-image he applies to the book, unless he refers to its handsome binding, in which case it is all the more strange that he should later call it a 'tablet' and a 'label'.

31. Compare the graveyard scene in *Hamlet*, which also seems to have been a late addition to the original script; see my *Unconformities in Shakespeare's Tragedies* (1989), pp. 83–5. There is an interesting similarity between the humour of the gravediggers and that of the gaolers in *Cym.* The repetition of the contents of the scroll and their explanation may be redundant, see Arden *Cym.*, p. 185, n. to lines 436–53.

32. *Cym.* has 3818 lines in Hinman's Norton Facsimile, *Ham.* 3904, *R3* 3887, *Ant.* 3636, *WT* 3369.

33. Thus II.i has been thought superfluous, see n. 10 above.

34. Expository and explanatory speeches include that of the First Gentleman at I.i.28–54, of Cornelius at I.iv.31–44, of Belarius at III.iii.55–107, of Posthumus at V.iii.3–51 and of Iachimo at V.v.170–208, this last recounting events with which we are already familiar.

35. The Norwegian composer Arne Eggen's opera *Cymbeline* was successfully produced at the National Theatre in Oslo in 1951, see Smidt, 'A Norwegian Operatic *Cymbeline*', *SQ* III.3 (1952), p. 284.

9   LIKE AN OLD TALE

1. 'By deliberately drawing the audience's attention to technique Shakespeare was able to distance his story and to convey a continual reminder that his play was after all only a play', Bethell, 'Antiquated Technique and the Planes of Reality', quoted from Muir (ed.), *Shakespeare: 'The Winter's Tale'* (1968), p.120. See also Mowat, *The Dramaturgy of Shakespeare's Romances* (1976), pp. 60–1, and Muir, *Shakespeare's Comic Sequence* (1979), p. 172.
2. See especially Bethell, op. cit. Bethell speaks of 'a deliberate creaking of the dramatic machinery' and instances the famous stage direction '*Exit, pursued by a bear*' and the 'crudely amateur device' of drawing characters aside merely to redirect the dialogue (pp. 116–25). Coghill, in 'Six Points of Stage-Craft in *The Winter's Tale*' (*SS* 11, 1958, pp. 31–41), rebuts Bethell's suggestion of intentional comic naivety, arguing the mastery of theatrical effect evidenced by some of the examples of alleged crudity. With regard to the bear see also Matchett, 'Some Dramatic Techniques in "The Winter's Tale"', *SS* 22 (1969), pp. 98–9.
3. 'Of all Shakespeare's *coups de théâtre*, the descent of Hermione from her pedestal is perhaps the most spectacular and affecting', Coghill, op. cit., p. 39. Muir testifies to the 'tremendous effect' of this scene in the theatre, op. cit., pp. 169–70.
4. See also Evans, *Shakespeare's Comedies* (1960), pp. 296–7, and Muir, op. cit., pp. 166–7.
5. Evans, op. cit., pp. 312–13. The clearest hint may be found in the following exchange between Leontes and Paulina:

> *Leon.*   My true Paulina,
> We shall not marry till thou bid'st us.
> *Paul.*   That
> Shall be when your first queen's again in breath.
> Never till then.
>
> (V.i.81–4)

6. Muir, op.cit., p. 164.
7. Bergeron, 'The Restoration of Hermione in *The Winter's Tale*', in Kay and Jacobs (eds), *Shakespeare's Romances Reconsidered* (1978), p. 126. See also Rees, *Shakespeare and the Story* (1978), p. 152.
8. Pafford reminds us that I. Gollancz in 1894 also found parallels with Euripides' *Alcestis*, see Arden *WT*, p. xxxiv. Bergeron suggests a link with the civic pageant written by Anthony Munday for the Lord Mayor's Show in London in 1611, in which a resurrection from the dead is enacted; and with funeral statuary such as that which may have been made for the interment of Prince Henry in 1612, op. cit., pp. 126–32. Glynne Wickham had previously, as Muir points out, 'shown that the "statue" of Hermione would have resembled the

painted effigies on Elizabethan and Jacobean tombs and would have been a familiar sight to Shakespeare's original audience', Muir, op. cit., p. 171.

9. Schanzer finds 'structural parallel and thematic contrast' in the two halves of *WT*; see 'The Structural Pattern of "The Winter's Tale"', *REL*, V.2 (1964), pp. 72–82.

10. Coghill, op. cit., p. 40.

11. Mowat, op. cit., pp. 77–8. In Mowat's view:

> The fact that the expository scene never mentions Hermione, that the celebrated friendship immediately explodes into attempted murder and that Mamillius, about whom much of the opening exposition centers, simply disappears from the action and dies, is almost as startling – in terms of Shakespeare's normal dramaturgical practices – as is the later deliberate deception of the audience concerning Hermione's death. (p. 78)

See also Rees, op. cit., p. 153.

12. *Pace* Pafford, Arden *WT*, p. lxxvi. Tillyard thinks that 'the continued existence of Leontes and Hermione is a matter of subordinate expediency; and it is Florizel and Perdita and the countryside where they meet which make the new life'. Perdita, he says, 'is one of Shakespeare's richest characters' and 'the play's main symbol of the powers of creation', *Shakespeare's Last Plays* (1938, 1964), pp. 42, 44. Contrast Evans's view that 'the best in Perdita's affair was exploited before the fleeing lovers first reached Leontes' court', op. cit., p. 312.

13. Transcript as rendered in the Arden *WT*, pp. xxi–xxii.

14. Coghill, op. cit., p. 39. Arden *WT*, p. lii. Coghill goes on to applaud Peter Brook's production of *WT* at the Phoenix Theatre in 1951–2. Against G. G. Gervinus (*Shakespeare Commentaries*, 1863), 'Q' maintains that 'the greatest fault of all' in *WT* 'is the manner in which the play mishandles Leontes' recognition of Perdita' (Cam. *WT*, 1931, 1980, p. xxiii). In a similar vein, R. S. White finds that 'the reconciliation between father and daughter is presented in a mode very close to parody'. He thinks Shakespeare recognised that this incident was 'potentially emotionally distracting' and was 'carefully skirting the problem' (*Shakespeare and the Romance Ending*, 1981, p. 108). Other adverse critics of the scene are Johnson in the eighteenth century and Bethell in the twentieth. Muir takes issue with both and refers to his own experience, and that of other eminent Shakespearians, of the effectiveness of the scene on the stage (op.cit. p. 171). Both Muir and Evans (op. cit., p. 312) think the narrative method a useful choice in that it reserves the central climactic position for Hermione.

15. See the Arden *WT*, p. 165. Some of Autolycus' function is probably borrowed from Capnio in *Pandosto*, see *Sources*, VIII, pp. 188–9.

16. In Pafford's opinion, 'The fact that he had been Florizel's servant but that there is no recognition when they meet . . . is purely conventional', Arden *WT*, p. xxvi.

17. This is a small problem but is perhaps too easily brushed aside by Pafford with the usual explanation: 'Perdita considers that Florizel's attire demeans him...and it is clearly a country swain's clothes.... Shepherd and Clown think it is court dress...but that is mere dramatic convenience and no more puzzling than they they do not then recognize the clothes or Autolycus', Arden note to IV.iv.1.

18. See J. E. Bullard's and W. M. Fox's Letter to the Editor, *TLS*, 14 March 1952:

> At the end of the fourth act there is some elaborate stage business, including a change of clothes with Florizel, the effect of which is to transport Autolycus, along with the shepherd and his son, to Sicily, where it is clearly intended that he should be associated in some way...with the recognition of Perdita. This recognition we take to have been the main stage-business of the original fifth act. Autolycus does indeed appear in that act, but his only considerable speech is a lame apology for the failure to carry out expectations created by the fourth act....

Incidentally, there is another loose end in that Camillo does not keep his promise, given at IV. iv. 621–4, to provide letters which will satisfy both Leontes and Polixenes as to Florizel's romance. Florizel after arrival in Sicilia even has reason to suspect that Camillo has betrayed him, see V.i. 192. Perhaps we should recognise that Camillo is less than candid in his dealings with the young lovers, in which case we may have to change our impression of his character. He has a revealing aside at IV.iv.662–7:

> What I do next, shall be to tell the king
> Of this escape and whither they are bound;
> Wherein my hope is I shall so prevail
> To force him after: in whose company
> I shall re-view Sicilia, for whose sight
> I have a woman's longing.

Mowat comments on the Bohemia section of *WT* (op. cit., pp. 25–6):

> Into the realm of fairy-tale princesses, shepherds, and true love come the rage of a suddenly cruel Polixenes and the treachery of a seemingly helpful Camillo, who seems a 'preserver' to Florizel, who furnishes letters and secret advice to 'save' the young couple, but who, as he tells us in an aside, frames the entire business to serve his own ends, and gives no thought to the fate of the young couple....

19. See Pafford's discussion of this problem in his Arden Introduction, pp. 1vii–1viii.

20. See Trienens, 'The Inception of Leontes' Jealousy in *The Winter's Tale*', *SQ* IV.3 (1953), pp. 321–6, esp. p. 324; Coghill, op. cit., pp. 31–3; Arden *WT*, p. 1vii, n.3.

21. See Styan's comments on various productions of the play quoted by Wright in *ES* 70.3 (1989) p. 225, n.3 (from Styan's 'Understanding Shakespeare in Performance', *Shakespeare in Southern Africa*, 1, 1987, p. 21).
22. See e.g. Matchett, op. cit., pp. 94–8; Coghill, op. cit., pp. 31–3; Muir, op. cit., p. 165. All three point to the nine months' duration of Polixenes' visit (I.ii.1–3) and the fact that Hermione must be visibly pregnant as one way of preparing us for Leontes' suspicion.
23. Holbrook, *The Quest for Love* (1964), p. 136. There is a speech by Leontes at I.ii.137–46 which exegetes have found particularly difficult and which is discussed by Pafford in an Appendix (Arden *WT*, pp. 165–7). It begins in F:

> Most dear'st, my Collop. Can thy Dam, may't be
> Affection?

Latching on to Pafford's discussion, Laurence Wright thinks the word 'Affection' has been misinterpreted by most critics. He finds the appropriate meaning in an observation by Hallett Smith:

> Munro and all the other editors think 'Affection' means love or lust, the feeling Hermione has for Polixenes (supposedly). I maintain that 'Affection' here means *Affectio*, that is, a sudden mental seizure, and that the passage describes the feeling of Leontes, his own suspicion or jealousy, and not his wife's supposed feeling at all. (*SQ* XIV.2 (1963), p. 163, n. 6)

In Wright's view Leontes suffers 'a psychological aberration which overwhelms his rationality and has no evident moral significance at all' ('When Does the Tragi-Comic Disruption Start?: *The Winter's Tale* and Leontes' "Affection"', *ES*, 70.3 [1989], pp. 225–32).
24. Knight, *The Crown of Life* (1947, 1965), p. 84.
25. It is Polixenes' flight more than anything else which serves to motivate Leontes' cruelty to Hermione.
26. Mowat, op. cit., pp. 7–20; Knight, op. cit., p. 96.
27. Pafford observes that 'things have to happen quickly on the stage' and thinks 'this demand for speed can also explain Paulina's reconciliation with Leontes at the end of III.ii, though there are slight signs of hurried composition or alteration in this scene', Arden *WT*, p. xxvi.
28. Like Marina in *Pericles*, Paulina is given in marriage by arbitrary decision of the king. Neither lady is consulted and neither is allowed a verbal response.
29. As she summons Hermione back to life, Paulina declares that 'her actions shall be as holy as/ You hear my spell is lawful', V.iii. 104–5.
30. Tillyard counts the mention of 'Bright Phoebus in his strength' as a significant reference to Apollo in Perdita's famous flower speech, but this is surely far-fetched, op.cit., p. 46.
31. There is only a passing reference to the Oracle at V.ii.126. And it was Venus, not Apollo, who gave life to Pygmalion's statue in Ovid.

32. A few minor inconsistencies are listed in Arden *WT*, pp. 1i–1ii.
33. I see no point in trying to explain away the false evidence by making Paulina more elaborately deceitful or Antigonus (in the seacoast scene) more imaginative than the text makes them appear to be – this would be looking outside the play for unnecessary comfort.

10 PROSPERO'S PROJECT

1. See also Mowat, *The Dramaturgy of Shakespeare's Romances* (1976), p. 81; and Righter, Penguin *Tmp.*, pp. 11–12.
2. See also Penguin *Tmp.*, pp. 12–19.
3. A critical survey of different ways of reading *Tmp.* is presented by Powell in *Shakespeare and the Critics' Debate* (1980), pp. 74–84.
4. Mowat, op. cit., p. 117. See also pp. 98–9, 103.
5. Powell, op. cit., pp. 83–4.
6. Rees, *Shakespeare and the Story* (1978), pp. 166–9. See also Leech, 'The Structure of the Last Plays', *SS* 11 (1958), pp. 19–30. In the opinion of Leech as reported by Mowat (op. cit., p. 94), 'both *Cymbeline* and *The Tempest* suffer from Shakespeare's inability to force cyclic experience into crisis form'.
7. Mowat, op. cit., p. 94.
8. See Rees, op. cit., pp. 161–2.
9. Powell sees two different Prosperos, op. cit., p. 89.
10. See West for a survey of views and a discussion of Prospero's character ('Ceremonial Magic in *The Tempest*' in Thaler and Sanders, eds., *Shakespearean Essays* [1964], pp. 63–78, esp. p. 71).
11. Compare IV.i.144–5: 'Never till this day/Saw I him touch'd with anger, so distemper'd.'
12. I.ii.457–9, 463. See Breight's article referred to below.
13. Breight, '"Treason doth never prosper": *The Tempest* and the Discourse of Treason', *SQ* 41.1 (1990), pp. 1–28.
14. Ibid., p. 14.
15. Cf. Breight, op. cit., pp. 25–6.
16. Powell, op. cit., p. 97. Powell has an interesting discussion of Prospero's character and intentions, pp. 89–99. See also Righter's comments, Penguin *Tmp.*, p. 12:

> If his [Prospero's] thoughts were directed initially towards revenge, towards exacting due punishment for the high wrongs he had suffered, why did he carefully arrange the meeting of Ferdinand and Miranda in Act I? Harsh behaviour to Alonso would hardly be compatible with this marriage. Was he perhaps undecided, still unsure of his own mind when, at the urgent prompting of Fortune, he devised the shipwreck? If so, why is the audience given no hint of this state of indecision? A Prospero explicitly torn between the rival impulses of anger and forgiveness in the early Acts, debating alternative courses of action in soliloquy, would certainly have added to the dra-

matic tension of a play often criticized for its singular lack of suspense.

17. What he means by calling her in the preceding line 'a third of mine own life' has puzzled critics and remains uncertain – see the Arden n. to IV.i.3.
18. See Caliban's speech at III.ii.51–3.
19. 'Equally disturbing is the fact that Alonso is never, apparently, to know about his own brother's attempt to kill him', Righter, Penguin *Tmp.*, p. 38.
20. '[T]he possibility suggests itself that he intended to subject them to a twelve-year purgatory to atone for their crimes', Corfield, 'Why Does Prospero Abjure His "Rough Magic"?', *SQ* 36.1 (1985), p. 41. Ariel's warning to the malefactors in the Harpy scene definitely suggests detention 'in this most desolate isle' (III.iii.79–81).
21. Alonso does seem to begin another apology, addressed to Miranda, at V.i.197–8, but is interrupted by Prospero, who wants to hear no more of 'a heaviness that's gone' (198–200).
22. F reads '(Whose inward pinches *therefore* are most strong)' (my italics), where the Arden editor adopts Tannenbaum's 'helpful modernization' to 'therefor'. If an ambiguity is sensed in the spoken word it is unproblematic. The syntax of these lines is awkward and may seem to refer the 'inward pinches' to Sebastian, but the logic directs them to the 'brother mine', Antonio.
23. See also Corfield, op. cit., p. 40.
24. Dobrée, 'The Tempest', in Muir (ed.), *Shakespeare: The Comedies* (1965), p. 165.
25. Curry, *Shakespeare's Philosophical Patterns* (1937, 1959), esp. p. 180.
26. Corfield, op. cit., pp. 42–3, 46–8. West argues the basic badness and illicitness of Prospero's' 'spirit magic', op. cit.
27. Egan, 'This Rough Magic: Perspectives of Art and Morality in *The Tempest*', *SQ* XXIII.2 (1972), pp. 171–82, quoted from pp. 177, 180–1. Similarly, Theodore Spencer finds that 'Prospero abjures his magic not to become like the gods, but to return to humanity', 'Shakespeare and the Nature of Man: *The Tempest*', in Dean (ed.), *Shakespeare: Modern Essays in Criticism* (1957, 1967), p. 459. See also Felperin, 'Romance and Romanticism. Some Reflections on *The Tempest* and *Heart of Darkness*', in Kay and Jacobs (eds), *Shakespeare's Romances Reconsidered* (1978), pp. 66–7; and Righter, Penguin *Tmp.*, p. 44.
28. Egan and Righter regard the Epilogue as part of the play; see Egan, op. cit., p. 173, and Penguin *Tmp.* pp. 50–1. But Spencer disagrees, both implicitly with them and explicitly with Curry and Middleton Murry, who interpret the Epilogue in religous terms; see op. cit., p. 461, n.2.
29. The deletion of the boatswain's blasphemy must have been due to censorship. Sebastian's curse of this outspoken individual – 'A pox o' your throat, you bawling, blasphemous, incharitable dog!' (I.i.40–1) – and Gonzalo's welcome to him in the last scene – 'Now, blasphemy,/That swear'st grace o'erboard' (218–19) – make it clear that in the draft of the play, at least, the boatswain was volubly profane.

30. Curry, op. cit., pp. 174, 192.
31. Ibid., pp. 198–9.
32. Ibid., pp. 196–7.
33. West, op. cit., pp. 65, 75.
34. Kermode says that 'At I.ii.301 Prospero gives Ariel the purposeless order to dress up as a nymph of the sea' (Arden *Tmp.*, p. xviii), but obviously the order is not purposeless if we are to see Ariel leading a chorus of nymphs.
35. Arden *Tmp.*, pp. xx–xxiv, 171–2. Kermode, following Chambers, controverts the theory of H. D. Gray concerning the masque as a late addition.
36. See Cam. *Tmp.*, pp. 80–1 and Smith, 'Ariel and the Masque in *The Tempest*', SQ XXI.3 (1970), pp. 213–22.
37. '[W]hen I presented Ceres', IV.i.167. I see no reason to think of Ariel as a mere 'presenter'. He is elsewhere very much an actor in his own little spectacles. See also Smith, op. cit., p. 213.
38. IV.i.128–38. In line 131 it would be 'Ceres [not Juno] does command'.
39. Cam. *Tmp.*, pp. 83–4. The Arden edition, with one small exception, follows the F lineation of I.ii.298–308, but Kermode by adding and omitting some small words suggests an improved sense and rhythm, p. 161. It is also possible to retain the F wording and still improve the lineation:

> Go make thyself like a nymph o' the sea:
> Be subject to no sight but thine and mine;
> Invisible to every eyeball else.
> Go take this shape, and hither come in it:
> Go: hence with diligence. Awake, dear heart,
> Awake! thou hast slept well; awake!

The only change I have made to the F wording, apart from using the modern spelling of the Arden edition, is the expansion of the syncopated forms 'th'' and 'in't'.
40. There is an interesting ambiguity in I.ii.281–5, where F reads:

> *Pro* . . . . Then was this Island
> (Saue for the Son, that he did littour heere,
> A frekelld whelpe, hag-borne) not honour'd with
> A human shape.
> *Ar.* Yes: *Caliban* her sonne.
> *Pro.* Dull thing, I say so:

Does Ariel mean to contradict Prospero or to confirm his statement? If a contradiction is intended it seems he misunderstands Prospero's remark, which would explain the latter's irritation. In either case the passage insists on the information about Caliban's 'human shape', assuming the F punctuation is correct.
41. A few minor anomalies in I.ii may be mentioned briefly. Line 29 – 'So safely ordered that there is no soul–' – seems to call for a continuation which is missing. Line 253 – 'Of the salt deepe; ' – is metrically incom-

plete and Cam. *Tmp.* comments: 'Strongly suggestive of a "cut"; the F semi-colon increasing the probability.' At lines 28–31 Prospero assures Miranda that everyone on board the wrecked ship is safe, 'not so much perdition as a hair/ Betid to any creature in the vessel', but at 217 he has to ask Ariel if all are safe, and Ariel assures him in Prospero's own words, 'Not a hair perish'd'. At lines 316–17, when Caliban objects that 'There's wood enough within', Prospero retorts, 'there's other business for thee' but, at 368, Caliban is nevertheless commanded to 'Fetch us in fuel'. There is again mention of 'other business' for Caliban in line 369, but we are not told what.

42. Smith, op. cit., p. 219.
43. 'It is practically certain that some intervening scene has been deleted between 4.1 and 5.1', Wilson in Cam. *Tmp.*, p. 85.
44. Greg took the reappearance of Ariel and Prospero after an emptying of the stage as evidence 'that the act division is original', *The Shakespeare First Folio* (1955), p. 418, n. 1.
45. The plots against the rulers in this section may even be said to include a revolt on Miranda's part: on revealing her name to Ferdinand, she exclaims, 'O my father,/I have broke your hest to say so!' (III.i.36–7) (though of course we have heard nothing of this 'hest' before).
46. See my *Unconformities in Shakespeare's Early Comedies* (1986), p. 7 and Marvin T. Herrick, *Comic Theory in the Sixteenth Century* (1950, 1964), p. 119.
47. One might suspect an abridgement to compensate for the addition of the masque, but *Tmp.* is Shakespeare's fourth shortest play.
48. In addition to the minor anomalies mentioned in n. 41 above the following obscurities and inconsistencies may be observed.

The geographical location of the island seems to have been left deliberately vague, but there are conflicting suggestions of the Mediterranean (Alonso's return voyage from Tunis to Naples) and the Atlantic (Ariel's errand to 'the still-vex'd Bermoothes', Caliban as a native of the New World, etc.).

The shipwreck as dramatised realistically in the first scene has none of the supernatural phenomena described by Ariel at I.ii.195–215. Ariel at I.ii.226 assures Prospero that the ship is 'safely in harbour' (after Miranda had seen it 'dash'd all to pieces') but at V.i.222–6 we learn that Ariel apparently has had to repair it. When sent to fetch the master and the boatswain Ariel promises Prospero to return 'Or ere your pulse beat twice' (V.i.102–3) but he does not return till over 100 lines later. Although the master is fetched as well as the boatswain, it is only the latter who is given a speaking part. (The master is noticeably absent from the opening scene, though both Alonso and Antonio call for him.)

Miranda has seen the people in the ship swallowed up by the sea (I.ii.5–13, 31–2) and she remembers 'Four or five women once that tended me' (I.ii.47). She speaks knowingly of 'good wombs [having] borne bad sons' (I.ii.120). Yet we are told later that she has seen no other men than her father, Caliban and Ferdinand (see above, p. 158) and she remembers 'no woman's face... /Save, from my glass, mine own' (III.i.49–50).

Ariel is eager to do Prospero's bidding at I.ii.189–93 but unwilling shortly afterwards (242–50).

Francisco tries to persuade Alonso that Ferdinand is alive (II.i.109–118) but Antonio says it was Gonzalo who tried to persuade him (227–31). Francisco subsequently speaks only three words (at III.iii.40) and one may wonder whether there is any need for him. Wilson thinks he appears 'seemingly by accident rather than design' (Cam. *Tmp.*, p. 79).

There is a curious repetition in two places of Alonso's words at III.iii.100–3:

Therefor my son i' th'ooze is bedded; and
I'll seek him deeper than e'er plummet sounded,
And with him there lie mudded.

At V.i.56:

And deeper than did ever plummet sound
I'll drown my book.

At V.i.150–2:

                    I wish
Myself were mudded in that oozy bed
Where my son lies.

49. See e.g. Arden *Tmp.*, pp. xxii–xxiii.

11 CONCLUSION

1. *Julius Cæsar*, which was probably Shakespeare's first tragedy presented at the Globe, may be seen as a forerunner of *Hamlet*, which properly initiated the sequence of great tragedies.
2. The possibility has been suggested of partial censorship operative in *As You Like It* and *Twelfth Night*, see pp. 55, 72.
3. Examples have been indexed in my earlier *Unconformities* books – see Bibliography. See also my article 'Repetition, Revision, and Editorial Greed in Shakespeare's Play Texts', *Cahiers élisabéthains* 34 (1988), pp. 25–37.
4. See Smidt, *Unconformities in Shakespeare's Early Comedies* (1986), p. 173.

Bibliography

Dates are those of first publication and of the editions consulted.

Shakespeare's Plays

The Arden Shakespeare (London: Methuen):
  Much Ado About Nothing, ed. A. R. Humphreys (1981).
  As You Like It, ed. Agnes Latham (1975).
  Twelfth Night, ed. J. M. Lothian and T. W. Craik (1975).
  All's Well That Ends Well, ed. G. K. Hunter (1959, 1977).
  Measure for Measure, ed. J. W. Lever (1965, 1976).
  Pericles, ed. F. D. Hoeniger (1963, 1969).
  Cymbeline, ed. J. M. Nosworthy (1955, 1976).
  The Winter's Tale, ed. J. H. P. Pafford (1963, 1976).
  The Tempest, ed. Frank Kermode (1958, 1979).

Other editions with inclusive dates of first publication of the above plays

The New Shakespeare, ed. Arthur Quiller-Couch, J. Dover Wilson, J. C. Maxwell (Cambridge University Press, 1921–60).
The New Penguin Shakespeare (Penguin Books, 1968–76).
The Complete Signet Classic Shakespeare (New York, etc.: Harcourt Brace Jovanovich, 1963–5, 1972).
The Riverside Shakespeare (Boston: Houghton Mifflin, 1974).
The Oxford Shakespeare (Oxford: Clarendon Press, 1986–).
The New Cambridge Shakespeare (Cambridge University Press, 1985–).

General

Allen, John A., 'Dogberry', *SQ* XXIV.1 (1973), pp. 35–53.
Baldwin, T. W., *Shakspere's Five-Act Structure* (Urbana: University of Illinois Press, 1947, 1963).
Barber, C. L., *Shakespeare's Festive Comedy* (Princeton: Princeton University Press, 1959).
Barnet, Sylvan, '"Strange Events": Improbability in *As You Like It*', *SSt* IV (1968), pp. 119–31.

Barton, Anne, Introduction to *AYLI*, Riverside Shakespeare, pp. 365–8.

Battenhouse, Roy W., '*Measure for Measure* and Christian Doctrine of the Atonement', *PMLA* LXI (1946), pp. 1029–59.

Beaumont, Francis, and John Fletcher, *The Woman Hater* (1607) in Fredson Bowers (ed.), *The Dramatic Works in the Beaumont and Fletcher Canon*, Vol. I (Cambridge: Cambridge University Press, 1966), pp. 156–235.

Berger, Harry, Jr, 'Against the Sink-a-Pace: Sexual and Family Politics in *Much Ado About Nothing*', *SQ* 33.3 (1982), pp. 302–13.

Bergeron, David M., 'The Restoration of Hermione in *The Winter's Tale*', in Kay and Jacobs (eds), *Shakespeare's Romances Reconsidered*, pp. 125–33.

Bethell, S. L., *Shakespeare and the Popular Dramatic Tradition* (London and New York: Staples Press, 1944, 1948).

——, 'Antiquated Technique and the Planes of Reality' (1947), in Muir (ed.), *Shakespeare: 'The Winter's Tale'*, pp.116–35.

Billington, Michael (ed.), *Directors' Shakespeare: Approaches to 'Twelfth Night'* (London: Nick Hern Books, 1990).

Boas, Frederick S., *Shakspere and His Predecessors* (New York: Scribner's, 1896).

Bradbrook, Muriel C., *Shakepere and Elizabethan Poetry* (London: Chatto & Windus, 1951).

——, 'Virtue is the True Nobility', in Muir (ed.), *Shakespeare: The Comedies*, pp. 119–32.

——, *The Growth and Structure of Elizabethan Comedy*, New edn (Cambridge: Cambridge University Press, 1973, 1979).

Bradley, A. C., 'Feste the Jester', in Palmer (ed.), *Twelfth Night: A Casebook*, pp. 63–71.

Breight, Curt, '"Treason doth never prosper": *The Tempest* and the Discourse of Treason', *SQ* 41.1 (1990), pp. 1–28.

Brissenden, A. T., 'The Case for Balthasar', *N&Q* n.s. 26 (1979), pp. 116–17.

Bullard, J. E., and W. M. Fox, Letter to the Editor, *TLS* 14 March 1952, p. 189.

Bullough, Geoffrey, *Narrative and Dramatic Sources of Shakespeare*, Vols II, VI, VIII (London and Henley: Routledge & Kegan Paul; New York: Columbia University Press; 1958, 1968; 1966, 1977; 1975).

Bulman, James C., *The Heroic Idiom of Shakespearean Tragedy* (Newark: University of Delaware Press, 1985).

Carroll, Lewis, Letter to Ellen Terry, 20 March 1883, in Mares (ed.), New Cam. *Ado*, pp. 157–8.

Carter, A. H., 'In Defense of Bertram', *SQ* VII.1 (1956), pp. 21–31.

Chambers, E. K., *Shakespeare: A Survey* (London: Sidgwick & Jackson, 1925, 1948).

——, *William Shakespeare: A Study of Facts and Problems*, II (Oxford University Press, 1930).

Coghill, Nevill, 'Comic Form in *Measure for Measure*', *SS* 8 (1955), pp. 14–27.

——, 'Six Points of Stage-Craft in *The Winter's Tale*', *SS* ll (1958), pp. 31–41.

Coleridge, S. T., *The Collected Works*, Vol. 5, ed. Kathleen Coburn (Princeton: Princeton University Press., 1987).

Corfield, Cosmo, 'Why Does Prospero Abjure His "Rough Magic"?', *SQ* 36.1 (1985), pp. 31–48.

Cox, C. B., and D. J. Palmer (eds), *Shakespeare's Wide and Universal Stage* (Manchester: Manchester University Press, 1984).

Craik, T. W. (ed.), *Twelfth Night*, see Lothian.

Curry, Walter C., *Shakespeare's Philosophical Patterns* (Baton Rouge: Louisiana State University Press, 1937, 1959).

Davies, Neville, '*Pericles* and the Sherley brothers', in Honigmann (ed.), *Shakespeare and his Contemporaries*, pp. 94–113.

Dean, Leonard F. (ed.), *Shakespeare: Modern Essays in Criticism*, Rev. edn (London, Oxford, New York: Oxford University Press, 1967).

Dobrée, Bonamy, '*The Tempest*', in Muir (ed.), *Shakespeare: The Comedies*, pp. 164–75.

Doran, Madeleine, *Endeavors of Art: A Study of Form in Elizabethan Drama* (Madison: University of Wisconsin Press, 1954).

Edwards, Philip (ed.), New Peng. *Per.* (1976).

Egan, Robert, 'This Rough Magic: Perspectives of Art and Morality in *The Tempest*', *SQ* XXIII.2 (1972), pp. 171–82.

Evans, Bertrand, *Shakespeare's Comedies* (Oxford: Clarendon Press, 1960).

Everett, Barbara, (ed.), New Peng. *AWW* (1970).

Felperin, Howard, 'Romance and Romanticism: Some Reflections on *The Tempest* and *Heart of Darkness*', in Kay and Jacobs (eds), *Shakespeare's Romances Reconsidered*, pp. 60–76.

Foakes, R. A. (ed.), New Peng. *Ado* (1968).

——, *Shakespeare: The dark comedies to the last plays* (London: Routledge & Kegan Paul, 1971).

Fox, W. M., see Bullard.

Frye, Northrop, *A Natural Perspective* (New York and London: Columbia University Press, 1965).

———, *The Myth of Deliverance* (Toronto: University of Toronto Press, 1983).

Gervinus, G. G., *Shakespeare Commentaries* (1863).

Gesner, Carol, *Shakespeare and the Greek Romance: A Study of Origins* (Lexington: University Press of Kentucky, 1970).

Gower, John, *Confessio Amantis* (1554), in Bullough, *Sources*, VI, pp. 375–423.

Granville-Barker, H., *Prefaces to Shakespeare*, 10 (Vol. II) (London: Batsford, 1930, 1963).

Graves, Robert, 'Making sound sense of Shakespeare', *The Sunday Times*, 14 February 1965.

Greg, W. W., *The Shakespeare First Folio* (Oxford: Clarendon Press, 1955).

Halio, Jay L., 'All's Well That Ends Well', *SQ* XV.1 (1964), pp. 33–43.

Hapgood, Robert, 'Shakespeare's *As You Like It*, III.ii', *Explicator* XXIV.7 (1966), Note 60.

Harbage, Alfred, 'Shakespeare and the Myth of Perfection', *SQ* XV.2 (1964), pp. 1–10.

Hawkins, Harriett, '"The Devil's Party": Virtues and Vices in "Measure for Measure"', *SS* 31 (1978), pp. 105–13.

Herrick, Marvin T., *Comic Theory in the Sixteenth Century* (Urbana: University of Illinois Press, 1950, 1964).

Hinman, Charlton, *The First Folio of Shakespeare*: The Norton Facsimile (London, New York, Sydney, Toronto: Paul Hamlyn, 1968).

Hoeniger, F. D. (ed.), Arden *Per.* (1963, 1969).

Holbrook, David, *The Quest for Love* (London: Methuen, 1964).

Honigmann, E. A. J., *The Stability of Shakespeare's Text* (London: Edward Arnold, 1965).

———, 'Shakespeare's Revised Plays: *King Lear* and *Othello*', *Library*, Sixth Series, 4.2 (1982), pp. 142–73.

———, ed., *Shakespeare and his Contemporaries* (Manchester: Manchester University Press, 1986).

Humphreys, A. R. (ed.), Arden *Ado* (1981).

Hunter, G. K. (ed.), Arden *AWW* (1959, 1977).

Huston, J. D., *Shakespeare's Comedies of Play* (New York: Columbia University Press, 1981).

Jacobs, H. E., see Kay.

Jenkins, Harold, '*As You Like It*', *SS* 8 (1955) pp. 40–51.

Jones, Emrys, *Scenic Form in Shakespeare* (Oxford: Clarendon Press, 1971, 1985).

Jowett, John, see Wells.

Kay, Carol M., and H. E. Jacobs (eds), *Shakespeare's Romances Reconsidered* (Lincoln and London: University of Nebraska Press, 1978).

Kermode, Frank (ed.), Arden *Tmp.* (1954, 1979).

Kirsch, Arthur C., 'The Integrity of "Measure for Measure"', *SS* 28 (1975), pp. 89–105.

Knight, G. Wilson, *The Wheel of Fire* (Oxford: Oxford University Press, 1930; Methuen's University Paperbacks, 1960).

——, *The Crown of Life* (Oxford: Oxford University Press, 1947; Methuen's University Paperbacks, 1965).

Lawrence, William W., *Shakespeare's Problem Comedies* (1931; Penguin Books, 1969).

Leavis, F. R., 'The Greatness of *Measure for Measure*', *Scrutiny*, 10 (1941–2), pp. 234–47.

Leech, Clifford, 'The "Meaning" of *Measure for Measure*', *SS* 3 (1950), pp. 66–73.

——, 'The Structure of the Last Plays', *SS* II (1958), pp. 19–30.

Leggatt, Alexander, *Shakespeare's Comedy of Love* (London: Methuen, 1974).

Lever, J. W. (ed.) Arden *MM* (1965, 1976).

Levin, Richard, *Love and Society in Shakespearean Comedy* (Newark: University of Delaware Press; London and Toronto: Associated University Presses; 1985).

Lothian, J. M., and T. W. Craik (eds), Arden *TN* (1975).

McCollom, William G., 'The Role of Wit in *Much Ado Nothing*', *SQ*, XIX.2 (1968), pp. 165–74.

McIntosh, Angus, '"As You Like It": a grammatical clue to character', *REL*, 4.2 (1963), pp. 68–81.

Mahood, Molly M. (ed.), New Peng. *TN* (1968).

Mares, F. H. (ed.), New Cam. *Ado* (1988).

Matchett, William H., 'Some Dramatic Techniques in *The Winter's Tale*', *SS* 22 (1969), pp. 93–107.

Maxwell, J. C. (ed.), Cam. *Per.* (1956, 1969).

——, (ed.), Cam. *Cym.* (1960, 1968).

Mowat, Barbara A., *The Dramaturgy of Shakespeare's Romances* (Athens: University of Georgia Press, 1976).

Mueschke, Paul and Miriam, 'Illusion and Metamorphosis in *Much Ado About Nothing*', *SQ* XVIII.I (1967), pp. 53–65.

Muir, Kenneth, 'The Problem of *Pericles*', *ES* XXX (1949), pp. 65–83.

——, *Shakespeare: The Comedies* (Englewood Cliffs: Prentice Hall, 1965, 1976).

—— (ed.), *Shakespeare: "The Winter's Tale"*. *A Casebook* (London: Macmillan, 1968).

——, *Shakespeare's Comic Sequence* (Liverpool University Press, 1979).

Musgrove, S., 'Some Composite Scenes in *Measure for Measure*', *SQ* XV.1 (1964), pp. 67–74.

Nagarajan, S., '*Measure for Measure* and Elizabethan Betrothals', *SQ* XIV.2 (1963), pp. 115–19.

Neill, Kerby, 'More Ado About Claudio: An Acquittal for the Slandered Groom' , *SQ* III.2 (1952), pp. 91–107.

Nosworthy, J. M. (ed.), Arden *Cym.* (1955, 1976).

Nuttall, A. D., ' "Measure for Measure": The Bed-Trick', *SS* 28 (1975) pp. 51–6.

Ormerod, David, 'Faith and Fashion in "Much Ado About Nothing" ', *SS* 25 (1972), pp. 93–105.

Pafford, J. H. P. (ed.), Arden *WT* (1963, 1976).

Palmer, D. J. (ed.), *Twelfth Night: A Casebook* (London: Macmillan, 1972).

——, see also Cox.

Palmer, John L., *Comic Characters of Shakespeare* (London: Macmillan, 1946).

Parrott, Thomas Marc, *Shakespearean Comedy* (New York: Russell & Russell, 1949, 1962).

Pettet, E. C., *Shakespeare and the Romance Tradition* (1949; London: Methuen's University Paperbacks, 1970).

Pope, Elizabeth M., 'The Renaissance Background of *Measure for Measure*', *SS* 2 (1949), pp. 66–82.

Powell, Raymond, *Shakespeare and the Critics' Debate* (London: Macmillan, 1980).

Price, Jonathan R., '*Measure for Measure* and the Critics: Towards a New Approach', *SQ* XX.2 (1969), pp. 179–204.

Quiller-Couch ('Q'), Arthur, ed. (Introductions), Cam. *Ado* (1923, 1980), *AYLI* (1926, 1948), *AWW* (1929, 1968), *WT* (1931, 1980).

Rees, Joan, *Shakespeare and the Story: Aspects of Creation* (London: Athlone Press, 1978).

Righter, Anne (Anne Barton) (ed.), New Peng. *Tmp.* (1968).

Rose, Mark, *Shakespearean Design* (Cambridge, Mass.: Harvard University Press, 1972).

Rossiter, A. P., *Angel with Horns* (London: Longman, 1961).

Salingar, Leo, *Shakespeare and the Traditions of Comedy* (London and New York: Cambridge University Press, 1974).

Schanzer, Ernest, 'The Structural Pattern of "The Winter's Tale"', *REL* V.2 (1964), pp. 72–82.

Schoff, Francis G., 'Claudio, Bertram, and a Note on Interpretation', *SQ* X.1 (1959), pp. 11–23.

Smallwood, Robert, 'The Design of *All's Well That Ends Well*', *SS* 25 (1972), pp. 56–61.

——, '*All's Well That Ends Well* at the Royal Shakespeare Theatre', in Cox and Palmer (eds), *Shakespeare's Wide and Universal Stage* (1984), pp. 98–103.

Smidt, Kristian, 'A Norwegian Operatic *Cymbeline*', *SQ* III.3 (1952), p. 284.

——, *Unconformities in Shakespeare's History Plays* (London: Macmillan, 1982).

——, *Unconformities in Shakespeare's Early Comedies* (London: Macmillan, 1986).

——, *Unconformities in Shakespeare's Tragedies* (London: Macmillan, 1989).

——, 'Repetition, Revision, and Editorial Greed in Shakespeare's Play Texts', *Cahiers élisabéthains*, 34 (1988), pp. 25–37.

Smith, Hallett, 'Leontes' *Affectio*', *SQ* XIV.2 (1963), pp. 163–6.

Smith, Irwin, 'Ariel and the Masque in *The Tempest*', *SQ* XXI.3 (1970), pp. 213–22.

Spencer, Theodore, 'Shakespeare and the Nature of Man: *The Tempest*' (1942), in Dean (ed.), *Shakespeare: Modern Essays in Criticism*, pp. 456–61.

Stevenson, David Lloyd, *The Achievement of Shakespeare's "Measure for Measure"* (Ithaca: Cornell University Press, 1966).

Styan, J. L., 'Understanding Shakespeare in Performance', *Shakespeare in Southern Africa*, 1 (1987).

Taylor, Gary, *Moment by Moment by Shakespeare* (London: Macmillan, 1985).

——, and Michael Warren (eds), *The Division of the Kingdoms: Shakespeare's Two Versions of 'King Lear'* (Oxford: Clarendon Press, 1983).

——, see also Wells.

Thaler, Alwin, and Norman Sanders (eds), *Shakespearean Essays* (Knoxville: University of Tennessee Press, 1964).

Thomson, Peter, *Shakespeare's Theatre* (London: Routledge & Kegan Paul, 1983).

Tillyard, E. M. W., *Shakespeare's Problem Plays* (1950; Harmondsworth: Penguin Books, 1970).

——, *Shakespeare's Last Plays* (London: Chatto & Windus, 1964).

Toole, William B., *Shakespeare's Problem Plays* (The Hague: Mouton & Co., 1966).

Traversi, Derek A., *An Approach to Shakespeare*, 3rd edn, Vol. 2 (London, Sydney, Toronto: Hollis & Carter, 1969).

Trienens, Roger J., 'The Inception of Leontes' Jealousy in *The Winter's Tale*', *SQ* IV.3 (1953), pp. 321–6.

Trousdale, Marion, 'A Second Look at Critical Bibliography and the Acting of Plays', *SQ* 41.1 (1990), pp. 87–96.

Turner, Robert K., 'The Text of *Twelfth Night*', *SQ* XXVI.2 (1975), pp. 128–38.

Twine, Laurence, *The Patterne of Painefull Adventures* (1594?), in Bullough, *Sources*, VI, pp. 423–82.

Ure, Peter, *Shakespeare: The Problem Plays* (Writers and Their Work, No. 140; London: Longmans, Green, 1961).

Van Doren, Mark, *Shakespeare* (1939; New York: Doubleday, 1953).

Walker, Roy, 'The Whirligig of Time: A Review of Recent Productions', *SS* 12 (1959), pp. 122–30.

Weil, Herbert S., 'Form and Contexts in *Measure for Measure*', *CQ* 12.1 (1970), pp. 61–7.

Wells, Stanley, and Gary Taylor with John Jowett and William Montgomery (eds.), *William Shakespeare: A Textual Companion* (Oxford: Clarendon Press, 1987).

Werstine, Paul, 'Narratives About Printed Shakespearean Texts', *SQ* 41.1(1990), pp. 65–86.

West, Robert H., 'Ceremonial Magic in *The Tempest*', in Thaler and Sanders (eds), *Shakespearean Essays*, pp. 63–78.

Whitaker, Virgil K., *Shakespeare's Use of Learning* (San Marino: Huntington Library, 1953).

White, R. S., *Shakespeare and the Romance Ending* (Newcastle-upon-Tyne, 1981).

Wiles, David, *Shakespeare's Clown* (Cambridge: Cambridge University Press, 1987).

Wilkins, George, *The Painfull Adventures of Pericles Prince of Tyre* (1608), in Bullough, *Sources*, VI, pp. 492–546.

Wilson, John Dover (ed.), Cam. *Tmp.* (1921, 1977), *MM* (1922), *Ado* (1923, 1980), *AYLI* (1926, 1948), *TN* (1930, 1974).

——, *Shakespeare's Happy Comedies* (London: Faber & Faber, 1962, 1963).

Wright, Laurence, 'When Does the Tragi-Comic Disruption Start?: *The Winter's Tale* and Leontes' "Affection"', *ES* 70.3 (1989), pp. 225–32.

Index

Act-division 7, 160
Act to Restrain Abuses 126, 165; *see also* Profanity
Addition iii, 84, 86, 95, 132–3, 169, 172, 213n31, 220n35
Address, forms of 24–5, 33, 53–5, 189n7, 192n34, 194n10, 11, 208n3; *see also* Titles
Alexander, B. 198n15
Allegory 81, 145–6
Allen, J. A. 29, 193n37, 43
Allusion 4, 195n17
Ambiguity 62, 80, 145, 190n23, 210n29, 220n40
Ambivalence 47
Anachronism 127, 212n10
Anomaly 5, 93, 220n41; *see also* Inconsistencies, Unconformities
Apollo 138, 143–4, 165–6, 209n22, 217n30, 31
Aristotle 7
Armin, R. 70–2, 86, 104, 169, 172, 198n15, 199n24, 207n36
Astrology 155
Atheism 102
Authorship viii, 2, 95, 107–8, 208n3–5, 209n8,21, 212n10, 213n22

Balance 136–7
Baldwin, T. W. 187n13
Bandello, M. 24–5, 33, 193n35
Barber, C. L. 10, 199n28
Barnet, S. 194n1
Barton, A. 196n21, 200n29,35, 218n1, 16, 219n27,28
Battenhouse, R. W. 205n20, 206n28
Beaumont and Fletcher 173, 188n35
   Philaster 15, 125, 128
   The Woman Hater 125, 190n26
Bed-trick 12–13, 79–80, 92, 105, 168
Berger, H. 35, 189n19, 193n43

Bergeron, D. 136, 214n8
Bethell, S. L. 67, 188n47, 198n13, 214n1, 2, 215n14
Betrayal 41, 216n18
Billington, M. x, 199n27
Blackfriars 19, 132, 172
Blank verse 54, 195n12, 207n39, 210n36
Boas, F. S. 12
Boccaccio, G. 77, 84, 125, 133, 186n1
Bogdanov, M. ix
Bond of Association 148
Bradbrook, M. C. 81, 89–90, 187n17, 189n18
Bradley, A. C. 199n25
Branagh, K. x, 200n36
Break in composition 50–5, 60, 96, 158, 161
Breight, C. 148, 218n13–15
Brissenden, A. T. 189n21
Brook, P. 215n14
Bullard, J. E. 216n18
Bullough, G. 31–2
Bulman, J. C. 4
Burbage, R. 19

Cabalism 156
Capell, E. 96
Carelessness 2, 44, 119, 171
Carroll, L. 32
Carter, A. H. 201n11
Censorship 54–5, 164, 219n29, 222n2
Chambers, E. K. 26–7, 187n6, 197n3
Chambers, R. W. 206n26
Change of mind x, 3, 39, 60–1, 66, 164
Changes (*see also* Substitution)
   character 100–1, 149, 152
   focus 98
   mode 13–14, 82, 97–8, 163
   TN 64